Sell your books at
World of Books!
.com
quote.
e

150 More Group Therapy
Activities & TIPS

Handouts • Activities • Worksheets

Judith A. Belmont, MS LPC

Copyright © 2016 by Judith Belmont

Published by
PESI Publishing & Media
PESI, Inc
3839 White Ave
Eau Claire, WI 54703

Cover: Amy Rubenzer
Layout: Bookmasters & Amy Rubenzer

ISBN: 9781683730156

All rights reserved.

Printed in the United States of America.

PESI
Publishing
& Media
www.pesipublishing.com

TABLE OF CONTENTS

Copyright © 2016 Judith Belmont. *150 More Group Therapy Activities & TIPS*, www.belmontwellness.com. All rights reserved.

ACKNOWLEDGEMENTS

This book would not have been possible without the expert help from two key members of the PESI publishing team, Linda Jackson and Amy Rubenzer.

As my publisher at PESI, Linda has been the ultimate professional in her expert leadership in keeping this book on track, tight, and well organized. She has contributed numerous astute insights and suggestions, always relayed in a kind, tactful and patient manner.

As PESI's graphic designer, Amy has outdone herself on this book. Her effort in making this book come alive with such a "user-friendly" layout makes this book easily accessible to mental health professionals and their clients. Serious therapeutic topics have been softened with compelling illustrations and design which has really made this book a treasury trove of TIPS, presented in an eye-catching fashion.

I am grateful to all the influential authors in the field that have laid the foundation for all the best practices and "hands on" exercises cited in this book. They have provided a wealth of insights and ideas that I have used as a springboard for these 150 tips.

I am also indebted to the many clients and group participants throughout my career who have inspired me with their courage and commitment to use life skills techniques to better their lives and improve the world around them.

*Lastly, thank **YOU** very much as proactive mental health professionals who intend to use this resource to promote the importance of life skills psycho-education. Thank you for your interest to give your clients the gift of learning practical life skills to help them help themselves.*

Judith Belmont, MS, LPC

www.belmontwellness.com
August, 2016

 **Judith Belmont,** MS, LPC has 40 years of experience in the mental health field as therapist, author, trainer and speaker. She is the author of 6 books designed to provide mental health professionals and their clients valuable life skills resources. She has been a national mental health trainer, offering continuing education programs on various mental health topics. She also promotes wellness and positive communication in the workplace through motivational and interactive presentations nationally. As the founder of Belmont Wellness (www.belmontwellness.com), she provides training, coaching and keynotes.

INTRODUCTION

The group experience is an ideal forum for psycho-educational learning. We are social beings, and a group situation allows opportunities to improve social skills, learn from others, practice skills with others, and develop confidence and improve self-esteem by mastering important life skills in a social context. Group activities provide the forum for skill building in a supportive environment to practice skills and get feedback and support. The group setting is not only an ideal forum for learning social skills and improving the ability to connect with others in a meaningful way, it is also a powerful backdrop for personal self-discovery and growth. Ironically, personal growth and self-discovery is so often best achieved not in isolation, but rather through relationships and support.

In this book you will find various tips and tools to use with your clients to help them master important therapeutic concepts that will help them in their everyday lives and empower them to gain control over their lives. Although all the tips and tools are presented as psycho-educational ideas to use in a group context, many of these tips can easily be applied to individual therapy. The self-help handouts and worksheets, and even many of the mini-lessons and exercises, can be easily used in the context of individual therapy, along with applications to adults and children.

Mental health professionals have a unique opportunity to help their clients not only with their support, empathetic listening and guidance, but actually serving as life skills educators, empowering clients to help themselves. It is important to note that teaching is not telling clients what to do! Rather, using psycho-education demonstrates a pro-active approach in which therapists teach skills so that clients can put them to use. Just as a piano teacher does not expect a student to learn how to play by figuring out how to read notes and play the corresponding keys by themselves, a therapist cannot expect clients to use skills they never learned or practiced. Much of the learning and progress is achieved by practicing between sessions. Likewise, in the psycho-educational group, assigning "homework" and practice between sessions are cornerstones of the psycho-educational approach. Providing information and various practice opportunities and creative ways to incorporate the teachings will help your clients be self-empowered with insight, knowledge and skills.

The role of a leader of psycho-educational groups can be a very exciting and rewarding one when you have the right tools. My goal is that *150 More Group Activities and TIPs* will provide you with a solid toolkit of ideas to use with your clients to educate and inspire.

Judith Belmont, MS, LPC

Author of bestselling: *103 Group Activities and TIPS, 86 TIPS for the Therapeutic Toolbox,* and *127 More Amazing TIPS & Tools*

Group
Beginnings

Tips 1-15

1

Using Psycho-Education as a Cornerstone of Your Groups

THEORY

For clinicians, regardless of theoretical orientation, the goal of treatment is not just to support, it is not just to talk, it is not just to listen, it is to **educate.** Most popular psychological theories, including Cognitive Behavior Therapy (CBT) and all Third Wave orientations such as Dialectical Behavior Therapy (DBT), Mindfulness Based Cognitive Therapy (MBCT), and Acceptance and Commitment Therapy (ACT), rely heavily on teaching and educating as part of treatment. Many of our clients come into treatment having learned unhealthy life lessons, lacking healthy coping skills, while listening to their unhealthy self-talk. It is not uncommon for them to come in with judgments and labels about themselves that are more like fiction than fact.

Psycho-education is not telling people what to do. It is educating them to give them valuable insight and skills they have never learned.

IMPLEMENTATION

The following are some of the types of psycho-educational tools to use in groups. Using the topic of communication skills training, listed are examples of how to use psycho-educational techniques with your clients.

Mini-lessons - Short teaching sessions in a group to offer new skills.

Example: Explaining the difference between Assertive, Non-Assertive, and Aggressive Communication.

Group Activities - Interactive activities that promote learning experientially.

Example: Exercises such as practicing handshaking assertively, so that group members can learn the importance of non-verbal communication to express themselves assertively.

Handouts - Written material that teaches life skills concepts and are for reading and reference.

Example: A handout that highlights the three types of communication.

Worksheets - Skill building material to reinforce life skills.

Example: Providing a worksheet that individuals can practice changing aggressive "You" statements into assertive "I" statements.

Visualizations - Mentally rehearsing and creating imagery to lower stress and emotional distress, as well as to create images of being successful and reaching positive goals.

Example: Imagine being successful, confident and self-assured while speaking up in a meeting or to a coworker.

 Copyright © 2016 Judith Belmont. *150 More Group Therapy Activities & TIPS*, www.belmontwellness.com. All rights reserved.

Using Metaphors and Analogies - Using objects, images or symbols to represent life skills concepts, to make the learning more relevant and memorable.

Example: Using a shaken unopened soda pop bottle as an example of tension rising from being non-assertive and keeping upsetting thoughts in rather than expressing them, letting things build until exploding aggressively once emotions are uncapped.

Role Play - Having group members practice interpersonal skills while you and group members play significant people in their lives.

Example: You (or others in the group) play the part of a difficult family member, providing practice for improving communication with the help of group feedback and support.

Homework Assignments - Group members are given self-help assignments to work on improving skills between sessions.

Examples: Reviewing communication handouts and filling out worksheets, as well as practicing assertive behavior skills with people in their lives outside of the group.

PROCESSING

Giving and receiving feedback from peers in a safe and supportive environment is a major advantage of group therapy. Group therapy taps the power of universality, in helping members feel that they are not alone, while feeling supported in a safe social context. Group therapy taps the power of healing and learning in a group setting. The group milieu provides a wonderful backdrop for life skills education and practice, empowering clients to gain skills to help themselves.

Copyright © 2016 Judith Belmont. *150 More Group Therapy Activities & TIPS*, www.belmontwellness.com. All rights reserved.

Group Beginnings

THEORY

Structuring a group with some common elements at the start of a session will help you organize your group sessions for maximum effectiveness. **Effective beginnings and endings are major determinants of the effectiveness of the group.** In this TIP, guidelines are offered in the way of a checklist to remember important elements of effective group beginnings.

IMPLEMENTATION

Most effective group sessions will include most of the following common elements for effective group beginnings.

For each session, check off the items that you are including in the beginning of your session:

_____ **Sharing Successes and Challenges:** Make time to allow members to share their successes and challenges during the week. See TIP #4 *Sharing Successes and Setting Agendas* for more detailed ideas on this topic.

_____ **Feedback from the Last Session:** It is often helpful to tie up loose ends from the last session, get feedback and clarify any issues from the previous session.

_____ **Do an Informal Mood Check:** Informal mood checks can be in the form of going around and asking group members how they feel today. A more formal way would be to use quick tests such as The Burns Mood Inventory (Burns, 1993, Ten Days To Self Esteem).

_____ **Homework Review:** The importance of reviewing homework at the beginning of each session cannot be over emphasized. It reinforces the importance of taking the homework seriously and will encourage practice between sessions. You can do this at first with the entire group, which can be followed by some breaking into small groups or pairs to go over the homework in more detail.

_____ **Agenda Setting:** For each session, state your agenda for the session so members know the psycho-educational topic of the day.

_____ **Establish Goals:** Within the context of the agenda, each member should consider at least one personal goal they have for the session. Setting goals can be simply done by asking for each member to go around and complete this sentence: For this topic, I would like to learn _____ or improve my skills to: _____.

_____ **Use Quick Self-Tests:** If you have quick self tests to help set the stage for the day's session, have members fill them out. For example, if the topic for the session is forgiveness, start with TIP #124, *What is Your Forgiveness IQ?*.

_____ **Take a Mindful Minute:** If you want to incorporate mindfulness in your group, the beginning of the session is a great way to remind members of the importance of practicing mindfulness as you lead a brief breathing exercise, guided imagery, or visualization.

PROCESSING

Each of these elements will bring structure to the group and consistency throughout the group duration. Although each group might not have all the elements suggested above, effective groups will have most of them. Use this checklist as a way to ensure your group is structured for maximum success.

     Copyright © 2016 Judith Belmont. *150 More Group Therapy Activities & TIPS*, www.belmontwellness.com. All rights reserved.

How is Your Emotional Wellness?

THEORY

Quick quizzes can introduce the session topic and help members get a quick snapshot of where they stand on a given topic. Inventories for anxiety, depression and general mood, such as those having been made popular by Aaron Beck and David Burns, are easily accessible on the internet.

The following quick quiz on emotional wellness is an example of one that you can use over and over again regardless of the topic for the day and type of group, as the topic of emotional wellness is universal and relevant to any topic. The following **Emotional Wellness Quiz** serves as a good general overall gauge as to one's sense of well-being in general or even serves as a mood check for each session.

IMPLEMENTATION

This quick quiz can be given out periodically, and even at every session. By giving out this inventory, you are helping your group members gauge their own emotional wellness on that day, and this sets the stage for motivating them to increase their "Emotional Wellness IQ."

You might want to collect and keep the past quizzes, so that towards the end of the group you can give back the weekly quizzes so that group members can review their progress over time.

PROCESSING

If this quiz is given out just once, it can serve as a great springboard for examining the main characteristics of the emotional healthy person. When used at each session as a mood screening, little discussion needs to be done each time after the first time it is filled out. If you do use them periodically and collect them, towards the end of the group, giving out a folder for each group member with their quizzes in chronological order will offer a snapshot of whether the group experience was able to help them improve their Emotional Wellness IQ!

Quiz — ## How is Your Emotional Wellness?

NAME:_____ DATE: _____

Below are items that you may agree with or disagree with. On a scale of 1 to 7, rate your level of agreement with each item, being honest and open with yourself.

7 — Strongly Agree
6 — Moderately Agree
5 — Slightly Agree
4 — Neither Agree or Disagree
3 — Slightly Disagree
2 — Moderately Disagree
1 — Strongly Disagree

_____ I feel satisfied with the person I am and practice self-compassion.

_____ I do not allow regrets and disappointments to interfere with "today."

_____ I am very connected with others and do not feel isolated.

_____ I am generally a rational and optimistic thinker.

_____ I refuse to hold grudges and am able to be forgiving.

_____ I feel in control of my emotions, thoughts and feelings.

_____ I enjoy a healthy sense of humor and am able to laugh at life's shortcomings.

_____ I am grateful for how my life is currently, without focusing on what is lacking.

Total your score here: _____

51-56 — Emotional Wellness is extraordinary!
46-50 — High Level of Emotional Wellness.
40-45 — Moderate Level of Emotional Wellness.
32-39 — Emotional Wellness needs some boosting!
24-31 — Emotional Wellness is posing problem for emotional health - needs attention!
16-23 — Needs improvement! Actively work on improving your Emotional Wellness.
Below 15 — Danger Zone! It is critical to get professional help for emotional health

 Copyright © 2016 Judith Belmont. *150 More Group Therapy Activities & TIPS*, www.belmontwellness.com. All rights reserved.

Sharing Successes and Setting Agendas

THEORY

An excellent program called SMART Recovery, (Self Management And Recovery Training) provides structured sessions for facilitators and group members for those going through substance abuse recovery and their families. No matter what type of group you are leading, it is a great model for using step-by-step manuals for group leaders along with versions for group members and families. SMART Recovery's focus on cognitive therapy and life skills techniques can be applied to any group with a psycho-educational focus. This tip is borrowed from their Sharing Success portion of their program, where they use the beginning of each group **to help group members focus on their successes that week**, such as how they improved their coping skills in handling adversity.

IMPLEMENTATION

Keep 5 minutes at the beginning of each session for success stories to help encourage improved problem solving, positive growth and increased motivation to change. As they say in the Smart Recovery program, "Success breeds success."

You can make the point that even when there is a setback in the week's events, we can always find a positive takeaway or learning lesson to experience success moving forward. Developing that resilient mindset itself can be a success! This is a good time to remind group members not to take their successes for granted, and celebrate each success, no matter how small it may seem.

It will be helpful in setting the agenda for the present session to also ask what did not work as well as they had hoped, and brainstorm how they could have handled it differently. Remind them that setbacks and even failures are necessary precursors for success.

You can make the point that success can not be measured in home runs, but in smaller hits and singles which add up to more than a couple home runs if they persist.

SMART Recovery also emphasizes the importance of talking about the agenda for the group at the beginning of the session. This sets the expectation of what the group will focus on and help provide clarity and structure to the group experience.

PROCESSING

Providing time to share successes and learn from the successes of others is one of the most valuable aspects of group therapy. Encourage members to share a couple minutes of their personal situations, not being overly detailed, and make it a point to use each member's examples to ask if any one else has experienced this struggle or success. This type of questioning taps into the healing power of universality where people realize they are not alone, as they share common struggles on their personal road to success.

Copyright © 2016 Judith Belmont. *150 More Group Therapy Activities & TIPS*, www.belmontwellness.com. All rights reserved.

Give Us a Pearl and an Onion

THEORY

Structured icebreakers to start off a group can offer valuable opportunities for sharing, building trust and establishing rapport in the group. The use of visual metaphors helps group members engage in the activity without feeling put on the spot or threatened. Even the quiet group members will find this metaphorical visualization a fun way to express themselves and self-disclose. As in many of the other activities in this book, **using metaphors makes it easier to share feelings and thoughts**, and encourages flexible and creative thinking that is necessary to find new solutions to old problems.

IMPLEMENTATION

Introduce the activity by explaining the metaphors of an onion and a pearl. You might actually have a toy pearl necklace and an actual onion to make the metaphor realistic.

Explain to the group that the image of an onion represents something with a strong and pungent aroma. They represent very tough life lessons that need to be peeled away to find solutions.

The pearl is a metaphor for something that is a rare find, and is valuable. Pearls they share with the group can be pearls of wisdom they have gained, or something special they learned.

It will be interesting to note to your group that a pearl is actually a result of irritation and adversity. Pearls are made from sand irritation formed in a mollusk shell, and it is the roughness that creates the beautiful gem. You can make the point that, likewise, challenges and adversity in our life can make us deeper, more empathetic and develop more character.

After explaining the metaphors, ask group members to share both a pearl and an onion with the group, i.e. share something special that happened in the week, and something that was a difficult or challenging experience.

This can be a nice group activity to start off the group each session for both children and adults.

PROCESSING

This activity is a nice "touch base" activity that promotes self-disclosure and group trust. Using it frequently as a session opener will help the group become more cohesive. Look for the common themes that group members share, tapping the power of universality which is so valuable in the group experience.

 Copyright © 2016 Judith Belmont. *150 More Group Therapy Activities & TIPS*, www.belmontwellness.com. All rights reserved.

Proverbs in a Jar

THEORY

Wise proverbial sayings and inspirational quotes can provide inspiration for group members when shared and discussed. Ancient proverbs, especially Roman and Chinese, provide many deep ideas that offer insight and therapeutic messages about life. Group members will enjoy this simple activity and be inspired along the way! It also **stimulates more creative abstract thinking** by encouraging group members to look at things in new ways, especially when they hear the perspective of others in the group.

IMPLEMENTATION

Here are some examples that would be fitting for a life skills group:

- "The journey of a thousand miles must begin with a single step."

- "A bird does not sing because it has an answer. It sings because it has a song."

- "I hear & I forget. I see & I remember. I do & I understand." —Confucius

- "Happiness depends upon ourselves." —Aristotle

- "You cannot prevent the birds of sorrow from flying over your head,
  but you can prevent them from building nests in your hair." —Chinese Proverb

- "Every path has its puddle." —English Proverb

- "When the going gets tough, the tough get going."

- "No man is an island."

- "People who live in glass houses should not throw stones."

- "Hope for the best, but prepare for the worst."

- "Better late than never."

- "You can't make an omelet without breaking a few eggs."

Write the sayings on notecards, and place in a hat, box or some container. You might have it decorated with the word PROVERBS or with images of philosophers like Confucius or Aristotle.

Copyright © 2016 Judith Belmont. *150 More Group Therapy Activities & TIPS*, www.belmontwellness.com. All rights reserved.

Have each group member take turns going around and pick out one card at a time.

After they read the proverb, they say what they think it means, and then how it applies to their own life.

After the reader gives their own answer, ask for other group members to offer their own interpretations and examples of how it relates to them.

Variations: Instead of proverbs, using quotes or affirmations in a jar can also be fun as well as inspirational! For variety, alternate between proverbs in a jar, quotes in a jar, and affirmations in a jar.

PROCESSING

Using proverbs and applying their relevance to everyday life situations can be very meaningful and therapeutic. The success of the activity is in the processing of the answers as a group and helping members see commonalities. You might have the group make up their own proverbs to add to the jar. After all, we all have wisdom within us!

Copyright © 2016 Judith Belmont. *150 More Group Therapy Activities & TIPS*, www.belmontwellness.com. All rights reserved.

These Are a Few Of My Favorite Things

THEORY

Sharing with others, as well as crystallizing personally, a list of everyone's favorite things can be a nice way to **self-disclose to the group** and learn about others in a way that can be quite uplifting.

IMPLEMENTATION

As a fun way to start the activity, you could play the song "My Favorite Things" from *Sound of Music,* or show a clip on YouTube.

Introduce the activity by handing out the accompanying worksheet and tell the group that we can find out a lot about others and ourselves by identifying and sharing with one another our favorite things.

After they complete the activity, take turns going around and have each person talk about their favorite things.

Ask the group to point out commonalities and universal themes.

At the end of each person's turn, summarize what the group learned about others based on their responses.

PROCESSING

This simple exercise can be very powerful in promoting group cohesiveness and supportive sharing. It is a nice way to share within a positive context. There will be many opportunities for group members to identify with one another and find commonalities. Helping group members process why they chose certain favorite things and asking pertinent questions will make the activity the most meaningful.

Copyright © 2016 Judith Belmont. *150 More Group Therapy Activities & TIPS,* www.belmontwellness.com. All rights reserved.

Activity

My Favorite Things

My favorite song is: _____

My favorite movie is: _____

My favorite hobby is: _____

My favorite sport is: _____

My favorite person is: _____

My favorite place is: _____

My favorite food is: _____

My favorite animal is: _____

Copyright © 2016 Judith Belmont. *150 More Group Therapy Activities & TIPS*, www.belmontwellness.com. All rights reserved.

Group Story Telling

THEORY

A great get-to-know-you activity entails telling a story as a group. Working together, **group members learn to bond and trust one another**. Telling a story together, with no one being judgmental of each other's contribution, increases trust and group cohesiveness. This stream of consciousness activity helps members also think on the spot without worrying if they are right or wrong. For the shy individual, exercises that promote self-expression in a relatively non-threatening and structured way can be very valuable in overcoming social anxiety.

IMPLEMENTATION

Tell members that the group will put together a group story.

Let them know that every contribution is valuable in making up a group story. Emphasize that there are no right or wrong contributions, and everything is acceptable, as long as there is no rude, cursing or offensive language. All contributions are valued.

Tell them that you will start off the story with a simple phrase, and then will go around the room and each person will add to the story with a phrase or a sentence or two.

Examples to start off are:

"It was a dark and stormy night. . ."

"Two children were walking down the street. . ..."

"When two friends walked unsuspectingly into a vacant
building. . ."

Make as many go-arounds as you need until the story has a
conclusion.

As each member shares their contribution, carefully listen to what they are expressing and the mood they are conveying, which might help with tailoring the rest of the group discussion or activities with those observations in mind.

PROCESSING

Ask the group their impressions of the story, how they felt being put on the spot to share their contribution, and what they learned. Reflecting on the activity is as important as the activity itself and can provide a foundation for members to share their thoughts within the context of the group support. This activity is especially helpful for group members who need help to overcome social anxiety or are fearful of speaking up in groups.

Make the point that everyone has a valuable contribution not only in this activity, but in the group as a whole. Likewise, everyone has something to contribute to whatever situation they find themselves in the world outside.

Copyright © 2016 Judith Belmont. *150 More Group Therapy Activities & TIPS*, www.belmontwellness.com. All rights reserved.

Tip #9

Name Games

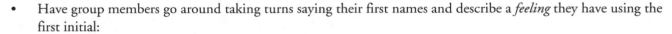

THEORY

In the initial group session, no matter what age, creative introductions set a light and fun tone, setting the stage for cohesiveness, creativity, and creating a safe place for self-disclosure and support.

Below are some examples of effective introductory exercises to help group members enjoy learning about one another and establishing rapport. Since most group members might understandably not want to disclose too much about themselves personally until trust is built, **these activities allow for light, non-threatening interaction**.

IMPLEMENTATION

The following are some Name Game variations:

- Have group members go around taking turns saying their first names and describe something *about themselves,* using the first letter of their name.

  For example, *"My name is Ellen, and I am energetic."*

- Have group members go around taking turns saying their first names and describe something they *like* that begins with the initial of their first name.

  For example, *"My name is Lenny and I like licorice."*

- Have group members go around taking turns saying their first names and describe a *feeling* they have using the first initial:

  For example, *"My name is Evelyn and I feel enthusiastic about the group."*

- Have members write their names with crayons or colored pencils and with the letters draw images inside or hanging down that describes something about themselves, sharing one at a time with the group.

- To practice each other's names, have members go around and say their name and repeat all the names before them until everyone gets a turn.

- Using a bean bag or a ball, after everyone learns each other's name, throw the bean bag or ball randomly and ask a question to the person you are throwing it to using their name, such as *"Jean, what is your favorite color?"* After Jean answers, she throws the beanbag or ball to someone else saying their name and asking another question. Make sure everyone gets a turn at least once.

- Paired introductions - Break into pairs and give them a few minutes to interview one another, and then each pair introduces their partner to the group.

 Copyright © 2016 Judith Belmont. *150 More Group Therapy Activities & TIPS,* www.belmontwellness.com. All rights reserved.

- Members go around and say their first name and one thing that few people know about them.

- Have members introduce themselves and say one thing that is true and one thing that is a lie, and the other members need to figure out which is the truth and which is the lie by asking questions.

- Pass around a package of M&Ms® or Skittles® and have members take two pieces of candy. Tell them to keep one for themselves and the other keep for the exercise. Then bring out a poster that asks a question for each color.

    For example, if they picked a brown M&M, they would first say their name and then answer the question like, *"What is the best thing you did this month?"*

- After learning everyone's names, have the group members line up in the alphabetical order of their first names.

- Using Scrabble® letters or other word game letters, like Banagrams®, members introduce themselves by picking a letter and using that letter to describe something about them or what they like.

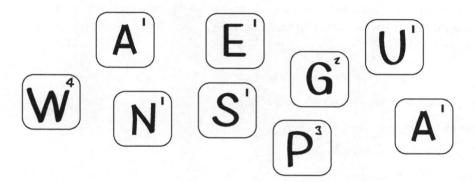

PROCESSING

These introduction variations all offer groups to start out getting to know one another in a fun, interactive way, which is relatively non-threatening. Spending a little time to explain answers will be helpful to help group members get to know one another. These light activities set a positive and creative tone for the rest of the group.

Copyright © 2016 Judith Belmont. *150 More Group Therapy Activities & TIPS*, www.belmontwellness.com. All rights reserved.

Questions for Building Trust and Self-Disclosure

THEORY

One advantage that groups offer is the opportunity for individuals to develop trust and comfort in being able to self-disclose. Sometimes **simply asking good questions can set the right platform for self-disclosure and group bonding**.

IMPLEMENTATION

The following are some effective questions that serve as a springboard for setting the stage for a group session. After everyone had an opportunity to touch base and share how they are feeling, and go over the homework for the week, asking a different question each session which all members take turns to answer can provide a nice opportunity for self-reflection and disclosure.

The following are some questions that are particularly effective:

- *What is something about you that very few people know?*
- *What is one thing that you secretly wish?*
- *What has been your biggest challenge lately?*
- *Who is the person you most admire?*

Questions can also be in the form of sentence completions. Group sentence completions can be a great way to give information in a relatively non- threatening way. Have notecards that they pick out of a box, or give them a sheet of about 15 items so they can pick one when it is their turn to fill in and complete the sentence. These are examples:

The one thing that people often do not understand about me is:

_____

I have always wanted to

_____

I dream of

_____

PROCESSING

Questions and prompting sentence completions such as the sampling above will provide opportunity to discuss meaningful thoughts. Group members get a chance to self-disclose things they would not ordinarily bring up, but are very important to them. Invariably this learning about each other will promote group cohesiveness and trust.

 Copyright © 2016 Judith Belmont. *150 More Group Therapy Activities & TIPS*, www.belmontwellness.com. All rights reserved.

Tip #11

Take a Humor Inventory

THEORY

Short mini-quizzes are a great way to begin a group to introduce a topic. Giving the group members a chance to see where they stand on a given topic before learning new skills, taking the short quiz again in subsequent sessions, will provide a good baseline to compare "before" and "after" the psycho-educational lessons.

Having group members find their "Humor Quotient" will give them a gauge of whether or not **they incorporate the benefits of humor in their lives.** Humor itself has been correlated with increased energy, elevated mood, lower blood pressure, lower anxiety, a healthier heart, an increased immune system, and increased sense of well-being. Therapy is serious stuff, but even so, injecting humor in treatment is therapeutic and helps your clients gain a more objective perspective of their situation.

IMPLEMENTATION

- Using the topic of humor is a light yet meaningful topic for setting the stage of group work. Introduce the topic by emphasizing that one of the most important characteristics of the stress resilient personality is having a sense of humor.

- Positive humor is not to be confused with sarcasm, which is really humor that is degrading to others and at their expense.
  Positive humor is not sarcastic or aggressive - it is having the ability to see the brighter side of life. Having a good sense of humor entails optimistic thinking, with the realization that, as author Oscar Wilde had said, "Life is too important to be taken seriously."

- Have group members fill out the quiz to get their "Humor Quotient" (see following page).
  You might ask how people scored by a show of hands, or if you think it is best with the particular group to not put them on the spot, ask them questions such as what was the one item that they scored the lowest in and what was the item they scored highest. This can lead to fruitful discussion about what prevents them from seeing the lighter side of life.

Just the act of taking this quiz will underscore the importance of having a sense of humor, and highlights some characteristics inherent in having a sense of humor.

PROCESSING

Brainstorm with the group members how they can raise their humor quotient. Looking at the areas in which they scored the lowest, review how they could develop a lighter perspective that would increase personal resiliency. Ask them to share with the group the role models in their lives that have used humor to handle even the most difficult times, and have been inspiring to them. The beauty of these short quizzes is that you can encourage members to retake the quiz periodically, to see if their "Humor Quotient" has increased. Even though people commonly think that a sense of humor should come naturally, improving one's sense of humor can take some serious intention to improve!

Copyright © 2016 Judith Belmont. *150 More Group Therapy Activities & TIPS*, www.belmontwellness.com. All rights reserved.

Where's Your Sense of Humor?

The following questions will help you take stock of your "humor inventory."

Rate each item on the following scale of 1 to 5:

False ⟵⟶ True

| 1 | 2 | 3 | 4 | 5 |

_____ I take myself too seriously.

_____ I am too busy to find the humor in things.

_____ I am too involved with "important things" to be able to see the lighter side of life.

_____ I am worried about what others think about me.

_____ On average, I do not laugh a lot.

_____ There is not much that strikes me as funny.

_____ I have not had a good laugh in quite some time.

Take your total score and divide it by 7:

Total score _____ divided by 7 equals your score: _____.

Interpretation of your score

1. Superb: Your Humor Quotient is unusually high! Keep up the good work!

2. Very Good: You have a very good ability to see the lightness in life!

3. Average: Your Humor Quotient could use some boosting.

4. Needs Work: Look for more opportunities to lighten your load.

5. Needs a Lot of Work: Life is too serious to be taken so seriously! Try to find more lightness in your life! If your mood is low, consider getting professional help.

What are some ways that you can improve your Humor Quotient?

_____

_____

From *The Therapist's Ultimate Solution Book: Essential Strategies, Tips and Tools to Empower Your Clients* by Judith Belmont. Copyright © 2015 by Judith Belmont. Used by permission of W.W. Norton & Company

 Copyright © 2016 Judith Belmont. *150 More Group Therapy Activities & TIPS*, www.belmontwellness.com. All rights reserved.

Describing in Pictures

THEORY

An interesting variation of self-disclosure through verbally sharing and questioning is to use art as a way to self-disclose and express thoughts and feelings to the group. Whether you are starting the group off with a "mood check" to encourage expression through pictures, or having them draw a success they had within the week, **drawing activities can provide an opportunity for creative expression**. Even for the very first group session, drawing activities can be a non-threatening way for group members to introduce themselves.

IMPLEMENTATION

Have paper, pens, pencils, crayons and/or colored pencils available. This activity is appropriate for all ages.

In the example of having them draw how they feel as a type of mood check, simply ask group members to draw how they feel right now.

Emphasize this is not an activity that requires artistic ability. Any imagery that expresses something meaningful is what's important. Suggest that even using easy-to-draw stick figures or faces can be helpful in conveying feelings, as well as figurative and symbolic representations of their feelings (such as a sun or a cloud).

If you want this to be just a "touch base" at the beginning of the session, make sure you structure this activity with a time limit, such as three to five minutes. When processing the drawings with the group, have a time frame in mind to make sure you have enough time for the general group activity for the session.

Other examples of using drawing to "touch base" at the beginning of the group session is to have group members draw one of their successes or challenges they experienced this week, drawing their goal for the session, or describing something about their week in pictures.

PROCESSING

Drawing is helpful with young children who are not verbally expressive. Children are also not generally as inhibited about using drawing and art for self-expression, and are less critical than adults about their artistic ability. Drawing with adults can be also quite therapeutic, as adults are often not used to self-expression non-verbally. Processing the drawings as a group, in small groups, or pairs can provide a creative outlet to express and share, and provide the basis for an enjoyable activity for people of all ages. If you find the drawing activity successful, in later group sessions you can pick another topic to draw, as a way to set the stage for the group topic you are introducing.

Copyright © 2016 Judith Belmont. *150 More Group Therapy Activities & TIPS*, www.belmontwellness.com. All rights reserved.

It's All in Our Perceptions

THEORY

These activities are some of my favorites that I use at the beginning of group sessions. They **introduce CBT principles that reinforce the notion that our take on the world is filtered by our perceptions**.

The demonstrations *show* that perceptions are powerful in determining our take on reality. By thinking more flexibly, we can change our perceptions, which in turn changes our world. When we change the way we look at the world, we change our lives. Demonstrations are much more effective than words alone.

IMPLEMENTATION

Introduce the concept that our world is filtered by our perceptions, and often our disturbing feelings result from unhealthy ways of thinking and perceiving. Aside from life threatening situations like physical abuse, it's our take on a situation that disturbs us, not generally the situation itself. Even in 130 AD, Greek philosopher Epictetus is reported to have said, *"People are not disturbed by things, but by the view they take of them."*

You might share Wayne Dyer's quote, *"If you change the way you look at things, the things you look at change."*

Hand and Arm Folding Exercise - My favorite way to introduce groups to the power of perception and the importance of staying flexible in their perceptions is a very quick exercise that is a crowd pleaser. I use it with every group and workplace wellness training and it never fails to enlighten people.

Directions:
Clasp your fingers so that your fingers interlock. Which thumb is on top?
In a group situation, about half have their left thumb on top and half the right, regardless of right or left-handedness. Note what is natural for some is not natural for another. This represents our perceptions - we think people see things the same way and by this "hands on" exercise we realize this is not true!

Now shift your fingers in the opposite way (make sure all fingers are clasped differently, not just the thumbs). How does it feel?

Common responses are "weird, strange, or uncomfortable." However, for some people it is effortless and natural! Thus, this "hands on" exercise serves as a metaphor for how we need to shift our thinking just so slightly in order to be able to change our perceptions. This is also a good exercise when addressing the concept of accepting differences in others. The exercise demonstrates that people don't always think like you, we all do things differently, and what is natural for some of us is not natural for others.

An advanced version of this is to have group members fold their arms, and this often makes even a greater impact since folding arms with the other arm on top feels very awkward for most, even though for about half of the group it will be most natural.

 Copyright © 2016 Judith Belmont. *150 More Group Therapy Activities & TIPS*, www.belmontwellness.com. All rights reserved.

We See What We Look For - Have group members look around the room and look at everything that is blue. Then have them close their eyes and tell you everything that they saw in red! You will hear groans because once they look for certain things; they do not pay attention to what else is around.

Practicing mindfulness helps people be more open to their surroundings and the present moment. All too often we ignore what is around us, living inside our own heads and pre-occupied with what we are thinking, thus limiting good observational skills and present awareness.

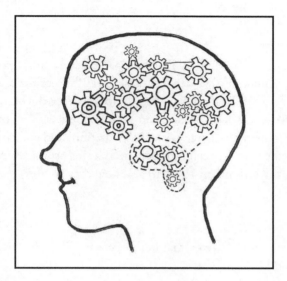

You might make the point that our perceptions filter our reality and reinforce some of our unhealthy ways of thinking. For example, someone with low self-esteem will tend to interpret the benign comments of others as being judgmental, serving as evidence that they are not liked.

In TIP #29, I demonstrate another example of how it's all about our perceptions in a group snowflake activity. In this activity, everyone listens to the same instructions on how to fold and cut a piece of paper, and all the snowflakes that result come out different!

PROCESSING

These few favorite perception-altering activities are great demonstrations that are quick and impactful and bring home the point that it's all in our perceptions! Use these exercises as a starting point to discuss how becoming more aware of various perceptions and personal differences can actually help us be more accepting and less judgmental of others.

These activities are good for the beginning of sessions, since they highlight the importance of thinking flexibly and will set the stage for starting off the group with an open mind.

Copyright © 2016 Judith Belmont. *150 More Group Therapy Activities & TIPS*, www.belmontwellness.com. All rights reserved.

Choices in a Jar

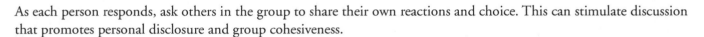

THEORY

This activity is directly taken from a great product by Free Spirit Publishing that I purchased online called *Choices in a Jar*. Although generally designed for children, this activity is also great for teens and adults. This jar includes 101 small cards which offer two alternatives and an individual picks the choice they like the best. Using *Choices in a Jar* encourages creativity, flexible thinking, self-discovery, self-disclosure and group cohesiveness. This is a great tool for the beginning stage of a group. People get to express themselves in hypothetical situations and make choices of two alternative concepts, some realistic and some imaginary (the concepts can be quite entertaining as well as therapeutic). Group members **learn about each other by learning what is important to them** and how they think.

IMPLEMENTATION

Introduce the Choices in a Jar to the group by saying that in this jar you will pick cards that offer two alternative choices, and pick the one you like the best and explain why.

Would you rather:

- *Always lose or never play?*
- *Be really bored or super stressed out?*
- *Always be loved or always be right?*
- *Live 200 years in the future or 200 years in the past?*
- *Know it all or have it all?*
- *Not be able to talk or not be able to hear for one day?*

One by one, have group members pick from the jar and explain their choices.

As each person responds, ask others in the group to share their own reactions and choice. This can stimulate discussion that promotes personal disclosure and group cohesiveness.

For an alternative activity, provide small notecards to the group members and ask them to write their own examples of choices and put them in a jar. Then have members pick the cards that others have written.

PROCESSING

Free Spirit Publishing's cards in a jar are great to introduce therapeutic topics. These reasonably priced jars offer various therapeutic opportunities for whatever life skills focus you want to discuss with your group. Other titles include: Healthy Me in a Jar, Temper Tamers In a Jar: Helping Kids Cool Off and Manage Anger, Chill Skills In a Jar: Anger Management Tips for Teens, and Feelings In a Jar.

Whatever topic you want to explore with your group, you can also make up your own notecards with choices, statements, things to act out, simple questions, etc. for a fun self-discovery and team building activity.

     Copyright © 2016 Judith Belmont. *150 More Group Therapy Activities & TIPS*, www.belmontwellness.com. All rights reserved.

The Many Ways I Am Precious

THEORY

Small shiny rocks and glass beads can represent the gem inside of all of us. These can be purchased inexpensively at craft stores. These **shiny gems can remind group members that we all are precious**, and the group situation is a great forum to discover each other's unique qualities. This activity helps set a positive tone for starting a group overall, or for any start of a group session.

IMPLEMENTATION

Use shiny craft stone gems of different colors that are inexpensively bought from craft superstores in multicolored packs.

At the first meeting, this can be one of the introductory exercises for group members to introduce themselves to the rest of the group.

Ask the group members to think about what is special about them, and take turns sharing answers with the rest of the group.

You might use this exercise when introducing names at the very beginning, in which each group member goes around and says their name and at least two reasons why they are special.

Make the point that real gemstones, including diamonds, are no more precious than human beings, no matter what the value - even if we forget that sometimes, or others do not treat us that way.

PROCESSING

This is a short, simple but powerful exercise for the first group meeting or the beginning of a weekly session. It starts things off on a high note by helping people think positively about themselves and others. Make the point that self-love is not being conceited or selfish, but about recognizing your specialness. Self-love is an important foundation for loving and being healthy to others. This activity will offer an opportunity to introduce group members to the importance of self-compassion, which entails being kind and accepting of oneself instead of being self-critical and judgmental.

Copyright © 2016 Judith Belmont. *150 More Group Therapy Activities & TIPS*, www.belmontwellness.com. All rights reserved.

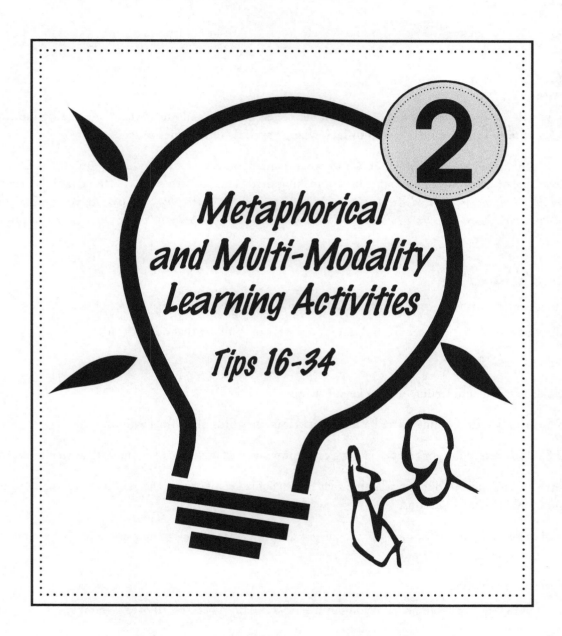

2

*Metaphorical
and Multi-Modality
Learning Activities*

Tips 16-34

Using Metaphors from Daily Life

THEORY

In this tip we will explore how everyday objects can be used as props in and out of the group. **Using familiar objects from everyday life to improve insight and unlock change appeals to all types of learners.**

Metaphors are frequently used in CBT, DBT and other contemporary orientations. DBT author Dr. Lane Pederson, writes of the value of using metaphor and stories in making therapeutic points. He uses this adage as an example, *"You can't control the winds but you can adjust your sails."* As Pederson writes, *"Metaphors facilitate learning, create a memorable visual, and are usually well received by clients as they communicate a personally relatable point in a non-confrontational manner."*

IMPLEMENTATION

Make the following points with your group. Metaphors in therapy, as in life, are so powerful because they:

- Allow us to shift our perspective and unlock old ways of thinking that do not work.

- Help us think flexibly.

- Evoke emotion, and feelings are the key to change.

- Help us understand things better because metaphors use words plus visualizations.

- Offer us increased insight by associating a concept with an example that we understand well in everyday life.

- Serve as reminders in our everyday life that helps clients keep positive and reinforce the therapeutic concepts and insights between sessions.

Metaphorical items as *therapeutic touchstones:* Giving group members the props to take home can be extremely beneficial to help keep in mind therapeutic points.

Here are some of my favorites:

- **A Toy Bowling Pin -** to make sure you stay assertive and don't get bowled over—and if you do get knocked down, get right back up!

- **A Toy Soldier -** reminds you to be brave and fight for what you believe in!

- **A Small Angel -** to remind you that there is hope and you are not alone.

- **A Hershey Kiss -** reminds group members of the importance of love and kindness and of giving "kisses" to others - and oneself!

 Copyright © 2016 Judith Belmont. *150 More Group Therapy Activities & TIPS*, www.belmontwellness.com. All rights reserved.

- **An Eraser** - reminds you that it's okay to make mistakes!

- **A Pencil or Pen** - can remind you to write yourself a happy life story!

- **A Small Bouncing Ball** - demonstrates the stress resilient personality that can bounce back!

- **A Marble** - in case you feel like you are losing your marbles, here is a spare!

- **A Button** - to remind you that no one can push your buttons!

- **A Dice** - reminds you that things happen that are out of our control, but we still can enjoy the game of life!

- **A Small Seashell** - to remind you of peaceful days on the beach.

- **A Little Pearl-like Object** - to remind you that you hold pearls of wisdom, and that wisdom often results from challenge and adversity like the process of irritation that results in creating a pearl.

- **A Bandage** - to help you heal and soothe your hurts.

- **A Sticky Note** - with a note to yourself on it, to remind yourself how special you are!

- **A Crayon** - to put more color into your world!

- **A Balloon** - to remind you to "lighten up!"

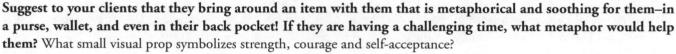

Can you and your clients add to this list?

Suggest to your clients that they bring around an item with them that is metaphorical and soothing for them–in a purse, wallet, and even in their back pocket! If they are having a challenging time, what metaphor would help them? What small visual prop symbolizes strength, courage and self-acceptance?

Another variation using metaphorical items is to bring in some household items that are larger, such as kitchen utensils (whisk, spatula, kitchen timer, etc). Put them in a bag or box, and have group members take turns pulling out an item and sharing a metaphorical meaning for the object they pick. This activity helps increase flexibility in thinking while having some fun at the same time!

PROCESSING

There is tremendous value in using metaphors to help group members think creatively and help learn new life skills. Giving time for processing and sharing metaphorical ideas will be one of the most effective tools you will use in helping clients gain valuable life skills.

Copyright © 2016 Judith Belmont. *150 More Group Therapy Activities & TIPS*, www.belmontwellness.com. All rights reserved.

Tip #17

Making a Calming Box

THEORY

Expanding upon the metaphorical toolkit idea, this activity gives group members the opportunity to create a tangible calming box. Using actual objects that serve to distract and self-soothe are great for both children and adults in times of distress. **It is one thing to think about something, but another to provide an alternate activity or tangible soothing touchstone.** Tangible objects are especially helpful in times of emotional upset to give immediate comfort and can serve as a distraction, as well as offering alternative activities.

IMPLEMENTATION

Supply boxes for each group member, or have them bring in their own. Boxes can be purchased reasonably at craft supply stores and even a dollar store. Small shoeboxes can also be used.

Introduce the activity by saying that in times of anger or any other emotional distress, having tangible reminders of life skills learned in the group will help them control their anger or other intense emotions.

Have a variety of objects on a table in the middle of the room, and go over with the group how these items can help soothe them. This can be a fun brainstorming activity, as there are no right or wrong answers.

Examples include:

- **Deck of Cards, Crossword Puzzles or Sudoku** – Rather than being just symbolic, these objects in the box can provide alternate activities to cope with upsetting events.

- **Stress Ball** – Serves as reminder that a stress ball is like a stress resilient personality - it retains its shape, it is soft, it has no rough edges and it always bounces back – and it feels good to squeeze!

- **A Hershey Kiss** – Reminds us being kind is more important than to be right and is yummy to eat!

- **Glitter Calming Jar** – A glitter calming jar, made up of water, glitter and glue, can be great resource to help calm and settle our minds while the glitter settles to the bottom slowly after the jar is shaken (many recipes can be found on the internet).

- **A Journal** – Having a "go to" place to write out our thoughts in times of crises can help us stay calm and process emotions in a healthy way. It also helps to look over past entries to develop a healthy perspective.

- **A Smiley Sticker** – Helps us remember to stay positive and optimistic and look at the brighter side of a situation.

- **Small Toy Kaleidoscope** – Watch the colors change and turn. It can be very calming!

- **Bubbles** – Encourages deep breathing while blowing bubbles and watching them disappear.

 Copyright © 2016 Judith Belmont. *150 More Group Therapy Activities & TIPS*, www.belmontwellness.com. All rights reserved.

- **Pinwheel** – Helps to focus on our breath as we blow slowly to turn the wheel by blowing slowly

- **Small Play Dough** – Good sensory outlet that you can mold and shape

- **Notecards with Pencils and Crayons** – Group members can draw some other reminders that have meaning or them, or even write some calming messages to themselves which basically serves as coping cards.

- **Decorative Note** – If time allows, you can have magazines, scissors and glue to decorate the box and even their notecards.

Encourage them to find other objects for their boxes when they go home that can offer them more resources when they need to "calm down."

Calming Boxes for Kids

When making calming boxes with children, you can use the following ideas to help children reflect on what they need to soothe themselves in times of distress. This will help them self-soothe in times of emotional arousal instead of acting out or acting impulsively.

Here are some ideas of things you might find calms kids down:

- **Personal photos** – as a baby, family members, friends and /or pets
- **An activity book** – word games, brainteasers, or Sudoku
- **A healthy snack** – like a granola bar or piece of fruit
- **Paper and pencil** – to write down thoughts
- **A favorite book**
- **Legos** – to build something
- **A bottle of bubbles** – to help breath deeply and slowly
- **A kaleidoscope** – to watch the changing design and embrace change
- **A glitter calming jar** – shake it up, and watch it settle
- **A balloon** – to blow up, tie and watch it float in the air
- **A stress ball** – to squeeze and bounce
- **A stuffed animal** – to hug
- **A deck of cards** – to play games like memory and solitaire

PROCESSING

During this activity, encourage sharing of ideas among group members. Sharing ideas of what is soothing can be quite therapeutic in itself. At the end of the project, have members share with the group what they chose to put in their boxes, and discuss how their items will be used in times of distress. Periodically ask for feedback in subsequent group sessions on how they are using their calming boxes.

Copyright © 2016 Judith Belmont. *150 More Group Therapy Activities & TIPS*, www.belmontwellness.com. All rights reserved.

Tip #18

The Power of Visualizations and Demonstrations

THEORY

Visualizations can be considered powerful metaphorical demonstrations. Visualizations make therapeutic points to represent a therapeutic concept. Along with metaphors, freely use visualizations and demonstrations in your groups. Group processing through talking is auditory, but by involving other types of learning, such as visual learning or kinesthetic learning, you can make more of an impact and make it more memorable. For example, watching the news on TV with the visuals of the story often makes more of an impact than listening to the radio and only hearing about it.

Some people are more **visual learners and remember a point more when they are SHOWN rather than when they are TOLD**. Cognitive therapy, dialectical behavior therapy, acceptance and commitment therapy, and impact therapy are all examples of modalities that heavily rely on "hands on" learning. Some of the examples below are just a tip of the iceberg of how to make some therapeutic points memorable.

IMPLEMENTATION

This is a representative sampling of how to use visual demonstrations to create life skills learning:

Impact Therapy founder, Dr. Ed Jacobs and his associate, Dr. Christine Schimmel (*Impact Therapy: The Courage to Counsel*) liberally use visualizations in their therapy techniques. They use simple diagrams and images from everyday life to teach important therapeutic points that truly make an "impact."

For example, to demonstrate unhealthy boundaries between a mother and son, they draw a simple diagram of overlapping circles. One circle represents the mother and the other the son, and the circles overlapping represent the invasion of personal boundaries and enmeshment between the child and parent.

They then draw separate circles right next to one another, showing healthy boundaries in which mother and son respect one another's personal boundaries.

———— • ————

Another example of a visualization used by Jacobs and Schimmel is when they use a shaken soda bottle to help clients visualize what happens when a person lets anger build up without healthy expression. Too much "bottled-in" emotion without healthy expression can make someone explode, just like in the case of the soda bottle that is shaken and then uncapped. Using an actual soda bottle, having the clients shake it or watching it be shook, can make quite an impact as they experience what happens when feelings are literally "bottled in." It can get a bit messy uncorking a bottle inside after it is shaken, but uncorking it outside can certainly make quite a memorable impact!

———— • ————

 Copyright © 2016 Judith Belmont. *150 More Group Therapy Activities & TIPS*, www.belmontwellness.com. All rights reserved.

Dale Carnegie recalls one of his most memorable experiences in school was when his teacher brought the students to the science lab sink and pushed over a container of milk and yelled "No use crying over spilled milk."

———— • ————

A drop of food coloring in a clear glass of water is useful to demonstrate the power of one negative thought to literally color your mind and your view of the world. Use many colors and show how the water gets dark and discolored, with too many negative thoughts.

———— • ————

To demonstrate the problem with denial or resistance in dealing with reality that can not be changed, use the example of a beach ball in a small tub of water - when you push the ball down, it keeps on springing back up!

———— • ————

To demonstrate the fragility of relationships, I bring in a few eggs - one is hard boiled and the other raw. For a more potent multi-sensory educational experience, I pass them both around rather than merely explain, and make the point of how careful everyone is passing the eggs around so they would not break. However, often people treat others like they are "hard boiled" and treat a raw egg better than they treat a real person! I then break the raw egg on a plastic tarp and emphasize the point that, just like Humpty Dumpty could not be put back together again, if you are not careful, some relationships can be damaged irreparably. *I call this activity treating someone as good as an egg!*

PROCESSING

Leave enough time at the end of the session to process how the group members felt about the visualizations that were used during the session, and brainstorm how using visualizations can help remember important therapeutic points. How can these visualizations make them better able to control impulsive behavior in times of extreme stress and how can they use the visualizations to remember important life lessons?

Make the point that advertisers spend billions of dollars a year using visuals to sell their products. How can they use the power of visualizations to help them stay focused on their personal therapeutic goals?

Copyright © 2016 Judith Belmont. *150 More Group Therapy Activities & TIPS*, www.belmontwellness.com. All rights reserved.

Are You More Like a Mentos® Mint—Or a Diet Cola?

Tip #19

THEORY

Using familiar items in this very dramatic activity makes an impact and will not be easily forgotten!

IMPLEMENTATION

This activity uses Mentos® mints and Diet Coke® or other sodas. Both of them seem to be quite mild mannered types of food, but when they are put together – watch out!

Do this demonstration outside or in a place that has a plastic tarp to limit the mess.

Using a bottle of diet cola, twist off the cap, and put in one or two Mentos.

When the ingredients of both items are put together there is a chemical reaction that causes a very impressive eruption!

This is a great visualization for demonstrating that when you have a catalyst in a situation, it can be explosive!

PROCESSING

These are some questions you can ask the group: *Are they more like a Mentos – an instigator – or are they more like a diet cola – someone who is easily triggered? Do they get explosive when triggered? Do they react to other's instigations? Or are they more like milk, refusing to let a catalyst trigger them into an explosion?* This demonstration is fun while meaningful and will likely lead to animated discussion.

NOTE: There are numerous demonstrations of adding a Mentos to diet cola and other sodas on YouTube.

 Copyright © 2016 Judith Belmont. *150 More Group Therapy Activities & TIPS*, www.belmontwellness.com. All rights reserved.

Paper Folding Exercise

THEORY

Demonstrations that emphasize therapeutic points are more powerful than just talking about the point without the visualization. **People learn more when they can experience using more senses than just hearing.** Furthermore, if they do the activity themselves, they learn more by "doing" than just watching. This paper folding exercise is an adaptation of author Debra Burdick's paper folding exercise in her mindfulness book, *Mindfulness Skills for Kids and Teens*.

IMPLEMENTATION

Pass out a blank piece of paper to each group member.

Ask them to fold it lengthwise or sideways, pressing down to accentuate the crease. Then have them repeat this to have 2 or 3 more folds again pressing on each crease.

Have them open up the paper and notice the creases, and then refold along the same lines.

Author Debra Burdick makes the point that it is easier to refold the same fold than start a new one, illustrating how "our neural pathways are 'worn' into the brain." She uses the example of learning to tie shoes. It becomes easier with practice once the pathways are already there. She makes the point that learning something for the first time takes more effort and, in the case of mindfulness, practicing mindfulness regularly will help people be more proficient at it.

Burdick makes the further point with this exercise that if we get stuck in negative patterns of thinking, it is easier for our neural pathways to go there again, which makes us stuck in negative interpretations. We need to practice looking at things in a fresh way to change the automatic pathways.

This demonstration can be a useful for a discussion of CBT principles addressed in the fourth chapter.

After this discussion, a follow-up activity is to pass out another piece of blank paper and have group members write some positive thoughts and choices that they want to practice, and for each point fold the paper once. This symbolizes making new neural pathways of positive choices and thoughts.

PROCESSING

The effectiveness of this demonstration is in the processing of the points made above. Have members personalize and express these points in the group, getting support and ideas of how to make changes by new practices. Exercises like these emphasize the importance of processing new skills to change our habits, and offers hope that we all can change our habits and automatic pathways with conscious intention.

Copyright © 2016 Judith Belmont. *150 More Group Therapy Activities & TIPS*, www.belmontwellness.com. All rights reserved.

Tip #21

Make an Impact!

THEORY

Impact Therapy is a creative counseling orientation developed by Ed Jacobs, Ph.D. and expanded upon by collaborators such as Christine J. Schimmel, Ed.D. and Danie Beaulieu, Ph.D. **Impact Therapy offers a multi-sensory approach to therapy**, with roots in Gestalt Therapy, Transactional Analysis, as well as Albert Ellis' Rational Emotive Therapy. Underlying Impact Therapy is the understanding that change happens when clients are involved kinesthetically. Impact Therapy uses props and metaphors liberally, along with visualizations and demonstrations, to unlock learning and insight. Both therapist and clients are active in this experiential model of treatment. The techniques of Impact Therapy fit in perfectly well in this section on multi-sensory learning.

IMPLEMENTATION

This TIP offers a sampling of some examples of props used in Impact Therapy's multi-sensory approach:

- **Use of a White Board** - A white board (or flip chart) is used in most group sessions to illustrate and demonstrate points. Using a board helps group members visualize through diagrams and drawings, making more of an impact than using words alone.

- **Bottle of Soda** - This demonstration shows that when we do not give ourselves time to cool off we can explode. Shake a bottle of soda and ask what will happen if it is open. Of course, it will fizzle and spray all over. Just like our anger, if we do not allow time to let it settle and if we react impulsively, we will be like that bottle of shaken soda.

- **Styrofoam Cup** - When addressing self-esteem issues, punch holes in a styrofoam cup to show how our negative thoughts can punch holes in self-esteem. This prop can help group members visualize and then share with one another what punches holes in their self-esteem.

- **Weights** - To help dramatize an issue of being weighed down, literally have weights that group members can hold to enact and dramatize the thoughts and behaviors that weigh them down.

- **Piece of Plexiglas** - This can be used as a shield between two people to emphasize the point that no one has a direct line into your emotions. Each person alone has control over their feelings.

- **Pieces of String or Rope** - Ask your group members if, when they are angry, how long is their fuse before they react? Have various lengths of string or rope and have group members pick one to symbolize their fuse. Have them brainstorm how they can lengthen their fuse.

 Copyright © 2016 Judith Belmont. *150 More Group Therapy Activities & TIPS*, www.belmontwellness.com. All rights reserved.

- **Child's Chair** - Instead of just talking about deep-seated issues, using a child's chair in group therapy will make it more real by allowing members to actually visualize and even address the little child within them.

- **Visual Diagrams** - Impact therapy makes use of diagrams on a white board or flip chart to illustrate points. For example, in addressing enmeshment of a mother and son, Jacobs and Schimmel draw 2 circles that are overlapping, and then draw two separate circles of healthy boundaries.

- **An Extra Chair** - Extra chairs are used often in Impact Therapy to represent to clients significant people in their lives. Even if the person chosen is not alive, there can still be a conversation enacted to work out deep-seated issues. The chair can also represent the irrational thoughts that clients need to challenge. In this case, group members are encouraged to change seats as they address and dispute their irrational self-talk, going back and forth between the chairs as they enact the two ways of thinking.

PROCESSING

In their book, *Group Counseling: Strategies and Skills*, Jacobs and Schimmel emphasize that the processing of any activity will determine the effectiveness of the technique. They see activities as merely a catalyst for discussion so the technique is not an end in itself. An activity in itself will not have the impact and meaningfulness if the processing of the activity is inadequate. They caution leaders to leave plenty of time to process an activity, and cite one of the major mistakes in leading groups is that the therapist does not leave enough time for processing, spending too much time on the exercise itself.

Copyright © 2016 Judith Belmont. *150 More Group Therapy Activities & TIPS*, www.belmontwellness.com. All rights reserved.

Effective Use of Metaphors in the ACT Theory

THEORY

Acceptance and Commitment Therapy (ACT) relies heavily on the use of metaphors to bring about therapeutic change. ACT is based on the idea that pain in life is inevitable and instead of fighting inevitable pain, **acceptance strategies can help clients make peace with it and detach from the intensity of the pain**. The use of metaphors helps clients conjure images of their unhealthy ways of thinking and this visualization helps them become more empowered. The following are a few of the popular uses of metaphors in ACT to help clients use metaphorical visualization to heal and move closer towards their life goals.

IMPLEMENTATION

ACT founder Stephen Hayes uses metaphorical visualizations to help clients learn the process of *cognitive defusion*, one of the cornerstones of ACT. *Cognitive defusion* is the act of objectifying your thoughts and "de-fusing" your irrational ways of thinking from your automatic thought processes.

An example of *cognitive defusion* is to replace the thought "I am a failure" with the thought that "I am having the thought that I am a failure." The latter helps individuals **be more objective about their thoughts rather than identify with them**.

The following are some of the popular metaphorical visualizations developed by Hayes:

Quicksand – When you struggle to get out of quicksand you sink in deeper. When you try to stop and resist your thoughts, they often make it worse. In ACT, he instructs clients to be more accepting of life's inevitable struggles and figuratively spread out in the quicksand, not resist it. Paradoxically, the less they resist, the less they sink in the quicksand. As the saying goes, *"What you resist will persist!"*

Passengers on the Bus – Clients imagine that they are driving a bus, and the cranky passengers represent their irrational and negative thoughts that sidetrack the driver from his goal. Instead of listening and getting sidetracked by these angry passengers (i.e. negative thoughts), the bus driver does not stop the bus or take the bus in the wrong direction. Rather, the driver keeps on driving towards a goal of living a more positive and healthier life, and commit themselves to stop getting sidetracked and manipulated by the behavior of others.

Thought Train – Ask clients to imagine a train is passing by, as they watch from a bridge, and each boxcar has a worry or negative thought written on it. Watching the train go by rather than getting on the train is an example of *cognitive defusion*. In essence, **instead of looking *from* your thoughts, you are looking *at* them**.

 Copyright © 2016 Judith Belmont. *150 More Group Therapy Activities & TIPS*, www.belmontwellness.com. All rights reserved.

Leaves Floating on a Stream – Clients imagine sitting by a stream and imagining themselves getting their thoughts out of their mind and on to the leaves that are floating on the stream. Using visualizations, instruct group members to put all their negative thoughts on these leaves and then watch them float downstream and out of sight. Instead of keeping the thoughts inside their heads, they can imagine how to *de-fuse* their thoughts and be more objective and detached.

The Yellow Jeep – This metaphor shows that when you resist thoughts, you will think of them more. In this exercise instruct clients to think of a yellow jeep and then tell them to stop. Of course, that image is hard to shut off, and clients will certainly be more likely to imagine a yellow jeep than they had before the exercise. This will help people stop resisting obtrusive thoughts and become more accepting of their pain and their thoughts, although with more detachment.

A Beach Ball – Resisting reality and ignoring one's issues is like pushing a beach ball into water, and having it pop up when you let go. This demonstrates that you can only suppress your thoughts and feelings for so long.

PROCESSING

Processing these images as a group is just as important of using the images and visualizations themselves. For example, ask group members how they felt putting their thoughts on the leaves and watching them disappear. How can they incorporate these visualizations in their everyday life? What thoughts are they "fused" with and how can they develop more objectivity and acceptance of inevitable struggles? How can they become more accepting of things out of their control, without giving up and feeling like their efforts are futile? Helping group members use these lessons and personalize to their own life situations will help them apply metaphors to their own lives.

Copyright © 2016 Judith Belmont. *150 More Group Therapy Activities & TIPS*, www.belmontwellness.com. All rights reserved.

Using Movie Clips to Educate and Heal

THEORY

Cinema-therapy can be a powerful tool in therapy, **as it can teach important life lessons in a way that evokes insights and emotion** through watching clips from movies. For every group topic and theme, you can find a movie clip on the internet - especially on YouTube - to support and encourage open discussion, insight and interaction. MovieClips on YouTube in particular is helpful in finding short clips to make your point. A short clip, rather than the whole movie, is generally sufficient and more to the point. YouTube has made it very easy to see little clips of movies that evoke an emotional response and make a therapeutic point. The power of movies is unlimited in its potential.

IMPLEMENTATION

There are certain film clips that I personally find very impactful to make certain therapeutic points. Here are some of my favorites:

Ordinary People – This is a very intense psychological movie about a family that is torn apart after the boating death of one son, in the aftermath of the other son's suicide attempt. One of my favorite scenes are the one in which the mom (Mary Tyler Moore) and son (Timothy Hutton) are outside talking about the dog next door, and the more the mom gets defensive in response to her son asking why they could never get a pet, the less she was able to "listen" and the more they talked AT each other and OVER each other. This is a great scene to depict what the difference between hearing and active listening. It is also a poignant scene depicting how the son's crazy behavior is triggered by invalidation and unhealthy family dynamics with an emotionally crippled mother.

Any Given Sunday – Al Pacino's memorable speech to a football team about how success is gained in inches is very moving and inspirational, and will serve to evoke emotion in the group to focus on how every inch we take means something. It makes the point that we can find purpose and meaning in our everyday efforts in life. After all, achieving greatness in life is measured not in touchdowns but in our smaller, everyday actions to pursue our goals.

Everybody's Fine – Robert Deniro plays a father who is well-meaning but very strict and judgmental with his children. There are quite a few scenes that group members will likely relate to in pinpointing the complex relationships between children and their parents. An exquisitely moving scene depicts DeNiro and his four adult children, played by children instead of adults, as he addresses each one about why they kept things from him. They explain in various ways they needed to avoid his disappointment and pretend that "everything's fine." Group members can often relate to the dynamics and tension shown in the family, gaining insight to a well-meaning but demanding parent, in which real issues in families are not addressed but kept underneath the surface in a collusion of denial to avoid judgement and criticism.

Rocky V – Sylvester Stallone has quite a few memorable clips in this movie, but I especially like his speech below. This message can be very inspirational for group members who have felt knocked down by life and need the motivation to keep on being hopeful and fighting back.

 Copyright © 2016 Judith Belmont. *150 More Group Therapy Activities & TIPS*, www.belmontwellness.com. All rights reserved.

"You, me or nobody is going to hit as hard as life. But it ain't about how hard you're hit, it's about how hard you can get hit and keep moving forward, how much you can take and keep moving forward. That's how winning is done! Now if you know what you're worth then go out and get what you're worth. But ya gotta be willing to take the hits, and not pointing fingers saying you ain't where you wanna be because of him, or her, or anybody! Cowards do that and that ain't you! You're better than that!"

PROCESSING

Using movie clips can provide many opportunities for discussion and make a significant impact. Cinema-therapy has an advantage over more traditional therapy in that one can experience and visualize concepts, and be emotionally triggered through memorable media. Watching even a few minute video clip and then processing it together can be quite eye opening. By processing the takeaways from the film clips, group members can help one another heal as well as using the lessons of the movie clip to heal themselves.

Copyright © 2016 Judith Belmont. *150 More Group Therapy Activities & TIPS*, www.belmontwellness.com. All rights reserved.

Tip #24

Using Songs to Educate and Heal

THEORY

Most people enjoy music, and music evokes emotions and imagery that often the spoken word cannot do alone. Using the power of music within the counseling group can be effective in helping members learn important life skills concepts.

IMPLEMENTATION

There are many ways to use music in groups. Here are some ideas which can make quite an impact in various ways:

- You can use music as background for a relaxation exercise or drawing activity.
- Have each group member take turns each week playing a song that is meaningful for them. They can be in charge of processing it with the group.
- You could also play a short clip of an irrational song to emphasize that some songs—even the ones that sound so romantic—are actually illogical, unhealthy and codependent!

"I Can't Stop Loving You" by Ray Charles

I make the point that using the word *can't* is irrational, and is also contradictory as the next sentence is "I made up my mind." The real sadness is this irrational thinking and the victim mentality. I then ask them to translate into a healthier message: "I am having a hard time being able to stop loving you!" Maybe it would not make a gold record, but it would be so much healthier!

"You Make Me So Very Happy" by Blood, Sweat, and Tears

The problem with this song is if one's happiness depends on someone else, others then have the power to cause misery and even suicidal behavior. A translation: "I am very happy when I am with you" or "my life is so much happier with you." I point out the difference that you are still in control of your happiness without being codependent!

It is fun to brainstorm other songs that they know. Other good "victim songs" are, "There Goes My Everything", by Englebert Humperdinck, which shows "all or nothing" thinking that one's self worth is only based on others, and "Because of You," by Kelly Clarkson in which she blames her parents and upbringing on all her problems now.

Can you and your clients think of more?

You can also use positive songs to play and discuss. For example, the "Greatest Love Of All" by Whitney Houston is a great song to address self-esteem.

PROCESSING

Using music to make therapeutic points, to develop insight, and to help clients gain insight and heal, can make quite an impact. Since so many people love music, incorporating music always makes for a fun and pleasant activity.

 Copyright © 2016 Judith Belmont. *150 More Group Therapy Activities & TIPS*, www.belmontwellness.com. All rights reserved.

Tip #25

Picture it!

THEORY

A group provides a perfect situation for self-expression within the context of a social milieu. Provide various opportunities for self-expression and creativity by incorporating drawing into your therapeutic toolbox. You don't have to be an art therapist to use art in groups, and group members do not need to be artistic. Rather, use of art is an experiential medium that allows for self expression for group members to express thoughts and feelings creatively.

IMPLEMENTATION

Supply your group with paper, crayons, pens, colored pencils. Let group members know this is a drawing activity for self-expression, not to prove artistic talent. There is no right or wrong way to express themselves - it can be realistic or abstract.

Have group members draw a picture, image, symbol or just colors representing:

- How they are feeling now
- Something of value and importance to them
- Their goals
- Something that describes them
- Their favorite activity
- Their view of the future
- An affirmation or mantra they can use to remind them of the lessons from the group
- How it feels to be them
- Someone or something that is meaningful to them
- Their relationship to others

You might have soft music on to serve as a relaxing background backdrop to the activity.

PROCESSING

Once they are finished drawing, have each member process the drawing and share what it represents. This act of sharing and processing is just as valuable as the activity itself. Drawing can provide a unique vehicle for self-disclosure and self-expression, while building group cohesiveness and gaining insights.

Copyright © 2016 Judith Belmont. *150 More Group Therapy Activities & TIPS*, www.belmontwellness.com. All rights reserved.

Using Metaphors to Illustrate Points

THEORY

In all my books, the use of metaphors and metaphorical life skills toolkits have been featured prominently, and they continue to be one of my most effective tools to teach life skills.

Using metaphors **keeps clients engaged and often invokes insight, positive emotion, smiles and even laughter**. Adding a visual image to a mental abstract concept will be more powerful than using just the words.

IMPLEMENTATION

For many of the activities that you do, think of props that will help make your point. Here are just a few examples, and the next few tips have more specific ideas of how to use metaphorical props to improve life skills.

Here are a few examples:

When talking about improving communication skills, show the group a **finger trap**. When people are in conflict trying to prove that they are right, they both pull and get stuck in the trap! To demonstrate this, I have one person take one side and I have my finger in the other, and when I walk and pull they get up and I lead them around. I make the point that when two people fight and try to prove they are right, they let the other people take control of them and their behavior, leading them around like a pony.

Miniature traffic signs can help remind us about lessons of improving relationships. For example: STOP reminds us to not be aggressive. The Yield sign reminds us to compromise and strive for a "win-win." The speed limit sign reminds us to set limits with others and be able to say "no." The use of these props help members learn to "obey the signs" in life and not just on the street!

An elastic band reminds group members of my demonstration on the topic of stress. I use an elastic band to represent stress - I show that stress can be positive and is desirable as long as it is pulled just enough so it does not "snap," and a limp rubber band represents boredom and lack of engagement. Being taut with elasticity represents the right life balance!

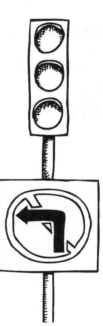

PROCESSING

I am always amazed at the variety of interpretations group members have of various metaphors. Learning from and sharing with others will increase everyone's ability to think "out of the box." Make the point that getting out of our problems often requires creative flexible thinking, so using metaphors and sharing creative ideas will increase everyone's ability to find new solutions to old problems.

To quote Einstein, *"We cannot solve our problems with the same thinking we used when we created them."*

 Copyright © 2016 Judith Belmont. *150 More Group Therapy Activities & TIPS*, www.belmontwellness.com. All rights reserved.

Assembling a Metaphorical Life Skills Toolkit

THEORY

Using metaphors in a life skills toolkit has been one of the most valuable activities I have done with therapy groups as well as workplace wellness groups. The beauty of this type of activity is that you can tailor the toolkit and the items to the purpose of the group or the theme of the session. Metaphors serve as tangible, visual reminders for life lessons.

IMPLEMENTATION

The following are types of toolkits that you might have for your groups, and some of the items will vary depending on the theme of the kit, although some metaphors would fit any kit. For example, a Hershey Kiss will remind people the importance of love and kindness, and sharing positive sentiments with others.

The following are ideas of life skills toolkit themes:

- The Happiness Toolkit
- The Life Skills Toolkit
- The Stress Management Toolkit
- The Substance Free Toolkit
- The Positive Living Toolkit
- The Relationship Toolkit
- The Anger Management Toolkit
- The Depression Relief Toolkit
- The Emotional Regulation Toolkit
- The Positive YOU Toolkit

To assemble a toolkit of metaphors, use plastic bags, paper bags, little buckets, or containers that you can get at a dollar store.

Example: **The Positive YOU Toolkit** – These are some items that I preassemble into bags for my wellness presentations for the following topics:

Be flexible and resilient in face of challenge

Lesson: Staying flexible and changing your perceptions will help you overcome obstacles.

Metaphorical suggestions:

- A bendable smiling person figurine - Stay flexible
- A small bouncing ball - Bounces back and goes in all different directions

Copyright © 2016 Judith Belmont. *150 More Group Therapy Activities & TIPS*, www.belmontwellness.com. All rights reserved.

Be a stress manager ... and not a stress carrier!

Lesson: Stress for success - use stress to motivate, not debilitate.

Metaphorical suggestions:

- An elastic band - I use the band to demonstrate positive and negative stress. Too much tension and you will snap it, but too little and it will be limp and lifeless.
- A stress ball - It is like the stress resilient personality. It bounces back, floats, rolls with the punches, retains its shape, and is soft.

Communicate assertively

Lesson: Use "I" Statements instead of "You" statements. Avoid rhetorical questions.

Metaphorical suggestions:

- A toy bowling pin - To make sure you stay assertive and don't get bowled over! And if you do get knocked down, get back upright!
- A finger trap - Don't get stuck in the trap of being aggressive and trying to prove you are right.

Use positive self -talk

Lesson: Our feelings are caused by our thoughts! No one makes us feel a certain way - we do!

Metaphorical suggestions:

- A toy magnifying glass - Be a thought detective!
- Smarties candies - Remember to be smart and stay rational.

Have an attitude of gratitude

Lesson: Choose kindness over being right.

Metaphorical suggestions:

- A Hershey Kiss® - Represents kindness and self-love. Spread positivity by giving kisses!
- A Hershey Hug® works too!

Group Toolkit

Lesson: Each person can assemble bags to represent lessons they learned from the group.

Metaphorical suggestions:

- Have people bring in their own metaphorical items for the group.
- Each person can print clip art of their favorite metaphor online and distribute to the group members.
- Have notecards handy so group members can draw their favorite metaphors.

PROCESSING

Assembling a metaphorical toolkit is a very impactful activity, and stimulates everyone's creative thinking. As you can see, there are many ways you can use the concept of the life skills toolkit, and you can adapt this metaphorical activity to any topic of your group.

Copyright © 2016 Judith Belmont. *150 More Group Therapy Activities & TIPS*, www.belmontwellness.com. All rights reserved.

The Practical Coping Skills Toolbox

THEORY

Sometimes people need practical tangible distractions to soothe and calm rather than metaphorical representations, and this toolbox fits the bill. For example, a real candy bar is certainly a lot tastier than a picture of one!

This toolkit would be an example of **an emotional regulation strategy of DBT, addressing the need to develop skills for increasing distress tolerance**. The group situation is a perfect forum to make up a Coping Skills Toolbox. The Coping Skills Toolbox limits the chance that self-destructive behavior, such as substance abuse or self-harm, which is seen as the only option in times of distress.

IMPLEMENTATION

Large colorful containers are ideal in making up Coping Skills Toolboxes. You can get them from a dollar store. The following are some examples of articles that group members might find soothing. Think of it like an emergency coping skills kit.

- A stuffed animal to hug
- A bottle of bubbles to blow out frustration
- Comics or joke books
- Book
- Scented candle
- Playing cards
- Notebook, journal or notecards to write out feelings
- Cards given to you from friends and family
- Calming oils to touch and smell
- Sudoku book
- Candy bar
- Stress ball
- Silly putty
- Yarn and needles for knitters

Have the group think of other examples of tangible items they can put in their Coping Skills Toolboxes and ask them to bring in other things from home for the next session to complete the project.

PROCESSING

Have group members take turns showing one another their Coping Skills Toolbox. In a group, people learn from one another and get some valuable ideas of coping skills from what fellow members have found successful.

Celebrating our Uniqueness with Snowflakes

THEORY

This activity uses the power of visualization with a hands-on activity that helps children and adults alike appreciate their uniqueness.

IMPLEMENTATION

Give paper, scissors, and colored pencils to each person.

To create a snowflake, have them fold the paper in half, and then fold again once or twice. Cut pieces around the edges or corners with a scissors. Unfold their paper to see their snowflake.

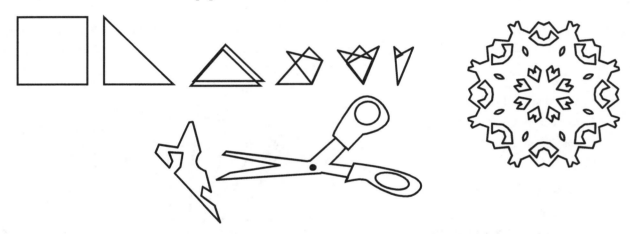

The group members can either write words, phrases or draw on their own snowflake and those of others in the group. For their own snowflake they can put how they are unique and special, and then can write on the snowflake of others (with their name in parenthesis) of what they appreciate about the other person's uniqueness.

Go around and have each group member display their creations, and share how just like the snowflake – where no two are alike – they are unique and special in their own ways.

PROCESSING

This simple activity/visualization makes the point that we are all unique and special. It can offer a celebration of sorts of each of our uniqueness. Hearing from others how they are unique, with the help of this creative activity, will help them be less likely to believe their negative self-talk.

Expressing Feelings Through Art

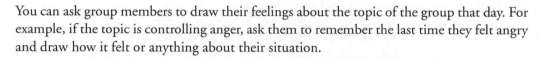

THEORY

Using art therapy techniques with children and adult groups can provide a wonderful opportunity to promote self-exploration and self-expression. **Artistic activities aid the process of personal self-discovery, growth and healing.**

IMPLEMENTATION

There are many ways you can incorporate art in your groups. Some group members will grunt at the thought of drawing as they feel they are not good at it, so reassure them that they can use words, abstract design, stick figures, or any method to express themselves without worrying about the quality of the art work. By setting the stage that it is not about the quality of the art, they will be less critical of their "work" and often find that they enjoy the process.

You can ask group members to draw their feelings about the topic of the group that day. For example, if the topic is controlling anger, ask them to remember the last time they felt angry and draw how it felt or anything about their situation.

You can use books that integrate CBT principles with art, such as *The CBT Art Activity Book* by Jennifer Guest. In this book, there are coloring and drawing activities with pertinent self-help topics, giving some structure to therapeutic drawing activities.

A popular activity for art therapists is to have group members create a mandala. The word mandala in Sanskrit means circle and is regarded as symbolizing unity and harmony. It is a spiritual symbol to help people get in touch with inner growth and healing. You can either provide a circle for each member by using a plate or compass, or use a more intricate mandala from the Internet that you can print out and have them color. There are also coloring books featuring various mandalas for adults and children alike that can be now found at gift shops and even supermarkets.

Ask group members to draw:

- What they like about themselves
- Their favorite things
- A self-portrait
- What love or happiness means to them
- Draw their goals and hopes

- A characteristic they like about themselves
- How they feel today
- Someone they admire
- What they learned in the session

PROCESSING

Creative activities such as expressive drawing can serve as a basis for great sharing and discussions. Have members go around and share their drawings and explain what it means to them. This self-disclosure helps group members develop more trust and cohesiveness with the others. They can learn more about others as well as themselves, and learn new ways to think about things by seeing the creative expressions of others.

Copyright © 2016 Judith Belmont. *150 More Group Therapy Activities & TIPS*, www.belmontwellness.com. All rights reserved.

Tip #31

Unleash Your Sunflower Power!

THEORY

A sunflower is a very powerful metaphor for growth, positive energy and transformation. To make this visualization come to life, bring in an actual or artificial sunflower.

IMPLEMENTATION

Who doesn't appreciate the beauty of a sunflower? The metaphor of the sunflower is introduced by making these points:

- Sunflowers grow tall, confident and strong, reflecting the warmth and energy from the sun.

- Even the huge head of the sunflower resembles the sun itself.

- As the sunflower grows tall and strong, it becomes more and more striking.

- The sunflower emerges from the dirt and needs the nutrients of the dirt to grow. In our lives, some of our own "dirt" and painful lessons in our life can provide the foundation for beautiful growth, just as the sunflower emerges bold and beautiful from the dirt.

- Similarly, as we bask in the warmth and positive energy of our own positive ways of thinking and emotional lightness, we grow more confident and stronger at our core.

- Just as sunflowers need to be planted in full sun, we as human beings do best and grow to our potential when we bask in positive ways of thinking and living.

Have the group members brainstorm other ideas using this metaphor.

Pass out the following activity to help show how members can grow.

PROCESSING

This activity provides learning on many levels. It is a springboard for self-discovery as well as self-disclosure. Make sure you leave enough time for everyone to share their sunflower drawings with the group.

 Copyright © 2016 Judith Belmont. *150 More Group Therapy Activities & TIPS*, www.belmontwellness.com. All rights reserved.

Activity

Unleash Your Sunflower Power!

In the image of the sunflower, fill in your examples of the following three parts:

THE DIRT – Write your difficult lessons, mistakes, adversity and challenges.

THE STEM – Write your values, characteristics, behaviors, and choices.

THE FLOWER – Write your hopes, goals, dreams, and aspirations.

Copyright © 2016 Judith Belmont. *150 More Group Therapy Activities & TIPS*, www.belmontwellness.com. All rights reserved.

Growing From your Roots

THEORY

Using the metaphor of a tree can **help group members visualize their roots, their values and what they need to grow**. Using metaphors from everyday life for important life lessons and self-exploration can provide a very meaningful experience that individuals are reminded of countless times in their day. What better image to use than a tree, which we all see in everyday life, no matter where we live?

IMPLEMENTATION

Introduce this activity asking the group to imagine a tree. Ask them to think of what this tree needs in order to grow tall and strong. Answers include water, nutrients, sun, air, nurturing environment, etc.

Make the point that all trees, like people, need good roots. In terms of people, our roots include the foundation from our families, friends and other relationships, education, lessons we learn, our values, and our morals.

The trunk represents one's strengths, healthy choices, habits and behaviors that arise from the roots, such as refraining from substance abuse, assertive communication, opening to others, asking for help, identifying rights, honesty, etc.

The leaves represent our goals, hopes, aspirations.

Ask them to use the following activity to fill in their own personal thoughts represented in the roots, the trunk and the leaves. How would they characterize their metaphorical roots, trunk and leaves?

When all have finished, have them take turns sharing their responses with the group.

PROCESSING

When group members share their work, look for both similarities and differences. Invite them to add to their trees based on hearing the responses of others, since by sharing we can learn from others. Using the analogy of the tree, ask them what happens when the roots and trunk images contain negative thoughts and behaviors that limit growth, such as aggressive behavior, irrational black and white thinking, conflict and substance abuse. In unhealthy environments, the tree will not grow big and strong.

 Copyright © 2016 Judith Belmont. *150 More Group Therapy Activities & TIPS*, www.belmontwellness.com. All rights reserved.

 **Activity** **Growing From Your Roots**

Using the tree as a metaphor:

Write in the root area of the tree what are the important elements of your own personal roots. What keeps you grounded? How do your relationships support you? What are your life lessons, values and morals to keep you grounded?

Write in the trunk area your strengths, healthy choices, habits and behaviors that arise from the roots, such as healthy communication, asking for help, and your other life choices that help you grow.

Write in the leaves your goals, hopes and aspirations.

Copyright © 2016 Judith Belmont. *150 More Group Therapy Activities & TIPS*, www.belmontwellness.com. All rights reserved.

Contain Your Worries in a Worry Doll!

THEORY

The idea of compartmentalizing your worries in an outside object, thereby releasing a person of their worry, is not new. Guatemalan Worry Dolls are small, colorful dolls that are quite popular with Guatemalans and tourists alike. The folklore behind these dolls is to help people (usually a child) **put their worries aside to go to sleep**. When the person wakes up in the morning, the worries do not return, as the doll has kept them. Parents in the Guatemalan culture often have their children make their own worry dolls, which underscores the healing powers of this visualization.

IMPLEMENTATION

Ask each group member to write down three worries they have. You might want to give them a few minutes to share their responses with a neighbor.

Give out a worry doll to each participant (These tiny dolls can be purchased inexpensively on the internet). Tell them the folklore of the worry doll and emphasize that containing worry is actually a psychological technique of compartmentalizing and objectifying worry.

You can be creative, especially with children, and have a ceremony in which they give their worries to their doll.

Help group members figure out ways they can use their doll at home to remind them that worry is in their control and can be contained.

You might have the group members write down the worries that they are giving to the doll.

Variation: You can also use a "worry box" to symbolize compartmentalizing and therefore controlling worry. Younger children especially enjoy decorating boxes.

PROCESSING

Using these dolls as metaphors for containing one's worries will appeal to children as well as adults. Since they can be purchased rather inexpensively online, these dolls will be a very meaningful metaphor to take home and use in a metaphorical toolkit. Follow up this TIP in later weeks to find out how the group members are using their worry dolls, and what are the worries that the dolls help them give up.

 Copyright © 2016 Judith Belmont. *150 More Group Therapy Activities & TIPS*, www.belmontwellness.com. All rights reserved.

Are You a Bucket Filler - or a Bucket Dipper?

THEORY

Using simple concepts from children's books can provide great metaphors for life skills learning for children and adults alike. My favorite example of this is the popular children's book, *New York Times* bestseller, *Have You Filled A Bucket Today?* by Carol McCloud. The premise of the book uses the **metaphor of a bucket that we all carry around invisibly, which needs to be filled with the kind acts of others and also towards yourself**. A smile, a good deed, a kind word, a kiss, a hug, helping someone, are all examples of bucket filling.

IMPLEMENTATION

Using the metaphor of a bucket, you can use the following worksheet to reinforce the importance of filling buckets instead of being a bucket dipper. A Bucket Dipper is a person who is unkind and takes away positive feelings with negative behavior, being inconsiderate, making rude comments, etc. When we have negative self-talk and undermine our sense of well-being, we also are serving as our own Bucket Dippers.

- With children, reading the book will help set the stage.

- With adults, mentioning the lessons of the book and having a copy on hand to show them will suffice.

- There are many other sequels to the book and depending on the population you might also use another book from the series.

- For follow up activities and handouts, refer to the bucket filler site to get many resources, activities ideas, etc. based on this concept. *http://bucketfillers101.com/bucket-lessons.php*

- Discuss with the group how the buckets are filled and how they are dipped into - make a list on the board.

Examples of Bucket Filling	Examples of Bucket Dipping
Kindness	Saying hurtful comments
Compliments	Criticizing
Being considerate	Being inconsiderate
Offering help	Being unhelpful
Expressing positive emotion	Being rude
Sharing	Not sharing
Hugging and kissing	Hitting, punching

Copyright © 2016 Judith Belmont. *150 More Group Therapy Activities & TIPS*, www.belmontwellness.com. All rights reserved.

Have each member write on separate note cards something nice and positive about each person in the group and put it in their respective buckets.

I purchased a heart punch at a craft store for clients to write their compliments for each other on the hearts. This limits the time you need to spend cutting with scissors. You can also purchase flower and star punchers.

This can spur a discussion about compliments, and how nice it is to compliment someone and reward the positive.

Discuss the difference between real, quality compliments rather than superficial ones. A quality compliment says something about the person and what you appreciate about them, not focusing on the superficial such as "I like your shirt."

This can be a segway to talk about how to take compliments assertively. You might make the point that people with low self-esteem have a hard time taking compliments, and often take compliments non-assertively with some self-disparagement, poor eye contact, and might even talk the person out of the compliment! You might want to have a short exercise in which each group member compliments the next person with a "quality" compliment as described above and have members practice how to take compliments assertively, with good eye contact and showing self confidence.

> **The focus on bucket filling and giving and receiving compliments emphasizes the importance of kindness to self and others in building relationships and developing compassion towards self and others.**

We all have buckets that need to be filled with loving and caring, positive messages. We also carry buckets with negative messages when people say hurtful things to us or we say hurtful things to ourselves.

Ask the group if they tend to be bucket fillers or bucket dippers to themselves and to others. Many times people are much kinder to others than they are to themselves.

Have them reframe or replace any negative messages they carry. This bucket activity helps group members' focus on holding and carrying around positive thoughts, to fill their own buckets as well as those of others!

You might find it helpful to ask the group members what they need to say to themselves to fill their own buckets with kindness!

Use the accompanying activity worksheet to help group members learn practical ways they can be expert bucket fillers!

An interesting variation to the bucket theme is to have some flat rocks and markers along with the paper punched shapes. On the rocks instruct them to write negative thoughts about themselves and on the paper punched hearts and stars, etc. write positive messages about themselves. The negative thoughts on the heavy rocks symbolize how negative thoughts weigh us down and make our hearts heavy, whereas there is always room for more light hearted and less cumbersome positive messages.

PROCESSING

Processing with the group using real-life examples of bucket filling and bucket dipping is important to help them relate personally to this concept of the invisible bucket. While processing this activity, recognize that we all are worthy and deserving of love and kindness. Everyone is responsible for being kind to others as well as themselves, and not be a bucket dipper to themselves or others. Putting the actual rocks in a bucket will help group members feel the weight of their negative thoughts!

Copyright © 2016 Judith Belmont. *150 More Group Therapy Activities & TIPS*, www.belmontwellness.com. All rights reserved.

Today I Am Going to Be a Bucket Filler!

These are names of two people who have buckets I want to fill with kindness. These are the things I plan to do to fill their bucket with kindness and why I want to do this.

I am filling a kindness bucket for: _____

What I plan to express _____

What I plan to do _____

Why I want to do this _____

I am filling a kindness bucket for: _____

What I plan to express _____

What I plan to do _____

Why I want to do this _____

I will also fill my own bucket today as I think of positive thoughts about myself and will do something positive for myself.

They are: _____

My positive thought to myself is: _____

I will do something I will be proud of: _____

This is an example of a healthy choice I can make for myself: _____

_____

Communication Skills

Tips 35-64

3

Tip #35

Basic Human Rights

THEORY

When introducing the topic of assertive communication, it is good to lay the foundation that **we all are worthy of being treated with respect**. The denial of basic human rights often leads to low self-esteem, anxiety and a lack of self-compassion. Using a guided visualization to help accept their undeniable rights is very powerful in a group situation.

IMPLEMENTATION

Introduce the concept of basic human rights by making the point that all too often people do not feel they have a "right" to think or feel a certain way, and therefore are very judgmental of their own behaviors, thoughts and feelings.

Those with low levels of self-compassion hold a shame-based filter, which results in harshly judging themselves and doubting that they are as worthy as others. Even though we theoretically know we are all created equal, many people with a lack of self-compassion just don't have that loving feeling towards themselves. To add insult to injury, people who do not identify and stand up for their rights allow people to treat them disrespectfully, which reinforces their tendency to call themselves names and beat themselves up.

After the introduction, brainstorm on a flip chart or white board what are some of our universal basic human rights. Here are some examples:

- I have a right to say "no" without feeling guilty.

- I have a right to be treated with respect.

- I have a right to make my needs as important as others.

- I have a right to be accepting of my mistakes and failures.

- I have a right to not meet others expectations of me that are unreasonable.

- I have a right to set healthy boundaries and limits with others, even if they do not like it.

- I have a right to set limits with my employees and make them more accountable.

- I have a right to be assertive even if they do not like it.

- I have a right to ask for more help.

- I have a right to not be "superboss" who is loved and revered by all.

After making the list, ask group members to identify one right that they have difficulty accepting.

 Copyright © 2016 Judith Belmont. *150 More Group Therapy Activities & TIPS*, www.belmontwellness.com. All rights reserved.

Ask them to close their eyes for a short visualization. Ask them to imagine what life would be like if they had the one right that they have trouble accepting.

You might want to have soft music in the background during the guided imagery.

You can have them imagine writing this human right on a cloud or on an imaginary board in a peaceful place.

Be creative in using imagery to set a relaxing and peaceful backdrop for imagining that they have this very special, undeniable right.

The following are some things you might want to include in the guided imagery when they visualize one right they would like to work on accepting:

- *What would life be like if you accepted that undeniable human right - how would you feel differently about yourself?*

- *How would your life be different?*

- *How would you act differently if you believed in that basic human right?*

- *How would you be able to be more authentic and less the person you think others want you to be?*

Have them open up their eyes, and ask them what the right was that they had chosen, and how it felt when they gave themselves permission to have this unquestionable right.

PROCESSING

Much of the success of this activity is in the processing. This is especially powerful in a group situation, as they will learn as much from one another as they learned from their own experience in this exercise. It always strikes me how people find peace and hope through this guided imagery. This exercise helps those with a critical inner voice to feel more deserving of being treated respectfully and consequently feel happier and more respectful of themselves.

Copyright © 2016 Judith Belmont. *150 More Group Therapy Activities & TIPS*, www.belmontwellness.com. All rights reserved.

You Have A Right...
and A Responsibility

THEORY

After visualizing their basic human rights in the previous TIP, this is a good time to introduce the concept of **corresponding responsibilities to those rights**.

IMPLEMENTATION

Before giving the group the accompanying handout, it would be helpful to brainstorm on a board or flip chart the basic human rights we have, and then balance them with the corresponding responsibilities.

To start the group off, here are a few rights and corresponding responsibilities.

I have a right to:	I have a responsibility to:
Be treated respectfully	Treat all others respectfully
Feel my feelings without judgment	Accept the feelings of others without judgment, ridicule and blame
Be human and make mistakes	Not judge the mistakes of others

Asking each group member what is one right that is particularly difficult for them to accept can be quite helpful tailoring the lesson to their own personal lives. Follow this question up by asking the group which responsibility is also hard for them to accept in dealing with others. Parents and those in leadership positions all too often use their power to be demanding and judgmental of those they try to control. **Make the point that just because you are a parent or a boss, does not mean you have a right to be bossy!**

Use the following handout to give out to the group members so they can have a reminder of the importance of their basic human rights and their corresponding responsibilities.

PROCESSING

In creating the list and using the accompanying handout, point out that in everyday life we allow ourselves to be violated and violate others because we think they deserve it or that we deserve it. There is tremendous power in the group process in recognizing the rights we all have universally. Elicit from members how they either violate their own rights or rights of others without even being aware. This can be quite an eye opener for group members and sets the stage for learning healthy communication skills. Those who tend to be more aggressive will become more aware of their need to be respectful of others while being true to themselves.

 Copyright © 2016 Judith Belmont. *150 More Group Therapy Activities & TIPS*, www.belmontwellness.com. All rights reserved.

My Human Bill Of Rights ...
and Corresponding Responsibilities

I have a right to:

I have a responsibility to:

Be treated with respect _____ Treat others respectfully

Not let others control me _____ Not control others

Accept my feelings without judgment _____ Accept the feelings of others

Stand up for my rights _____ Respect the rights of others

Express my needs and wants _____ Accept the wants and needs of others

Love myself unconditionally _____ Love others unconditionally

View my needs as important _____ Accept the needs of others

Accept myself for who I am _____ Accept others for who they are

Change myself _____ Not try to change others

Set boundaries and limits with others _____ Respect the boundaries of others

Accept my feelings without judgment _____ Be non-judgmental with others

Make mistakes and even fail _____ Not critique the failings of others

Ask for help _____ Offer help

Have privacy and my own personal space _____ Respect the personal space of others

Set my priorities _____ Respect the priorities of others

Say "no" without feeling selfish _____ Accept "no" from others

Follow my dreams, interests and passions _____ Support other's dreams and interests

Feel weak _____ Accept other's weaknesses

Not live up to others expectations _____ Not place demands on others

Be forgiving of myself_____ Forgive others

Seek others that support my growth _____ Support the growth of others

Copyright © 2016 Judith Belmont. *150 More Group Therapy Activities & TIPS*, www.belmontwellness.com. All rights reserved.

Common Irrational Assumptions that Violate Personal Rights

Tip #37

THEORY

The focus on basic human rights and corresponding responsibilities sets the stage to introduce cognitive therapy concepts of how our irrational thoughts lead us to deny our basic human rights. In this TIP we explore the underlying reasons of why it is difficult to accept personal rights. I have often been struck personally when my clients have questioned if they even have a right to feel a certain way. **Many of our clients hold irrational assumptions about themselves and others, which make it hard to embrace their basic human rights.** For example, they might feel inferior to others in the belief that others are more worthy and "better" than they are, and thus feel less deserving to be treated with respect. Those in verbally, emotionally and even physically abusive relationships surrender their self-esteem to others and subsequently allow themselves to be violated.

IMPLEMENTATION

Brainstorm with your group on a flip chart or white board some common irrational assumptions and distortions that make it difficult to accept basic human rights. Ask the group what thoughts go through their mind when their judgments about their opinions, thoughts and feelings limit their ability to express themselves freely with others. These are some of the responses you might get:

- *"I don't want to say the wrong thing."*

- *"I don't want them to think I am stupid."*

- *"I don't want to sound selfish."*

- *"It would be awful if they disapprove."*

- *"I should be polite and listen to them."*

- *"Maybe they're right and I am wrong - and that would be terrible!"*

- *"If someone is having a bad day and letting off steam, I don't want to make them more mad."*

After making the list, go over each item and brainstorm with the group more rational alternatives to these self-denying irrational assumptions.

"I don't want to say the wrong thing" can be replaced with *"I have a right to express myself without fear of being wrong. If I am wrong, that is okay. I don't need to be perfect."*

To personalize the learning, split the group into pairs to allow for more individualized work on replacing irrational assumptions that violate human rights with healthier alternatives.

 Copyright © 2016 Judith Belmont. *150 More Group Therapy Activities & TIPS*, www.belmontwellness.com. All rights reserved.

If time allows, give out notecards so that group members can make their own coping cards which remind them to challenge their basic erroneous assumptions that violate rights.

For example a card could look like this:

Side 1 – Erroneous assumption: *"What others think of me is more important than what I think."*

Side 2 – Objective Assumption: *"I choose not to live life worrying about what others think. Self-love underlies my ability to be healthy and I am worthy of love."*

PROCESSING

Accepting basic human rights due to healthier ways of thinking can literally change relationships. I have had clients who were able to be much more assertive and increase their limits and boundaries with others just by giving themselves "permission" to take their own rights more seriously. Examining the thought processes behind the concept of basic human rights is a great life skill as well as good introduction to cognitive therapy.

Emphasize to the group that no one knows you better than yourself, and no one can be the best judge of your thoughts and feelings than you.

To quote Oscar Wilde, ***"Be yourself; everyone else is already taken."***

Copyright © 2016 Judith Belmont. *150 More Group Therapy Activities & TIPS*, www.belmontwellness.com. All rights reserved.

Communication Skills Boot Camp

Tip #38

THEORY

The social milieu of the group situation is ideal in **helping people improve their relationships** and their ability to connect with others.

PROCESSING

Introduce the topic of communication skills using the following role-play exercise and the subsequent variety of handouts and worksheets. I offer clients various types of handouts and worksheets to help them build their skills with various resources that differ slightly in content to keep it fresh.

Make the point that we communicate all the time, yet are sorely lacking in instructions on how to communicate effectively. It is not uncommon for people to be misguided about healthy communication basics. Problematic and conflict-ridden relationships are the unfortunate fallout from miscommunication. Often these patterns are learned early on and often are a product of socialization. For example, women are more rewarded in society to be non-assertive, men to be more aggressive. Once the basics of communication are understood, one can readily differentiate between the aggressive "you" vs. the assertive "I" focus. In no time, healthier patterns are put into practice!

The following various handouts clearly differentiate between the three major types of communication, i.e. assertive, non-assertive and aggressive. These handouts will help improve the way clients come across to others and provide tools to express thoughts and feelings constructively.

In addition, ask for volunteers to role-play a personal situation they've experienced with a friend, co-worker or family member. I play the part of the volunteer or the other person so I can demonstrate assertive skills.

The following are the basic three types of behavior:

Aggressive - The focus is on changing the other person and is characterized by "you" statements. Honesty is geared towards controlling or changing the other person's mind or behavior, or "getting them to see" a point of view leading to disrespect of the other person and communication is tactless and blunt.

The Aggressive motto is *"I'm OK – You're not"*

———— • ————

 Copyright © 2016 Judith Belmont. *150 More Group Therapy Activities & TIPS*, www.belmontwellness.com. All rights reserved.

Non-Assertive - The focus is on protecting oneself and people pleasing. Fear of disapproval or conflict ends up with tension building and later blowing up or keeping feelings in, leading to depression and anxiety. Fear and inhibition reign.

The Non-Assertive motto is *"You're OK – but I'm not unless you like me!"*

———— • ————

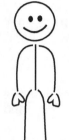

Assertive - The focus is on showing respect while expressing oneself. "I" statements are spoken, focusing on only expressing oneself, not changing others.

The Assertive motto is *"I'm OK – You're OK"*

———— • ————

You can give the example of parents who think it's perfectly fine to be dominating and controlling with their children since they are the parents (the "because I said so" mentality). However, make the point that intimidation leads to low self-esteem in children and is actually quite aggressive. Much more effective is an assertive, democratic approach where rights are respected and kindness and respect reign. All too often people might start out assertively, but if they do not get their way - watch out!

PROCESSING

With the help of the practical handouts in this chapter, clients can identify their patterns and style of communication. Once the basics of communication are understood, throughout the group you will find you can frequently revisit this topic, as most situations that group members want to work on requires healthy communication skills.

Copyright © 2016 Judith Belmont. *150 More Group Therapy Activities & TIPS*, www.belmontwellness.com. All rights reserved.

Using Role Plays to Introduce the Three Types of Communication

THEORY

Effective communication skills can make the difference between healthy relationships and unhealthy ones, as well as a happy life vs. an unhappy one. There is a strong correlation between having strong interpersonal relationships and life satisfaction, and even longevity.

IMPLEMENTATION

Using any of the variety of the following handouts to reinforce the communication lesson in this TIP , I introduce the topic with a role-play demonstration. As obvious as it seems, when starting out with a role play to demonstrate the differences between the types of the three behaviors, many group members think I am acting assertively when I am actually making a lot of "You" statements and acting rudely and dismissively.

The canned role-play opens up the stage for group members to choose their own scenarios to role-play. The power of the group cannot be over-emphasized in using various group members to enact scenes from each other's own lives.

Since this differentiation is so important, included are many different versions of communication handouts following this introduction. Some are simpler versions, better for children, while others are detailed for adults.

A volunteer from the group reads canned lines to which I respond, and I model for the group both ineffective and effective ways of handling a difficult situation.

Since the volunteer only reads canned lines, no one feels put on the spot, and the attention is just focused on you/the therapist. The only instruction to the group is to decide if communication is assertive, non-assertive or aggressive, while referring to their handouts.

Role-play Scenario

Give a volunteer from the group the following canned lines to play the friend who is constantly 15 minutes late picking you up for a meeting you both attend.

Copyright © 2016 Judith Belmont. *150 More Group Therapy Activities & TIPS*, www.belmontwellness.com. All rights reserved.

Meeting Scene for Assertiveness Example

Friend: *Hi – Are you ready to go?*

My response: _____

Friend: *Oh, I hadn't noticed the time!*

My response: _____

Friend: *You're much too sensitive – I'm only 15 minutes late!*

My response: _____

Friend: *Come on, you're being petty. It's not a big deal!*

My response:_____

Friend: *You shouldn't feel that way!*

My response: _____

Friend: *I didn't realize it was important to you – I'll try to be on time next time.*

Now I will fill in some representative things I say for each of the different types of communication. I start with the aggressive communication, which most people think is assertive.

Aggressive Scenario

Friend: *Hi – Are you ready to go?*

My response: *Yes – I've been ready for 15 minutes – Where have you been?* (NOTE: Rhetorical questions are aggressive)

Friend: *Oh, I hadn't noticed the time!*

My response: *You should be wearing a watch!*

Friend: *You're much too sensitive – I'm only 15 minutes late!*

My response: *How could you say that? (Another rhetorical question!) A lot happens at the beginning of the meetings, like the announcements!*

Friend: *Come on, you're being petty. It's not a big deal!*

My response: *Well, that's being petty – 15 minutes is very important!*

Friend: *You shouldn't feel that way!*

My response: *You shouldn't tell me how I should feel!* (I make the point never to "*should*" on others – and I double should her – i.e. I *should* on her twice!)

Friend: *I didn't realize it was important to you – I'll try to be on time next time.*

Copyright © 2016 Judith Belmont. *150 More Group Therapy Activities & TIPS*, www.belmontwellness.com. All rights reserved.

To my surprise, most groups think I am being assertive because I am just standing up for myself! And surprisingly, many people think the canned lines are also assertive or even non-assertive - Note they are actually quite aggressive (notice the name calling and labeling)!

If time allows, I then do a non-assertive scenario, or if I am pressed for time I just skip to the assertive role-play.

Non-Assertive Scenario

Friend: *Hi – Are you ready to go?*

> **My response:** *Yeah, I kind of have been waiting a while.*

Friend: *Oh, I hadn't noticed the time!*

> **My response:** *No big deal – it is just a few minutes late.*

Friend: *You're much too sensitive – I'm only 15 minutes late!*

> **My response:** *Sorry – I didn't mean to be a stickler for time.*

Friend: *Come on, you're being petty. It's not a big deal!*

> **My response:** *Sorry – I'm not trying to make a big deal about it – I'm just a stickler for time!*

Friend: *You shouldn't feel that way!*

> **My response:** *I know – I'm sorry – I get uptight about dumb stuff.*

Friend: *I didn't realize it was important to you – I'll try to be on time next time.*

Point out that in the non-assertive role-play, the other person is late but I am the one apologizing! I am belittling myself, labeling myself as a stickler and allowing myself to be disrespected!

Now, model for the group assertive skills using "I" statements:

Assertive Scenario

Friend: Hi – *Are you ready to go?*

> **My response:** *Yes – I have been waiting for a while now.*

Friend: *Oh, I hadn't noticed the time!*

> **My response:** *I have been bothered that we miss the announcements at the beginning of the meeting.*

Friend: *You're much too sensitive – I'm only 15 minutes late!*

> **My response:** *A lot goes on in the first 15 minutes. From now on if you are not here by 5:30 I will just meet you there.*

Friend: *Come on, you're being petty. It's not such a big deal!*

> **My response:** *I don't think that is fair to me. I just wanted to let you know.*

Copyright © 2016 Judith Belmont. *150 More Group Therapy Activities & TIPS*, www.belmontwellness.com. All rights reserved.

Friend: *You shouldn't feel that way!*

My response: *This is the way I feel.*

Friend: *I didn't realize it was important to you – I'll try to be on time next time.*

I have the group notice how I do not attack or focus on the other person, but rather focus on my needs and do not get sidetracked by what they are saying. I stick to the point without going letting the other person's aggressive statements lead me down a wrong path. I then ask for volunteers to try their assertive skills. Even after watching me, many people find they are either aggressive or non-assertive! It makes it very entertaining when group members try their skills in this role-play – or during another role-play such as the example below using a situation in which someone is rude or calls you a name. This time let the group members ham it up! In this activity there is usually a lot of laughter as group members try their hand at it!

2nd Role Play Scenario

Family member: *You're never there when I need you! You're selfish!*

Response: _____

Family member: *All you think about is yourself!*

Response: _____

Family member: *You always hurt my feelings!*

My Response: _____

In this example, communication stoppers would be *"That's not true!"* and *"You hurt my feelings too!"*

Assertive statements would be *"I am sorry you are hurt, but do not appreciate being talked down to like that"* and *"I am sorry you feel like I am not there for you."*

Emphasize you do not have to defend if you are verbally attacked, but rather you can simply reflect the feelings you are hearing and state your own.

PROCESSING

The success of the processing and learning will depend on the group leaders' proficiency and understanding of the three types of behavior. The following handouts offer a variety of resources to accompany this tip and reinforce the lessons. Since the topic of communication sills is so important, I offer numerous variations of communication skills handouts and worksheets in the following TIPS, some simply written for children and some more informative for adults. This way, instead of using only one or two worksheets for this very important topic, you have many to choose from at various times of the group to help your clients work on healthy communication skills. I use these type of communication TIPS also with almost all my individual clients, as invariably the issues they present involve some communication challenge.

Use role-playing regularly throughout the group's duration, so that members get to practice new skills learned, gaining valuable feedback and practice in the group as they fine tune their communication skills. The ability to role-play, along with support and feedback, is one of the most powerful experiences in a group.

Copyright © 2016 Judith Belmont. *150 More Group Therapy Activities & TIPS*, www.belmontwellness.com. All rights reserved.

The Three Types of Communication

Nonassertive Behavior	Assertive Behavior	Aggressive Behavior
• Inhibited • Lets others violate rights • Does not stand up for rights • Afraid of "making waves" • Lets others choose • Unconfident, nervous	• "I" statements • Expresses and asserts own rights, needs, desires • Stands up for legitimate rights without violating rights of others • Emotionally honest, direct, expressive	• "You" statements • Expresses own rights at expense of others • Has inappropriate outbursts or hostile overreactions • Emotionally honest and direct at others' expense

Feelings That Result

• Hurt, anxious, disappointed in self at the time and possibly angry later	• Confident, self respecting; feels good about self and others	• Angry, then righteous; superior, resentful, possibly guilty later

Effects

• Individual avoids unpleasant and potentially conflictual situations • Individual feels "used," accumulates anger, feels nonvalued	• Individual feels good, validated by self and others • Individual experiences improved self-confidence, gets needs met: relationships are freer and more honest	• Saved-up anger "justifies" a blowup • Individual has emotional outbursts "to get even"

Nonassertive - behavior is being like a turtle: hiding and being protective to be on the "safe" side, avoidant.	**Assertive** - communication is being like a wise owl: thinking rationally, standing upright, being confident, and showing wisdom without impulsivity.	**Aggressive** - behavior is represented by a lion: powerful, mighty, strong, threatening, while violating the rights of others.

From *The Therapist's Ultimate Solution Book: Essential Strategies, Tips and Tools To Empower Your Clients* by Judith Belmont. Copyright © 2015 by Judith Belmont. Used by permission of W.W. Norton & Company

 Copyright © 2016 Judith Belmont. *150 More Group Therapy Activities & TIPS*, www.belmontwellness.com. All rights reserved.

Communication Skills Made Easy

Assertive

Wise Communicator

"I" Statements: "I think ... ""I feel ... "

"It is important to me ..."

Respects self and others

"I'm O.K., you're O.K."

Non-Assertive

Passive

"You're O.K., I stink!"

"I need your approval."

"I can't stand conflict."

"Don't make waves."

Indirect, beats around the bush

Aggressive

"I'm O.K., but not too sure about you!"

"Because I said so!"

"I've kept things in too long so no wonder why I explode!"

Might makes right!

"You" statements!

"You make me so mad!"

Copyright © 2016 Judith Belmont. *150 More Group Therapy Activities & TIPS*, www.belmontwellness.com. All rights reserved.

Tip #42

Communication Style Comparison

Non-Assertive Behavior	Assertive Behavior	Aggressive Behavior
Keeps things in, does not speak up	Shares thoughts and feelings with tact	States thoughts and feelings without tact
Suppresses rights and needs	Asserts own rights, needs, desires	Expresses own rights at expense of others
Denies needs in order to make others like them or approve	Tries to get needs met while not violating rights of others	Gets needs met, but at the expense of others
Permits others to infringe on his/her rights	Set limits and priorities	Violates rights of others
Emotionally dishonest, indirect, inhibited, approval seeking	Confident, calm, secure	Honest without tact, bluntly direct, self-righteous
Self-denying	Chooses for self	Chooses for others
Emotional Costs	**Emotional Benefits**	**Emotional Costs**
Feels hurt, anxious, afraid of others' reactions	Confident, self-respecting, feels good about self	Angry, indignant, righteous
Self-Blaming	Does not blame	Blames others, judgmental, critical of others
	Outcome	
Low self-esteem, goals not met	May achieve desired goal(s), feels self-assured no matter what	Feels alienated, possibly guilty, negative
Feels non-valued	Feels valued	Power hides insecurity
	Payoffs	
Does not "make waves"	Relationships are open and honest	Feeling like justice is served
Avoids conflict	Feels satisfied about expressing self	Feels superior to others
Shying away from initiating relationships	Confident in enlisting support of others	Keeps others at a distance
People pleasing	Striving for a win-win	Focused on getting their own way

 Copyright © 2016 Judith Belmont. *150 More Group Therapy Activities & TIPS*, www.belmontwellness.com. All rights reserved.

Are you a Turtle, Tiger or Owl?

Non-Assertive Behavior is being like a Turtle	Aggressive Behavior is being like a Tiger	Assertive Behavior is being like an Owl
Hides, avoids, fearful of rejection or the anger of others	Rude, bossy and controlling of others	Wise, calm and collected, more observant than reactive
Goal: To Play It Safe and Be "liked"	Goal: To be right and prove it!	Goal: To express self honestly and tactfully.
Fearful of being yelled at or of others using physical force	Uses verbal and even physical force	Refrains from verbal or physical force
Remains quiet to not make mistakes or "get into trouble"	Uses "You" Statements	Uses "I" statements
Sensitive to disapproval and rejection	Insensitive to others	Sensitive to both self and others
Disrespectful to oneself	Disrespectful to others	Respectful to self and others
Allows right to be violated	Violates rights of others	Balances rights with responsibilities
Accepts others more than themselves	Is judgemental of others	Accepting of self and others
Keeps feelings in	Free to express angry feelings	Expresses feelings tactfully
Is fearful of being "wrong" or seeming "stupid"	Needs to be "right"	Is most concerned with being kind - not right
Dishonest and indirect	Bluntly honest without regard for others	Tactfully open and honest
Might feel anxious, sad, isolated and misunderstood	Feels superior over others, over-confident and gets angry easily	Feels secure, confident and loving

Copyright © 2016 Judith Belmont. *150 More Group Therapy Activities & TIPS*, www.belmontwellness.com. All rights reserved.

Understanding Your Communication Style

This worksheet will help you identify if you communicate like a turtle, a tiger or an owl.

Turtles represent people who are non-assertive.

Non-Assertive people hide feelings and thoughts, tend to be shy, and avoid expressing themselves in fear of disapproval or others getting angry. They do not speak up when others do not treat them with respect. This is tied to low self-esteem and sadness.

> **Non-Assertive motto:** *"You're O.K. - I'm Not!"*
> **Example:** Feeling upset but remaining silent and not standing up for yourself.

Tigers represent people who are aggressive.

Aggressive people tend to be bossy and argumentative, expressing thoughts and feelings without being considerate to others. They use "You" statements where they decide for others how they "should" be, and care more about being right than being kind. They do not treat others with respect and label others. Hitting is an example of physical aggression.

> **Aggressive motto:** *"I'm O.K. - You're Not!"*
> **Example:** *"You shouldn't feel that way! That's stupid!"*

Owls represent people who are assertive

Assertive people tend to be mature, sensitive, kind and respectful to themselves and others. They treat others like they themselves like to be treated. They express their thoughts and feelings honestly but with tact and show empathy to how others feel. They use "I" Statements.

> **Assertive motto:** *"I'm O.K. - You're OK!"*
> **Example:** *"I do not like how you are talking to me. I feel disrespected."*

Most people show all these behaviors at different times with different people. For example, some children are well behaved in school (assertive) but fight with siblings or parents (aggressive). The important thing to note is that when dealing with others, assertive behavior is the healthiest and most mature way to act, and is kindest to yourself and others.

Below, give an example of a time you were:

Non-Assertive _____

Aggressive _____

Assertive _____

For the times that you were non-assertive and aggressive, think of an "I" statement you could have used:

Aggressive example: _____

Non-assertive example: _____

 Copyright © 2016 Judith Belmont. *150 More Group Therapy Activities & TIPS*, www.belmontwellness.com. All rights reserved.

Communication Skills:
Quick Tips for Kids

Type of Communication	Non-Assertive	Aggressive	Assertive
Animals representing the type of communication	**The Turtle** Turtles protect themselves and hide from others	**The Tiger** Tigers are fierce and mighty	**The Owl** Owls are wise
Type of Statements	Does not express feelings - keeps things in	"You" Statements	"I" Statements
Goal	"Plays it safe" Avoids conflict at all costs	To control and get your own way	To express yourself and state your opinion, wants and needs
Common Feelings	Fearful, anxious, unconfident, sensitive to criticism, afraid to be wrong	Quick to anger, frustrated, impatient	Calm, self-confident, patient
Common Thoughts	"I need them to like me" "They are better than me." "I should be better."	"I am better than them" "I am right and will make sure they know it!" "They should act better."	"I accept and like myself and like them too." "I treat people as I want to be treated."
Common Behaviors	Shy, quiet behavior. Keeps things in, sometime exploding into aggression later on.	Disrespectful of others, lacking empathy. Tends to argue. Proves they are right.	Respectful behavior to self and others. Is more concerned with being kind than right.

Copyright © 2016 Judith Belmont. *150 More Group Therapy Activities & TIPS*, www.belmontwellness.com. All rights reserved.

Communication Stop Light

THEORY

Applying life skills lessons to common things we see in everyday life will make the lesson more meaningful. One common image that everybody comes into contact with many times a day is a stoplight. Whether you are a driver, passenger, or pedestrian, we all obey traffic signals frequently. **I have found the STOPLIGHT to be a great metaphor to use in helping clients improve their clients communication skills.**

INTEGRATION

Using the image of the stoplight for your demonstration, explain the three types of communication. The three colors in the stoplight represent the three types of communication.

RED - Aggressive Communication - STOP!

> This reminds you to STOP! Don't do it! Don't even go there! In everyday interpersonal communication there is no place for it. That means no arguing, You-messages, putting others down, being bossy or rude, or using physical force.

YELLOW - Non-Assertive Communication - CAUTION!

> Watch out for signs that you are anxious *and fearful, and suppressing your true thoughts and feelings in order to please others and gain approval.* Be aware of tension growing due to lack of self-expression. Tension and stress builds and you might end up exploding and acting aggressive. So pay attention to your thoughts and physical sensations - don't let things build! Stand up for yourself if you feel you have been treated disrespectfully.

GREEN - Assertive Communication - GO!

> Remember you have a right to express your thoughts and feelings, and also remember your responsibilities to be respectful to others. Strive for a win- win when everyone feels good. Stay confident and use stress to feel engaged and involved!

PROCESSING

Using this metaphor can make your communication skills lessons compelling. For example, you can suggest to your group members when they get angry, "Remember to STOP (Red) and decide how to proceed," i.e. GO (Green)! After giving one of my miniature stoplights to a very bright 10-year-old, he incorporated the metaphor by making on his own handout (included in this TIP) to remind himself of when to GO, STOP and use CAUTION!

 Copyright © 2016 Judith Belmont. *150 More Group Therapy Activities & TIPS*, www.belmontwellness.com. All rights reserved.

Activity

The Way Of Life

This is a transcription of my 10 year old client's chart he made up for himself after a session in which he learned the three types of communication. A worksheet with the three columns inspired him to make up his own. This life skills lesson significantly helped him manage his anger and control his temper.

Non-Assertive Behavior	Assertive Behavior	Aggressive Behavior
Keeping your feelings to yourself. When it is a bad feeling you need to talk about it, and relax.	You might be mad but you're not over-reacting, but expressing your feelings and being kind of calm.	Screaming or saying bad words, or over-reacting. Taking your troubles out on someone else.
Do not do this. It's just gonna be worse.	DO IT!	DON'T DO IT!
Fearful of being yelled at or of others using physical force	Refrains from verbal or physical force	Uses verbal and even physical force
Yellow Light	Green Light	STOP
Slow Down	GO!	

Copyright © 2016 Judith Belmont. *150 More Group Therapy Activities & TIPS*, www.belmontwellness.com. All rights reserved.

Activity

Communication Stoplight

RED - Aggressive Behavior...Stop!

YELLOW- Non-Assertive Behavior ...Caution!

GREEN- Assertive Behavior ...Go!

Give an example of your behavior in the past week which was:

Aggressive (Red):

_____

Non-Assertive (Yellow):

_____

Assertive (Green):

_____

Now think of ways that you can change your aggressive and non-assertive behavior to assertive behavior.

Turning my aggressive behavior into assertive behavior.

_____

_____

Turning my non-assertive behavior into assertive behavior.

_____

_____

Now think of how other people acted in the past week. Can you identify all three types of communication by others? Give examples:

_____

_____

 Copyright © 2016 Judith Belmont. *150 More Group Therapy Activities & TIPS*, www.belmontwellness.com. All rights reserved.

Activity

Stop, Caution and GO!

Aggressive Behavior RED - STOP!	Non-Assertive Behavior YELLOW - CAUTION!	Assertive Behavior GREEN - GO!
Watch out when you are seeing **RED!**	*Watch out for signs that you are anxious and fearful!*	**Speak freely and feel confident!**
Don't do it! Don't even go there! In everyday communication there is no place for aggression. That means no arguing, putting others down, using physical force or being bossy or rude.	Be aware of tension growing due to lack of self-expression. Tension and stress builds and you might end up exploding and acting aggressive - So pay attention to your thoughts and physical sensations - don't let things build. Stand up for yourself if you feel treated disrespectfully.	Remember you have a right to express yourself, and also remember your responsibilities to be respectful for others. Strive for a win-win when everyone feels good. Stay confident and use stress to feel engaged and involved!

Below, write some reminders for yourself about how they are different.

Aggressive Behavior	Non-Assertive Behavior	Assertive Behavior
STOP!	*CAUTION!*	*GO!*

Copyright © 2016 Judith Belmont. *150 More Group Therapy Activities & TIPS*, www.belmontwellness.com. All rights reserved.

I-Messages vs. You-Messages

THEORY

I-Messages are honest, direct, and assertive, whereas You-Messages are controlling, disrespectful and aggressive. Dr. Thomas Gordon, a prominent clinical psychologist and originator of Parent Effectiveness Training (P.E.T), Teacher Effectiveness Training, (T.E.T) and Leadership Effectiveness Training (L.E.T) is credited with developing the concept of I-Messages.

IMPLEMENTATION

Educate the group about the importance of using *I-Messages*. **You-Statements are aggressive, judgmental, disrespectful and controlling, I-Statements are assertive, respectful, honest but tactful**.

Practicing I-Statements though role-play is going to make the lessons effective. Just as taking a piano lesson and understanding the notes will not improve playing without practice, it is important to use various role play activities to put the learning into practice.

There are many ways to practice I-Statements using the accompanying handouts as reference:

Be A Translator! Have one group member say a You-Statement and then the person next to them translates it into an I-Statement. Then that person says a You-Statement to the next person, and so on until everyone has gotten a chance to both say an I-Statement and a You-Statement that is translated by the next person.

After this whole group activity, you can break the group up into pairs in which the two partners help one another re-enact their real life situations using I-Statements. After a short exchange, encourage them to give feedback to one another on how they felt in the interaction and suggest alternative ways of communicating if relevant.

Practice You-Statements Disguised As I-Statements. Make the point that even though you use the word "I" it does not mean you are "home free." Statements that start with "I" can be actually You-Statements. Take the example "I think you stink!" Just because you start with an "I" does not mean it is assertive!

It does not mean that you can no longer use the word "*you.*" When I have client's role play, they are often afraid of using the word "*you,*" fearing it sounds aggressive. If you are descriptive, the word "*you*" is fine to use such as "I really enjoy being with you." Problems occur when "*you*" is designed to blame others, such as "You made me so mad."

Use Personalized Role Plays. Have group members take turns sharing a real life situation that poses an assertive issue, and have volunteers play the other person or people in their lives. Role-playing, although often awkward and intimidating at first, is one of the best tools for giving group members practice refining communication skills.

PROCESSING

Using the previous handouts in this section as guides, these variations of role-play situations offer endless possibilities for processing. Ask members how it felt learning how to express themselves with I-Statements - how would it change their relationships with others? How would it change the self-talk in their heads?

After a session on I-Statements and assertive communication, follow it with a homework assignment, asking group members to bring in an example from the week that posed an assertive issue that they can practice with the group the next session.

 Copyright © 2016 Judith Belmont. *150 More Group Therapy Activities & TIPS*, www.belmontwellness.com. All rights reserved.

Activity

Replacing You-Messages with I-Messages

You-Statements are rude, disrespectful and lead to arguments and conflict. Even if someone is rude, such as in the example below, it is not appropriate to retaliate with aggressive words. Just because someone *"starts it"* doesn't mean you can't *"end it."*

Situation: A family member calls me a "loser."

Example of a You-Statement:

"You have no right to say that to me - you're the loser! How do you have such nerve?"
> Notice the labeling and attempt to put down, control and retaliate. Also notice the rhetorical question which is a put down disguised as a question.

Example of an I-Statement:

I felt ___*upset and angry*___ (describe feeling) when *you called me a "loser"* (describe event) and *would like for you to be more* *respectful and would appreciate an apology.* (ask for a change)

> Notice this is not at all like a You-statement. This time the person remains calm, confident and self-respecting and does not retaliate. There is no further name calling and put downs - the conflict stops with assertive behavior.

YOUR TURN TO PRACTICE:

Describe a challenging interpersonal situation in which you would like to be more assertive.

_____

Write an I-Statement to handle it effectively

I feel (or felt) _____ when _____
                     (describe feeling)   (describe event specifically)

and I would like _____.
                                       (ask for a change)

REMEMBER:

The goal of using I-Statements is to change yourself, not others.

Learning to use I-Statements takes practice!

Using I-Statements seems logical and simple, but many people find them so hard to do! Keep practicing!

Copyright © 2016 Judith Belmont. *150 More Group Therapy Activities & TIPS*, www.belmontwellness.com. All rights reserved.

The ability to use I-Statements reflects positive self-esteem, self-confidence, healthy thinking and self-respect as well as respect for others.

Can you think of other examples from your own life?

You-Message: _____

I-Message: _____

You-Message: _____

I-Message: _____

You-Message: _____

I-Message: _____

You-Message: _____

I-Message: _____

You-Message: _____

I-Message: _____

 Copyright © 2016 Judith Belmont. *150 More Group Therapy Activities & TIPS*, www.belmontwellness.com. All rights reserved.

Victim vs. Victor Self-Talk

It is also important for your internal self-talk to be assertive. When you <u>think</u> assertively, you <u>think</u> like a victor. When your self-talk is aggressive, you end up being a victim. Shift your thinking to become a victor instead of a victim! Stick to the facts, and not your negative interpretations! *Don't you want to be your own best friend?*

Aggressive/Victim Self-Talk

I'm a failure.

He made me so angry.
I'll never get over this!

Assertive/Victor Self-Talk

I am human and I make mistakes and learn from them.

I was angry with him when he said that.
It's a setback, but I have faith in myself and my resilience.

Think in I-Messages: Your Turn to Use Assertive Self-Talk!

Below, write examples of your Victim Self-Talk, and then think of how to change that aggression directed towards yourself to Victor Self-Talk. All too often people will talk to themselves in a way that they never would talk to others. If you find yourself doing this, **remind yourself to get rid of that inner bully!**

<u>Aggressive/Victim Self-Talk</u>	<u>Assertive/Victor Self-Talk</u>
_____	_____
_____	_____
_____	_____
_____	_____
_____	_____
_____	_____

Copyright © 2016 Judith Belmont. *150 More Group Therapy Activities & TIPS*, www.belmontwellness.com. All rights reserved.

Note Cards to Practice I-Messages

THEORY

I-Messages are a fundamental cornerstone of assertive communication and were developed by Thomas Gordon, author of *Parent Effectiveness Training*. There are different variations so you have plenty of communication tools in your toolbox to give out at various times that provide various skill-building opportunities.

IMPLEMENTATION

After group members are introduced to the three types of communication, practicing specific skills such as how to use I-Messages instead of You-Messages will help them apply these skills to their own situations.

The following are examples of You-Messages. Note that some of the You-Messages are commands and do not necessarily have a "You" in them. **Also point out that rhetorical questions are You-Messages.**

- *You are too sensitive!*
- *Didn't you listen the first time?*
- *You hurt my feelings again!*
- *That's enough - STOP!*

- *You have no right to say that to me!*
- *Why can't you be nicer to me?*
- *You're not listening to me!*
- *Why can't you consider my feelings?*

Make up note cards with some You-Messages and pass them out randomly. Each member takes turns reading the You-Message note card and then turns it into an I-Message. When members get stuck about how to change the You-Messages into I-Messages, the group leader and other group members can model for them alternative responses.

After the exercise, give each group member a blank card and have them write a You-Message that they either have said themselves or have heard from others.

Then collect the cards from the two halves of the group into two separate piles, and then give out the cards randomly to the other half of the group so they don't get their own back.

After a group member reads the card and thinks of an I-Message translation, have the originator of the card identity him/herself and briefly explain the situation.

For the next group session, or if there is time in this session, the cards are a good jump-off point for paired role plays in which members enact real life situations.

PROCESSING

Using note cards to reinforce I-Messages is a fun and easy way to help group members boost their Communication IQ! This is a very structured form of behavioral rehearsal that is less threatening than more involved role plays, and gives all members in the group a chance to practice improving their communication.

 Copyright © 2016 Judith Belmont. *150 More Group Therapy Activities & TIPS*, www.belmontwellness.com. All rights reserved.

Tip #49

Practicing Turning You-Messages into I-Messages

You-Statements lead to relationship problems including hurt feelings and arguments since the goal is to change someone else or put them down, and is disrespectful and rude. You-Statements are aggressive.

I-Statements help you communicate effectively because you're being factual, descriptive, and are respectful to yourself and others. They focus on expressing yourself instead of changing others. Using I-Messages are an example of assertive communication.

Here are some other examples:

You-Statement: *"Why are you being so nosy? It's none of your business!"*
I-Statement: *"I do not feel comfortable sharing something so personal."*

You-Statement: *"Stop acting like a jerk!"*
I-Statement: *"I do not like the way you are acting and will not talk with you until you can treat me more respectfully."*

You-Statement: *"You make me so mad!"*
I-Statement: *"I was mad when you said that."*

Practice turning aggressive *You-Statements* into assertive *I-Statements*:

You-Message: *"You have no right to say that to me!"*
I-Message:_____

You-Message: *"You never listen to me!"*
I-Message:_____

You-Message: *"You shouldn't feel that way!"*
I-Message:_____

You-Message: *"You're too sensitive!"*
I-Message:_____

You-Message: *"You should know better!"*
I-Message:_____

Copyright © 2016 Judith Belmont. *150 More Group Therapy Activities & TIPS*, www.belmontwellness.com. All rights reserved.

 **Activity**

Understanding I-Messages

These are good starters for I-Messages

I feel _____

I want _____

I would like _____

I think _____

I believe _____

I wish _____

I am asking you _____

Watch out for You-Messages disguised as I-Messages! Just because you start with an "I" does not mean you are home free!

Example of You-Messages disguised as I-Messages:

"I think you stink!"

"I wish you would get lost!"

"I can't stand you!"

"I think you are so rude!"

"I can't believe you are so selfish – all you think about is yourself!"

"I think you should take a good look at yourself!"

Notice the exaggerated thinking that includes labeling, all or nothing thinking and judgmental thinking. How would you change these statements into I-Statements?

_____

_____

 Copyright © 2016 Judith Belmont. *150 More Group Therapy Activities & TIPS*, www.belmontwellness.com. All rights reserved.

 **Activity**

I-Messages for Kids

I-Messages are respectful, and truthfully state your thoughts and feelings in a tactful way. They avoid blaming others and only state feelings and ask for a change, without demanding it.

The I-Message formula:

I feel (or felt) _____ (name an emotion)

when you _____ (describe a behavior).

I would like (or I am asking you to) _____ (request a change.)

At times, if the behavior is very upsetting, you might want to add a limit or consequence.

If it happens again, I will _____ (set limits and have a consequence).

The following example was given as a suggestion to a 10-year-old client who was bullied in school occasionally. He found that telling them to "STOP" made things worse. Once he used this statement, there were no longer problems and he was no longer fearful of going to school. With his I-Messages to them, he bully-proofed his life!

I-Statement response: *"I feel upset when you call me names. I am asking you to stop.*

If this happens again, I will tell the teacher."

Now it's your turn:

Can you think of a situation where you can use an I-Statement instead of keeping quiet or using a You-Statement?

I feel (or felt) _____, (name an emotion)

when you _____. (describe a behavior)

I would like (or I am asking you to) _____. (request a change)

At times, if the behavior is very upsetting, you might want to add a limit or consequence.

If it happens again, I will _____.

Copyright © 2016 Judith Belmont. *150 More Group Therapy Activities & TIPS*, www.belmontwellness.com. All rights reserved.

Helping Children Identify Feelings

THEORY

Often children - as well as adults - have trouble identifying basic feelings, and therefore act out emotions instead of identifying and understanding them. Having the ability to be self-aware and have self-control and express feelings is highly correlated with positive life skills and self-esteem. This activity can help children understand their feelings.

IMPLEMENTATION

Hand out the following worksheet to help children identify a variety of feelings.

Have them think of a general situation that upsets them, such as fighting over video games with siblings.

Ask them to circle their feelings.

Then have them go to the next section and circle or write in what they are upset about, and how they can ask for a change.

Then ask them to circle or write a consequence if the other person is not willing to make a change.

This TIP is in part a lesson about I-Messages and assertiveness, and is reinforced in the chapter focusing on building self-esteem.

PROCESSING

Ask the children how their relationship would be different with their family and friends if they had the ability to identify their feelings and control them in the way they learned from the worksheet. Ask them how they can remember this lesson in real life when they get emotional. Reinforce the point that these skills can be learned and are not dependent on anyone doing anything different as long as they themselves use good tools to deal with difficult situations.

 Copyright © 2016 Judith Belmont. *150 More Group Therapy Activities & TIPS*, www.belmontwellness.com. All rights reserved.

Activity

Identifying and Expressing Feelings Worksheet

Think of situations you find yourself upset. Imagine yourself in those moments. Can you imagine it?

First identify which feelings apply and circle those feelings, then go to each of the other sections and circle what applies. Write in any other answers in each of the sections that are not on the sheet.

I FEEL					
Angry	Sad	Frustrated	Upset	Confused	Disappointed
Overwhelmed	Furious	Out of control	Embarrassed	Disrespected	Stressed
Worried	Tense	Panicky	Nervous	Belittled	Afraid

When You					
Tease Me	Exclude Me	Hit Me	Hurt Me	Yell	Scream At Me
Don't Share	Make Annoying Noises	Laugh At Me	Don't Listen to Me	Are Mean To Me	Gang Up On Me
Are Rude	Disrespectful	Make Fun Of Me	Embarrass Me In Front Of Others	Call Me Names	Raise Your Voice

I Am Asking You To					
Stop Doing That	Be More Polite	Consider my Feelings	Stop Making Fun Of Me	Be Nicer To Me	Apologize
Give Me A Chance to ...	Leave Me Alone	Play Nicely With Me	Be More Respectful	Stop Calling Me Names	Show Respect

Or I Will					
Go Home	Not Play With You	Tell My Parents	Do Something Else	Not Want To Be Your Friend	Stop Playing The Game
Ask You To Go Home	Leave	Tell The Teacher	Stop Playing With You	Distance Myself	Not Ask You To Play Again

Copyright © 2016 Judith Belmont. *150 More Group Therapy Activities & TIPS*, www.belmontwellness.com. All rights reserved.

Rhetorical Questions: Is It Really A Question?

Some questions are really not questions - they are put downs disguised as questions! These are called rhetorical questions. Watch out for these types of questions, as they are actually aggressive statements!

"Can't you do anything right?"

> Translation - You can't do anything right!

"What were you thinking?"

> Translation - You weren't thinking and did something stupid!

"What's wrong with you?"

> Translation - There is something wrong with you!

"Are you kidding me?"

> Translation - You're not telling the truth!

"Why can't you listen?"

> Translation - You're not listening!

"Didn't I already tell you that?"

> Translation - You should know that already!

"What - are you crazy?"

> Translation - You're acting nuts!

"How many times do I need to tell you to put that away?

> Translation - Stop ignoring me and do what I want!

"Are you for real?"

> Translation - You are a piece of work!

YOUR TURN: Can you think of other rhetorical questions?

1. _____

   Translation: _____

2. _____

   Translation: _____

3. _____

   Translation: _____

 Copyright © 2016 Judith Belmont. *150 More Group Therapy Activities & TIPS*, www.belmontwellness.com. All rights reserved.

Tip #52

Hallmarks of Effective Communication

Effective Communication		Ineffective Communication
Use "I" Statements	instead of	**"You" Statements**
I'm uncomfortable when you raise your voice at me.		*You have no right to raise your voice at me!*
Use Descriptive Statements	instead of	**Inferential Statements**
I am frustrated that you do not seem to grasp my point.		*You're not listening to me!*
Be Kind	instead of	**Self Righteous**
I'm not sure if you heard me say that.		*I told you that already!*
Use statements	instead of	**Rhetorical Questions**
It took me aback when you said that.		*How could you say that?*
Show empathy	instead of	**Minimizing**
You seem real upset about that.		*There's nothing to worry about!*
Use Tact	instead of	**Tactless Statements**
I don't agree with what you said.		*That's ridiculous!*
Be Specific	instead of	**Over catastrophizing**
I am upset when you called me lazy.		*You're always criticizing me.*
Be respectful	instead of	**Labeling**
I don't feel comfortable when you act rudely to me.		*You're acting like a jerk!*
Ask for a change	instead of	**Demanding a Change**
Please stop saying that to me.		*Stop talking!*
Request	instead of	**"Shoulding"**
I would appreciate you not raising your voice.		*You shouldn't raise your voice*
Uses Active Listening	instead of	**Hearing and Defending**
It seems like you are disappointed in me.		*I never did that!*
Encourage	instead of	**Discourage**
Can you explain how you feel?		*That's a lie.*

Copyright © 2016 Judith Belmont. *150 More Group Therapy Activities & TIPS*, www.belmontwellness.com. All rights reserved.

Checklist for Communicating with Tact and Finesse

_____ Clarify your goal and make sure it is an assertive goal.

_____ Be aware of your own self-talk. Talk assertively to yourself!

_____ Avoid Rhetorical questions.

_____ Separate *Fact* from *Fiction* - Beware of your perceptions!

_____ Make sure you are listening, *not just hearing.*

_____ Be aware of non-verbal communication in both yourself and others.

_____ Clarify thoughts and feelings and avoid irrational thoughts.

_____ Identify your personal rights and corresponding responsibilities.

_____ Weigh benefits/risks of being assertive to decide if you do want assert yourself.

_____ Rehearse and practice good communication, asking for feedback.

… AND REMEMBER

_____ Use "I" statements.

_____ Avoid rhetorical questions.

_____ Be *in control - not controlling!*

_____ At times, it is an assertive choice not to assert yourself.

_____ Don't over-explain or over-apologize.

_____ Don't get sidetracked, always keeping your goal in mind.

_____ Be descriptive, not judgmental.

_____ Do not label others.

_____ Watch out for over- personalizing or over-catastrophizing.

_____ Another's aggression does not justify counter-aggression.

_____ Don't let someone else's negativity set the tone for your own behavior.

_____ Be conscious of expressing sincere praise and positive feedback.

The goal of good communication is to:

Express, not impress!

Explain what's on your mind, without trying to change theirs!

 Copyright © 2016 Judith Belmont. *150 More Group Therapy Activities & TIPS*, www.belmontwellness.com. All rights reserved.

What is your "Assertiveness IQ?"

NAME:_____ DATE: _____

Communication is important in all areas of our lives, and determines the quality of our relationships. This quiz identifies 7 keys to assertiveness. Take this quick quiz to get your *Assertiveness IQ!*

Directions: On a scale of 1 to 7, rate your level of agreement with each item.

> 7 — Strongly Agree
> 6 — Agree
> 5 — Slightly Agree
> 4 — Neither Agree or Disagree
> 3 — Slightly Disagree
> 2 — Disagree
> 1 — Strongly Disagree

_____ I am able to think flexibly and look at things from other points of view.

_____ I do not try to change other people's perceptions.

_____ I express my thoughts and feelings honestly with tact, using "I" statements and not "You" statements.

_____ In times of conflict and disagreement, I make sure I "listen" by validating, empathizing and summarizing instead of defending myself.

_____ I think rationally and can differentiate between facts and interpretations.

_____ I am more concerned with being kind rather than proving that I am right.

_____ I tend to think positively and optimistically.

Total your score here: _____

44 - 49 — GENIUS: Assertiveness IQ is extraordinary!

38 - 43 — MASTER: High level of Assertiveness

32 - 37 — PRO: Moderate level of Assertiveness

26 - 31 — INTERMEDIATE: Assertiveness needs some boosting!

20 - 25 — AMATEUR: Assertiveness IQ is low.

14 - 19 — DABBLER: Assertiveness IQ is dangerously low.

Below 14 — DANGER ZONE!: Assertiveness Skills in need of help!

Copyright © 2016 Judith Belmont. *150 More Group Therapy Activities & TIPS*, www.belmontwellness.com. All rights reserved.

Are You A Nay-Sayer?

THEORY

Healthy interpersonal relationships are a cornerstone of mental health and life satisfaction. The quality of our ability to develop healthy relationships is correlated with our general life happiness and life adjustment. **Those who are kind and positive to others will have healthier relationships**, and negativity interferes with developing close relationships. This exercise emphasizes and demonstrates well how the negativity of "nay-sayers" pushes others away. On the flip side, it also shows the power of treating others with positivity.

IMPLEMENTATION

Ask for group members to break up into pairs. The exercise consists of a few minute role play in which two friends are deciding on where to go for their planned weekend away.

Have the partners take turns being the person suggesting a weekend plan and the other being a *Nay Sayer*.

For example if one person wants to go to the beach, the other person finds all sorts of reasons why not, such as, *"I hate the sand in my toes"* and *"It's so far to drive."*

After taking turns being the *Nay-Sayer* a few minutes each, the *Nay-Sayers* change their tune and become more like cheerleaders. For every suggestion made by their partner, they delightfully and positively add to it, showing enthusiasm and encouragement for their partner's various ideas. For example, *"It will be great spending time with you! Can't wait!"*

Expect a lot of laughter and smiles as the pairs experience a much more positive interchange. Then have the pairs switch roles so they can each have a turn being on both sides of the role-play.

Get feedback from the group after the pairs have finished the activities and process how it felt both being the *Nay-Sayer* and being on the other end of the other's negativity.

PROCESSING

Even though negativity is exaggerated in this activity, it does bring home the point of how important it is not to be a "wet blanket." Process with the group how it felt to be on both sides of the conversation, and what they can learn from this exercise about how they come across to others. Help them use this exercise to develop more of an awareness of how they come across in everyday life, and what changes they can make in their lives to stay positive with others instead of promoting negativity.

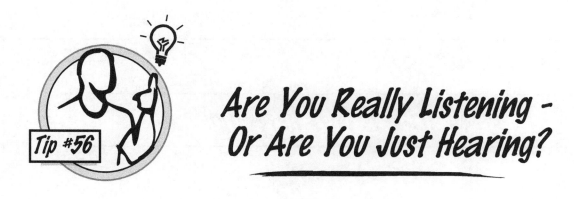

Are You Really Listening - Or Are You Just Hearing?

Tip #56

THEORY

Now that your group members have had plenty of opportunity to learn assertive communication skills with the various materials in this section, their knowledge will be incomplete if they do not learn about how to listen effectively, i.e. how to be an active listener. Many people think that communication is only talking, but knowing how to listen effectively is just as important. **Educating your clients about the difference between hearing and listening can be quite eye-opening.** This mini-lesson and the subsequent handouts/worksheets will teach your client how to be effective listeners.

IMPLEMENTATION

Emphasize that being a good listener is just as important as speaking effectively. The term "Active Listening" was coined by Thomas Gordon in his book, *Leader Effectiveness Training*. Hearing and listening are not the same. Hearing suggests merely taking in audible sounds, but listening is much more active.

In "Active Listening" one hears not just what they want, but understands more what message is being conveyed. When one actively listens they do not take words at face value but clarify, reflect and restate what they are hearing, taking into account the feelings behind the words.

Listening can be one of the greatest gifts you give to someone. Listening requires more active attention to both non-verbal and verbal messages when someone speaks, as one deciphers actively the message being expressed both verbally and emotionally.

Active listening is not passive nor judgmental, but rather validating. It is not self-absorbed and insensitive. By feeding back what you hear on a verbal as well as feeling level, the person can then clarify and sense that they are being valued.

After this introduction, pick from the following worksheets that focus on differentiating hearing vs listening. Have members work on the worksheets during the session or between sessions, followed by a discussion to personalize the information.

Have group members share their own examples from their own lives when they and others used both active listening and hearing. Have them recall a time in which they did use active listening and it was helpful, or times they did not and what was the result, as well as how they could have handled things differently. Have them role-play situations with one another in which one either "listens" or just "hears."

PROCESSING

Use the subsequent handouts and worksheets to help group members determine if they are just hearing or using active listening. Ask them to think of how many altercations and misunderstandings could be avoided just by using good listening skills!

Copyright © 2016 Judith Belmont. *150 More Group Therapy Activities & TIPS*, www.belmontwellness.com. All rights reserved.

Hearing is NOT listening!

Now let's learn about active listening. As you can see below, hearing and listening are not the same! Learn the difference!

Hearing	Actively Listening
Takes in audible sounds	Listening is more active, focusing on what is and is not being said.
Does not show interpretation or insight	Relies on paraphrasing, summarizing interpretation and insight
Focused on being heard	Focused on developing understanding
Does not show you care	Shows you care
Can be dismissive and disrespectful	Empathetic - it is a gift to others
Can be invalidating	Is validating
Talks AT	Talks WITH
Focused on what is being said	Attune to non-verbal and emotional content
Shuts down communication	Opens up communication
Leads to confrontation and anger	Leads to peace and healthy relationships
In times of conflict, goal is to prove a point	In times of conflict, goal is to compromise.
Focused on impressing a point on others	Focused on expressing and sharing
Shows you value yourself	Shows you value yourself and the other person
Goal is to be right	Goal is to be kind

**Just think of how many altercations and misunderstandings
we can avoid just by using good listening skills! Remember that good listening skills
actually require some talking which is focused on summarizing, validating
and empathizing with the other person.**

 Copyright © 2016 Judith Belmont. *150 More Group Therapy Activities & TIPS*, www.belmontwellness.com. All rights reserved.

Activity

Checklist For Active Listening

As you are listening, did you:

_____ Show empathy?

_____ Show respect?

_____ Show good eye contact and have attentive non-verbals?

_____ Summarize, clarify and paraphrase both the verbal message and the underlying message?

_____ Interpret how they seem to feel?

_____ Accept the other person's feelings without judgment?

_____ Listen for the message behind the words?

_____ Refrain from arguing back and setting the record straight?

_____ Show respect for the person without put downs, rhetorical questions, etc.?

_____ Use assertive "I" statements?

_____ Focus on being kind rather than right?

_____ Refrain from telling them what to do, how to be, and what they "should" say and do?

_____ Use open-ended questions rather than leading or rhetorical ones?

_____ Give the person space when they were finished?

How did you do? Is there anything you would like to work on to increase your ability to actively listen? Write it here.

_____

_____

_____

Copyright © 2016 Judith Belmont. *150 More Group Therapy Activities & TIPS*, www.belmontwellness.com. All rights reserved.

Practice, Practice, Practice!

THEORY

After group members learn about communication basics and active listening, **role-play is a great way to reinforce the learning.** Throughout the group's duration, role-play should be a staple. No other activity we do in groups brings about such valuable insights and skill building. When I ask at the end of a group what was most valuable, most people will mention the role-playing – even though suggesting role playing is often met with grunts and resistance.

IMPLEMENTATION:

There are countless ways to do role-play with the group. The best role-plays are ones from real situations that group members are willing to share.

To prepare for the role-plays, it is helpful to ask the week prior to bring in a role-play example they would be willing to work on in the group. With the advance notice, you likely will get volunteers to share their real life situations to role-play.

Once the situation is explained, use the Checklist for Communicating with Tact and Finesse (TIP 53) as well as Are You Really Listening - Or Are You Just Hearing? (TIP 56) to help members keep in mind the main considerations for effective communication. First and foremost, remind group members to make sure that their goal is an assertive one, and that they do not "talk at" but rather "talk with" others. Many times in groups, members find out their communication has been problematic because their goal was aggressive - i.e. trying to change someone else's mind, or that they were not really listening at all while trying to push their own agenda.

The beauty of a group is that there are many people who could play the parts of significant people from a person's life. So, let's say the situation is with a girlfriend, one of the females in the group can be asked to volunteer. If it involves more than one person, you have other people to make the role play realistic.

Make sure the situation is a short and simple one that does not need to be explained in detail. When you give the assignment the week before, let them know the situation they pick must be one that needs limited explanation.

Often the role-play needs to be re-enacted a few times, after receiving group feedback and suggestions. Practice make perfect! Practice, practice, practice!

PROCESSING

Often members get over self-consciousness quickly, and the role play experience can be quite fun, especially with some sense of humor by "hamming it up!"

 Copyright © 2016 Judith Belmont. *150 More Group Therapy Activities & TIPS*, www.belmontwellness.com. All rights reserved.

Activity · Developing Social Skills in Group Situations

Many people find speaking up and feeling comfortable in group situations to be challenging, especially when there are people they do not know. No matter your age or situation, speaking assertively and feeling confident can help improve social skills and alleviate social anxiety.

To work on improving your social skills in group situations, find a specific goal you would like to work on. The more specific the goal, the better chance you have of achieving it. For example, instead of having a goal "To feel more comfortable" break it down into smaller goals such as
"To feel comfortable going up to people and initiating conversation."

My goal is: _____

Practical strategies to reach my goal (i.e. use a list of reminders or coping cards to help me when I am nervous.) Write at least three items or reminders here.

1. _____
2. _____
3. _____

What went well? Don't forget to reward yourself!

_____
_____

What I want to improve:

_____
_____

Coping card tips/reminders to use for next time:

_____
_____
_____
_____

Role-Playing Using Role Reversal

THEORY

A very effective way to role-play is through role reversal, which is switching roles, so the one with the assertive scenario plays the other person. This offers a chance to act out what they think the other person might do and see how others can respond. **It is often helpful to have the therapist modeling assertive behavior.**

IMPLEMENTATION

Have each group member think of an assertive situation in which they tend to be generally non-assertive or aggressive.

Have the first volunteer pick someone to actually play them and after explaining the situation, the volunteer ends up playing the other person. This way they get ideas from group members how they could respond.

For example, a female who is having problems with her jealous boyfriend will play the boyfriend, enacting how he acts in real life, and the partner representing her tries to handle him assertively.

Sometimes group members have a hard time using assertive skills, so be prepared to role model assertive skills.

After demonstrating a couple examples with volunteers from the group, you might break up into pairs or triads so that everyone can get a chance to enact their role plays using role reversal. Use the following Communication Feedback Checklist (TIP 59) to give out to each group member to help remind them of the guidelines for effective communication in their role play practice.

PROCESSING

Group members find that role-playing their own situation, but not playing themselves, is a very good way to gain perspective on their situation. It also limits a lot of explanation about what things the other person will say. Observing how the group leader and other group members model assertive behavior can offer a wealth of ideas they might have never considered.

 Copyright © 2016 Judith Belmont. *150 More Group Therapy Activities & TIPS*, www.belmontwellness.com. All rights reserved.

Communication Feedback CheckList

This list will help you stay focused in practicing role play, and make sure your communication is effective. It will remind you of the guidelines of assertive communication and will help keep your communication assertive and not aggressive or non-assertive. **The goal of assertive communication is to express yourself, not to change someone else!**

_____ Did the goal of the communication seem assertive?

_____ Was it focused on expressing instead of changing someone's mind or behavior?

_____ What were the main points that came across? Were they clear?

_____ Were I-Statements used?

_____ Did the person show respect for themselves and the other person?

_____ Was there good eye contact?

_____ Was the tone of voice firm and confident?

_____ How was the body language? Did it reflect what was being said?

_____ Did the verbal and non-verbal communication match?

_____ Did the person smile or seem relaxed and open?

_____ Were there any problematic statements such as "you" statements and rhetorical questions?

_____ Were there problematic non-verbal distractions such as too many "sort ofs" or "ummms"

_____ Did the communication show self-control without being controlling?

_____ What was the best thing about this communication?

_____ What are suggestions to improve for next time?

Copyright © 2016 Judith Belmont. *150 More Group Therapy Activities & TIPS*, www.belmontwellness.com. All rights reserved.

Do You Show You Care?

Do you show you CARE to people around you? It's all in how you communicate!

> **C**ommunicate
> **A**ssertively with
> **R**espect and
> **E**mpathy

TIPS to show you CARE!

Communicate **A**ssertively	- Use "I" statements No blaming, name-calling, labeling or "shoulding" Be honest but tactful
Respect	- Show respect to yourself and others Be accepting, not judgmental Be tolerant of differences in ideas and opinions
Empathy	- Show consideration for the feelings of others Look behind the words for the feelings being expressed Understand another's point of view from their perspective

  Copyright © 2016 Judith Belmont. *150 More Group Therapy Activities & TIPS*, www.belmontwellness.com. All rights reserved.

Don't Be A But-Head!

THEORY

This short exercise is designed to make group members aware of the way they communicate. Most of us are unaware that **the use of "<u>but</u>" often negates the rest of the message of what we say to others**, and ends up making a positive message turn negative.

IMPLEMENTATION

This exercise can be fun to do as a whole demonstration and then split into pairs for additional practice. First, introduce the point that use of "*<u>but</u>*" often serves as a negative communication stopper, where you undermine the first part of the communication.

For example, if you say, "*You are a great person, but you can be really inconsiderate*" the compliment becomes a criticism in the same sentence, and the communication becomes adversarial. "*But*" negates any positive message. Alternatively, a "Yes and" phrase could be, "*You are a great person, and I especially appreciate that you are speaking to me more assertively when we have different opinions.*"

Ask for a volunteer to use role play with you about where to go for dinner, with both you and the volunteer using "*Yes but*" at the beginning of each sentence. Then start again, replacing "*Yes but*" with "*Yes and.*"

After demonstrating the power of "*Yes and*" in place of "*Yes but*" have members break into pairs or small groups. Using examples from their own lives, they can take turns role-playing the two scenarios and experience the difference.

PROCESSING

After doing the role plays, process as a group how it felt to be met by "*Yes buts*" and then the "*Yes ands.*" Also process how it felt to be the one to say "*Yes and*" instead of "*Yes but.*"

You will likely get a lot of agreement that "*Yes and*" is certainly a lot more pleasant and positive!

REMEMBER: Don't Be A But-Head!

Copyright © 2016 Judith Belmont. *150 More Group Therapy Activities & TIPS*, www.belmontwellness.com. All rights reserved.

Other Role-Play Variations

THEORY

If time is limited for personalized role plays, sometimes quick and simple structured exercises will do the trick. **Various types of canned role-play with note cards offers opportunities to practice** without getting too involved in a particular personal situation.

IMPLEMENTATION

Using canned role-play cards with simple scenarios gives your group members plenty of practice to develop assertive skills in a relatively non-threatening and efficient way. Although there is certainly an important place for more lengthy personalized role-plays in which group members act out their own personal situations, using canned short role-play examples offer a skill building opportunity to tackle a variety of scenarios in a short period of time. With no need for potentially lengthy explanations of personal situations, these examples give all group members plenty of opportunity to practice assertive skills with one another, often providing some lighthearted and comical responses as members "ham it up!"

Below are three examples of role-plays which you can use as ideas to create your own. You can either pass out a notecard or two to each person or have members pick them out of a box.

Example #1 - Assertive One Liners

This card variation poses a conflictual scenario in which the group member reads an aggressive line from their card and then they try to respond *assertively* using just one line rather than retaliate in kind.

Assertive One Liner

Your family member says,

"You only care about yourself!" and you say:

 Copyright © 2016 Judith Belmont. *150 More Group Therapy Activities & Tips*, www.belmontwellness.com. All rights reserved.

Example #2 - Assertive, Non-Assertive and Aggressive Role-Play Cards

For these cards, write a scenario for a person to respond to with only one sentence. On the top of the card is the instruction on which of the three types of communication they should use to respond. Then the group tries to figure out what type of communication it is. For example, in the card below labeled Non-Assertive, a group member would ask for a raise non-assertively, such as, "Do you think…ah… that maybe you could ever think of giving me a raise?" (Non-verbals would include looking down, hesitating, trailing voice). Then group members give feedback on how it came across. In this case, what did they notice that was non-assertive in both verbal and non-verbal behavior?

Point out the importance of making sure our non-verbal communication matches our verbal message. Group members usually have a lot of fun hamming up their responses by exaggerating their non-verbal communication.

Non-Assertive

You ask your boss for a raise

Example #3 - Assertive Dilemma

These cards offer short role-play practice with a fellow group member which poses an assertive dilemma. Each card offers a challenging scenario where another group member plays a difficult person using the scenario on the card, and the group member who picks the card tries to use assertive skills to respond. TIP #53 (Checklist for Communicating with Tact and Finesse) is an ideal handout to accompany these type of role-play cards to help remember the guidelines to stay assertive.

Aggressive Dilemma

A friend asks you for a ride but you are busy. He questions why you can't change your plans since he helped you in a pinch last week.

The group members might enjoy having their role-plays taped on their phone by another group member, so they can view it later. If you have the capability to play the video on a TV or computer screen, that would be ideal to assist in group learning.

PROCESSING:

Quick canned role-plays can be fun, are generally not anxiety provoking, and relatively non-threatening. Even quiet members find it easy to participate in these structured exercises. Expect some of the members to relate to some of the topics raised to their own life. If you have time, you might use these exercises as springboards for some group members' real life situations.

Copyright © 2016 Judith Belmont. *150 More Group Therapy Activities & Tips*, www.belmontwellness.com. All rights reserved.

How to Push Others Away

Do you have any relationships with people that you want to be close to but end up pushing away?
Here is a tongue-in-cheek checklist to see if you are actually pushing someone away by your ineffective communication!

DID YOU:

_____ Show judgment?

_____ Show disrespect?

_____ Talk louder so they could hear you better?

_____ Tell them what they should think, feel, or should do?

_____ Did you "should" on them in other ways, setting yourself up as the standard?

_____ Roll your eyes, grunt, sigh or make other nonverbal gestures that were dismissive?

_____ Tell them the way it is and prove why they are wrong and you are right?

_____ Tell them what they think or feel?

_____ Regard your interpretations about what they are saying as facts, rather than realizing they are just your interpretations?

_____ Try to set the record straight and prove you were right, even though they kept getting more upset?

_____ Put them down, label them as things like "selfish," "too sensitive," "lying?"

_____ Did you use "You" statements?

_____ Focus on being right rather than being kind?

_____ Use leading or rhetorical statements?

_____ Make sure they don't stop until you finished?

_____ Say dismissive statements like, "Here we go again."

How did you do? If you are having problems in your relationships, can you identify why?

 Copyright © 2016 Judith Belmont. *150 More Group Therapy Activities & TIPS*, www.belmontwellness.com. All rights reserved.

Tip #64

Choosing a Corner

THEORY

This is an interactive and fun activity to get group members reflecting on their own communication style. **Any variations of activities in which people get to move around are welcome and gets members involved and engaged.**

IMPLEMENTATION

In three corners of the room tape a sign in each corner saying Assertive, Non-Assertive or Aggressive in their respective corners.

After going over the characteristics of the three types of behavior, ask group members to think of one family member (or person at work or school, or friend) with whom they have the most conflict, and identify what kind of behavior they generally exhibit in times of conflict with that person.

Once they decide, point to the three signs in 3 separate corners of the room, and have them go over to the corner that best represents how they tend to react.

For those who go to the assertive corner, ask them one at a time to share with the group an example of how they stay assertive.

Then go to the non-assertive corner, and ask for each person to tell a short scenario of a non-assertive communication with the family member (or chosen person) of their choice that they picked. Ask them to say one statement or way to react to be more assertive. Occasionally when they are stuck you might role play with you being the person they have trouble asserting themselves to in order to help them develop assertive skills.

Once someone has shown how they could handle themselves assertively, they "graduate" to the assertive corner to join the rest of the assertive bunch. Keep going on until all the members from the non-assertive as well as the aggressive group "graduate" to the assertive corner.

PROCESSING

When people are stuck with ideas of how to get out of the corner, encourage feedback and suggestions from group members for new solutions. The beauty of the group situation is to learn from one another. I do this particular exercise in my workplace wellness groups when we are on the topic of assertiveness, and people generally like this very simple yet very educational exercise.

Copyright © 2016 Judith Belmont. *150 More Group Therapy Activities & TIPS*, www.belmontwellness.com. All rights reserved.

4

Changing Thoughts To Change Lives

Tips 65-88

Cognitive Therapy Boot Camp – Helping Clients Change Their Thoughts

THEORY

Cognitive Behavior Therapy is widely used in individual and group psychotherapy to help clients make major life changes by **changing their thoughts to change their lives**.

IMPLEMENTATION

The goal of psycho-educational life skills groups is to learn and practice new skills. Many people come to group with issues of depression, anxiety, substance abuse and difficult interpersonal relationships, and **CBT offers many "hands on" tips and practical solutions to these common problems.** Clients feel empowered to change their lives by changing their thoughts and perceptions.

The following TIPs in this section offer life skills practice opportunities that your group members will find helpful between sessions and within the group. All of these materials can serve as a basis for discussion and mini-lessons on how to defeat irrational thoughts and replace unhealthy thinking with more rational thinking habits.

All the following handouts are stand alone and self-explanatory and offer some opportunity for tailoring the lesson to one's own situation. They can be used for in-session group work or between session assignments.

When used as homework assignments, make sure you reserve time the following week after it is assigned for review. By using the completed handouts as springboards to share with the group, the learning becomes relevant and memorable. You will often find that people have trouble filling in the sheets accurately, so feedback and support will be very helpful. Very often, clients confuse thoughts and feelings, and going over homework sheets can help them differentiate between them more accurately.

Much of the success in using the following handouts and worksheets is in the processing with the group.

When addressing the topic of healthy thinking skills, having a variety of handouts and worksheets will offer your clients skills to last a lifetime. Well after the group experience is over, group members will have very tangible reminders of the lessons learned in the group with the following handouts and worksheets in this section. The first few TIPs focus on the lesson of Albert Ellis' REBT – Rational Emotive Behavior Therapy – and then the remainder are handouts and worksheets that are reflective of both REBT and/or CBT – Cognitive Behavior Therapy. Both orientations focus on how distorted thinking leads to negative experiences and disturbed emotions, and only by limiting one's cognitive distortions and disturbed patterns of thinking can a person feel better and improve their emotional health.

PROCESSING

The common thread with all the following handouts is that many of our feelings are largely determined by our thoughts, and we must challenge irrational thoughts and learn to think in more rational ways if we want to change our mood. Giving and receiving feedback to group members through the various activities helps challenge unhelpful ways of thinking. Group members will enjoy learning and practicing skills within the comfort and camaraderie of a supportive environment.

REMEMBER: Stick to the Facts, Not Interpretations!

Copyright © 2016 Judith Belmont. *150 More Group Therapy Activities & TIPS*, www.belmontwellness.com. All rights reserved.

Teaching the Psychological ABCs

THEORY

Teach the group members to break down a situation into the Psychological ABC model, and then back up the lesson with the following TIPs to help them personalize what they learned to their own lives. This lesson is one of the most valuable models for **teaching clients how to take control of their lives by taking control of their thoughts**. It's based on the works of Albert Ellis, originating in the 1950s, and his model, Rational Emotive Behavior Therapy (REBT), which provides the cornerstone of Cognitive Behavior Therapy (CBT), established in the 1960s by Aaron Beck.

IMPLEMENTATION

Teach group members to break down a situation into this model, and then back up the lesson with TIPs 67 and 68.

To introduce the psychological ABCs you can use the following example:

A - **Activating event** - *My family member calls me "lazy"*

To better make my point, I skip the B for the time being and go right to C

C - **Consequences** - Comprised of feelings and behaviors
  Feelings: Angry and Vengeful, enraged
  Behaviors: Yell, tell them to "shut up" and name call back

I ask them if the family member made them yell back and be upset, and usually they respond, "Yes."

I ask them what the B stands for in the middle - they often say behavior, whereupon I remind them that behaviors are part of the consequence.

I explain to them that B stands for beliefs or thoughts. I use the example that the thought that led them to yell and retaliate could be:

B - **Belief**
  "He has no right to say that!"
  "What a jerk!"
  This way of thinking is what makes them yell, feel enraged and retaliate.
  I brainstorm ways of *disputing* and *de-escalating* the irrational thoughts.

After identifying the B and tying it to how it causes the C, I go on to D

Copyright © 2016 Judith Belmont. *150 More Group Therapy Activities & TIPS*, www.belmontwellness.com. All rights reserved.

D - Disputing

"I wish he did not say that, but it is not up to me to decide what he 'should' say."
"Just because I do not like somethings that he said, calling him a jerk is a bit far-fetched and labeling someone is not helpful or accurate."

E - Effect of disputing the irrational thoughts

Feeling calmer
Annoyed but not enraged
Expressing feelings and thoughts assertively, not vindictively
Feeling in control, not out of control

The following REBT and CBT handouts and worksheets will be valuable resources for group members to gain more clarity in how they upset themselves and what they can do to stop their emotional distress.

Make the point that breaking situations down into these Psychological ABCs will help differentiate their thoughts, feelings and behaviors, and help them be more in control of extreme emotions.

PROCESSING

Ask the group to share situations that are upsetting, and ask how they can dissect their situations into the psychological ABC's. By working with the whole group or splitting up into smaller groups for more individualized attention, helping members learn to dissect their emotionally charged situations with this model is quite an eye opener and for some, life changing.

Copyright © 2016 Judith Belmont. *150 More Group Therapy Activities & TIPS*, www.belmontwellness.com. All rights reserved.

MY Psychological ABCs

Fill out this chart to identify the ABCs of your own personal situations.

Think of a situation that causes extreme emotional upset, depression, anxiety or stress, and use this chart to help you separate your disturbing thoughts from your emotions and behaviors, and physiological reactions.

A - Activating Event	B - Belief (perceptions, interpretations and thoughts)	C - Consequence Feelings - Behaviors	D - Dispute and De-escalate	E- Effect of the Disputing and De-escalating
Example: Friend calls me a name	I can't stand him! He's a jerk!	Enraged - Yell and name call back	"He's a jerk" and "I can't stand him" shows all or nothing, extreme thinking. "I really can stand what I do not like - I need to stop dramatizing and labeling, and just stick to the facts that I do not like what he said."	Feel calmer, express myself assertively and tell him I do not like being called names

Copyright © 2016 Judith Belmont. *150 More Group Therapy Activities & TIPS*, www.belmontwellness.com. All rights reserved.

Tip #68

The 12 Basic Irrational Beliefs of Albert Ellis (REBT)

In the 1950s, Albert Ellis was one of the first psychologists to focus on the importance of changing thoughts to change lives. As one of the pioneers of cognitive therapy, he regarded **all irrational beliefs as stemming from these 12 basic irrational beliefs that underlie anxiety, depression and other disturbing emotions.** This list is adapted from Albert Ellis' basic list.

#1 Irrational Idea — It is a dire necessity to be loved and approved of by virtually everyone to really be happy.

Disputing Irrational Idea — This is impossible. If you expect to gain everyone's approval you will not be focused on getting your own approval and you are putting your self-esteem in the hands of others!

———— • ————

#2 Irrational Idea — To be worthwhile, one must be competent and achieving in virtually everything they do.

Disputing Irrational Idea — This is again impossible. We cannot be competent in everything and it is okay to be better at some things than others. It does not mean you are a FAILURE.

———— • ————

#3 Irrational Idea — People are to be blamed for being "bad" and punishment or blame is acceptable if people "deserve it."

Disputing Irrational Idea — People are not bad, but might be unhealthy. Even if they are disturbed and unhealthy, mental illness and bad behavior does not mean that people are to be hated and seen as wicked.

———— • ————

#4 Irrational Idea — It's TERRIBLE and catastrophic when things don't go as you want them to.

Disputing Irrational Idea — "Awfulizing" things that are short of death, maiming and life threatening is over-catastrophizing, Rather, things that are seen as TERRIBLE can be regarded as "unfortunate" and "disappointing."

———— • ————

#5 Irrational Idea — My happiness is controlled by events and other people outside of me - not myself. They are to be blamed - not me.

Disputing Irrational Idea — We are in charge of how we react to life's events and are in control of our happiness. We do not need to control and micromanage other people to ensure our happiness. We are not *victims* if we choose to be *victors*.

———— • ————

 Copyright © 2016 Judith Belmont. *150 More Group Therapy Activities & TIPS*, www.belmontwellness.com. All rights reserved.

#6 Irrational Idea – It's okay to worry and dwell on things if they are potentially fearsome and even dangerous.

Disputing Irrational Idea – Even though we can try to limit our exposure to danger, worrying about things that are out of our control by acting judiciously and cautiously will rob us of our mental stability. Crippling anxiety will result from our "what ifs."

———— • ————

#7 Irrational Idea – Rather than face challenges and difficulties, it is at times better to deny and avoid facing them.

Disputing Irrational Idea – Remember - What you resist will persist! Denying and refusing to face things head on and deal with them will make things worse in the long run. Taking the "easy way out" by denying and not addressing issues will come back to bite you and rob you of a healthy life.

———— • ————

#8 Irrational Idea – It's okay to be dependent on others who are stronger.

Disputing Irrational Idea – Except in the case of children who are helpless and dependent on good nurturing and parenting, as adults it is up to us to be strong. That does not mean we cannot ask for help. You should never depend on anyone for your happiness, as that neediness will undermine self-confidence and end up making you feel vulnerable and even desperate.

———— • ————

#9 Irrational Idea – My past will always affect me and will determine my thoughts and emotions today.

Disputing Irrational Idea – You certainly develop habits from your past, but it is up to us to change the way we deal with the past now. We can live in it or learn from it, it is our choice. Our past does not need to determine our present happiness.

———— • ————

#10 Irrational Idea – If someone is upset, one "should" be upset too.

Disputing Irrational Idea – Although it is nice to have empathy for others and show concern, we do not have to let other's unhappiness rob us of our own happiness. Our happiness should not rely on others and their unhappiness should not dictate our level of happiness. If the adage were really true that "you are only as happy as your least happy child" there would be many parents whose lives would be sunk!

———— • ————

#11 Irrational Idea – There is one right solution, and it is vital to be "right." Perfection is the goal.

Disputing Irrational Idea – That type of perfectionist thinking is rigid and limits flexibility. There is often no "right" solution to life's issues and too many people are crippled by the need to be perfect.

———— • ————

#12 Irrational Idea – To be worthy, people must be skilled and good at things.

Disputing Irrational Idea – Personal worth does not depend on doing things great. Average skills do not make someone inferior to another person who has above average skills. We are each good at various things and self-worth is not dependent on our performances.

Copyright © 2016 Judith Belmont. *150 More Group Therapy Activities & TIPS*, www.belmontwellness.com. All rights reserved.

My Irrational Beliefs

In the spaces below, for any item that applies, write your own personal interpretation of Ellis' irrational beliefs and offer a healthier alternative.

Irrational Idea #1 – It is a dire necessity to be loved and approved of by virtually everyone to really be happy.

My Personal Example: _____

_____

Disputing Personal Example #1: _____

_____

Irrational Idea #2 – To be worthwhile, one must be competent and achieving in virtually everything they do.

My Personal Example:_____

_____

Disputing Personal Example #2: _____

_____

Irrational Idea #3 – People are to be blamed for being "bad" and punishment or blame is acceptable if people "deserve it."

My Personal Example:_____

_____

Disputing Personal Example #3: _____

_____

Irrational Idea #4 – It's TERRIBLE and catastrophic when things don't go as you want them to.

My Personal Example:_____

_____

Disputing Personal Example #4: _____

_____

Irrational Idea #5 – My happiness is controlled by events outside of me and other people - not myself. They are to be blamed - not me.

My Personal Example:_____

_____

Disputing Personal Example #5: _____

_____

 Copyright © 2016 Judith Belmont. _150 More Group Therapy Activities & TIPS_, www.belmontwellness.com. All rights reserved.

Irrational Idea #6 — It's okay to worry and dwell on things if they are potentially fearsome and even dangerous.

My Personal Example:_____

_____

Disputing Personal Example #6: _____

_____

Irrational Idea #7 — Rather than face challenges and difficulties, it is at times better to deny and avoid facing them.

My Personal Example:_____

_____

Disputing Personal Example #7: _____

_____

Irrational Idea #8 — I should be dependent and rely on others who are stronger.

My Personal Example:_____

_____

Disputing Personal Example #8: _____

_____

Irrational Idea #9 — My past will always affect me and determines my thoughts and emotions now.

My Personal Example:_____

_____

Disputing Personal Example #9: _____

_____

Irrational Idea #10 — If someone is upset, I "should" be upset too.

My Personal Example:_____

_____

Disputing Personal Example #10: _____

_____

Irrational Idea #11 — There is one right solution, and it is vital to be "right." Perfection is the goal.

My Personal Example:_____

_____

Disputing Personal Example #11: _____

_____

Irrational Idea #12 — To be worthy, people *must* be skilled and good at things.

My Personal Example:_____

_____

Disputing Personal Example #12: _____

_____

Copyright © 2016 Judith Belmont. *150 More Group Therapy Activities & TIPS*, www.belmontwellness.com. All rights reserved.

Tip #69

Types of Cognitive Errors

These are some of the common thought habits that cause distress, including anxiety and depression, based on the works of CBT notables Aaron Beck and David Burns.

All or Nothing Thinking – Things are seen as black and white terms, where there are no shades of gray. If you make a mistake, you think that you "failed" and/or are a "failure." **Example:** *"I am a bad mother."*

Blaming - You blame yourself or others for the problems in your life, giving up control of your feelings and reactions. This is "victim" mentality. **Example:** *"He makes me miserable!"*

Discounting the Positive – In a given situation, you focus only on the negative. **Example:** *"Even though she asked me to mentor a coworker because of my competence, she does not realize I really do not know a lot."*

Emotional Reasoning – You lose objectivity and stick to your interpretations based on your emotions and negative self-image rather than sticking to the objective facts. **Example:** *"I feel like a stupid person so I AM a stupid person."*

Fallacy of Fairness – You expect life to be fair. **Example:** *"Life should be fair and I should get what I deserve."*

Fortune Telling – You predict a negative outcome in the future based on your distorted way of thinking. You think you know what will happen without any real evidence. **Example:** *"I'll never love again."*

Jumping to Conclusions – Without checking the facts, your conclusions immediately interpret a situation idiosyncratically in line with your negative way of thinking. **Example:** *"He didn't call me - He must be breaking up with me."*

Labeling – You label yourself or others by terms such as *"lazy" "fat" "stupid" "loser" "jerk"*, stating them like they are facts. A label becomes erroneously an evaluation of self-worth. **Example:** *"I'm just fat and lazy"* and *"He is a jerk.*

Magnification or Minimization – You either blow things out of proportion or deny something is a problem when it is. **Examples:** *"It's nothing - Not a big deal (when it really is to you)."* and *"It's AWFUL that she said that!"*

Mental Filter – You pick out a negative single issue and dwell on it, like a drop of ink that discolors a whole beaker of water. **Example:** *"My big nose makes me so unattractive."*

Mind Reading – You think with certainty that you know what and why others think and feel. **Example:** *"He is just trying to show me up!"*

 Copyright © 2016 Judith Belmont. *150 More Group Therapy Activities & TIPS*, www.belmontwellness.com. All rights reserved.

Over-Catastrophizing – This is when people assume the worst and exaggerate an issue. If you made a mistake you see yourself as a failure. **Example:** *"She's mad at me - I can't ever face her again."*

Overgeneralization – You generalize from a specific. You think in absolutes, like "always" "never"and see a single negative event as a never-ending pattern. **Example:** *"Nobody likes me."*

Personalization – Interpretations are distorted and you think things are about you when it is just an interpretation. You think if someone is angry or negative you take responsibility for things out of your control. **Example:** *"It's my fault that my child is depressed"*

Playing the Comparison Game – Comparing yourself to others and needing to keep up with or outshine others to feel good about yourself. **Example:** *"He is so much smarter than me - I'm stupid."*

Should Statements – Having pre-conditions on how you and other people "should" be. Judgmental and unforgiving expectations using "musts" and "shoulds" create a lot of anxiety. **Examples:** *"I shouldn't be so upset about this." "He should know that already!"*

Write some examples of your own unhealthy thoughts and note which one or more cognitive errors fit.

COGNITIVE ERRORS

Irrational Thoughts	Type of Cognitive Errors
Example: *I am weird and always will be*	Labeling, Fortune Telling, All or Nothing Thinking

Copyright © 2016 Judith Belmont. *150 More Group Therapy Activities & TIPS*, www.belmontwellness.com. All rights reserved.

Activity

My Cognitive Errors Diary

This worksheet can serve as an ongoing diary throughout the week whenever you identify a cognitive error. Below, write some examples of your unhealthy thoughts and on the right side of the column choose one or more cognitive errors that you can Identify.

My Cognitive Errors Diary	
Irrational Thoughts	**Type of Cognitive Errors**

 Copyright © 2016 Judith Belmont. *150 More Group Therapy Activities & TIPS*, www.belmontwellness.com. All rights reserved.

Tip #70

Cracking the NUTS
and Eliminating the ANTS

THEORY

Psychologists Elisha Goldstein, Aaron Beck and David Burns use catchy acronyms to help clients uncover and eliminate their unhealthy thoughts. Their "user-friendly" techniques offer visualizations to help clients become more mindful of their unhealthy thinking patterns.

In his book *Uncovering Happiness*, Goldstein uses the image of **NUTS** to refer to **N**egative **U**nconscious **T**hought**S**. He suggests that by **being mindful of those intrusive thoughts, and by bringing them into awareness**, we can stop driving ourselves "NUTS." He found using this acronym injects some humor with his clients, who get a laugh out of the NUTS that are making them NUTS!

Beck used the acronym **ANTS** to refer to the **A**utomatic **N**egative **T**hought**S** that result in anxiety and depression, leading to low self esteem and self doubt. Burns popularized this acronym in his book, *Feeling Good*. NUTS and ANTS sabotage self-esteem and happiness, and are characterized by the cognitive errors highlighted earlier in this chapter, such as all or nothing thinking, jumping to conclusions, emotional reasoning and labeling.

IMPLEMENTATION

Offer group members a mini-lesson on the concept behind these two acronyms: NUTS and ANTS. The acronyms are essentially interchangeable for representing habitual self-sabotaging thought habits.

After introducing the concepts, here are some ways to incorporate in the group. Use the following activity to help members *crack* the NUTS and *eliminate* the ANTS!

Name – the *NUTS* and *ANTS* - Have group members write down 5 phrases that put words to the NUTS and ANTS, such as *"I'm no good," "I'll never find someone to love," "There's something wrong with me," "I'm unlikeable."* After naming the NUTS, reflect on the general themes that tie them together.

Crack – the *NUTS* and step on the *ANTS* - Have group members ask themselves how certain they are of the truth of these NUTS and ANTS. Have them challenge the truth of their self-sabotaging statements. Where's the evidence? What are more factual ways to reframe them?

Count – the NUTS and ANTS - Give group members a few minutes to identify the NUTS and ANTS that go through their head, or write them down, and count how many they identify in a certain period of time.

PROCESSING

Using these two visual acronyms adds humor into the group while helping tackle irrational thought habits by cracking the NUTS and stepping on the ANTS! Identifying ANTS and NUTS can be an effective homework assignment to bring in for processing at the next group. How many were they able to identify in the past week? Did they count them? How many NUTS did they crack? How many ANTS did they step on?

Copyright © 2016 Judith Belmont. *150 More Group Therapy Activities & TIPS*, www.belmontwellness.com. All rights reserved.

Activity

Stop Going NUTS!

Learning to identify negative unhealthy thoughts will help you stop going NUTS or buggy!

Psychologist Elisha Goldstein uses the acronym **NUTS** to refer to our **N**egative **U**nconscious **T**hought**S**. Psychologists Aaron Beck and David Burns refer to those disturbing self-sabotaging thoughts as **ANTS** - **A**utomatic **N**egative **T**hought**S**. They both use different images for the same problem we experience when we think in self-sabotaging ways -- which rob us of self-esteem and happiness.

Name your top 5 NUTS:
Example: "I'm unlikeable"

1. _____
2. _____
3. _____
4. _____
5. _____

What ANTS do you want to eliminate?
Example: "No one will ever love me."

1. _____
2. _____
3. _____
4. _____
5. _____

What are some cognitive errors what make you nutty and drive you buggy?
Example: All or nothing thinking

1. _____
2. _____
3. _____

 Copyright © 2016 Judith Belmont. *150 More Group Therapy Activities & TIPS*, www.belmontwellness.com. All rights reserved.

Stick to the Facts - Not Interpretations!

Do you upset yourself?

All too often we use irrational patterns of thinking that are disturbing, illogical and unhelpful, causing an endless supply of upsetting emotions, depression and anxiety. **You can improve your thinking habits by learning to separate fact from fiction.** The following are examples of unhelpful fictitious thinking and how to transform these statements into the facts.

There is nothing wrong with making interpretations - just know they are fictitious and not fact! Notice the words in bold are exaggerations.

Fiction	Type of Error	Fact
I **can't** stand it!	All or nothing thinking	I have trouble handling it.
It's **awful** that he said that!	Over-catastrophizing	It is disappointing he said that.
He **shouldn't** act that way!	"Shoulding"	I wish he did not act that way.
Things **never** work out!	All or nothing thinking	Things often do not work out like I hope.
I will **never** find anyone to love.	Fortune telling	I do not know the future - I will try my best.
I am such a **loser**.	Labeling	I am unhappy with myself and will change.
She drives people **crazy**!	Blaming	People find her challenging.
I am to **blame** that my child is unhappy.	Personalization	I tried my best and blaming myself is illogical.
I am upset, but it's **no big deal**.	Minimizing	I am upset and will not minimize it.
He thinks it's **my fault**!	Jumping to conclusions	I do not know what is inside his head.
I am ugly **because** I have a large nose.	Mental filter	One feature does not negate all my others.
"I'm **doomed**."	All or nothing thinking	I'm struggling - let's not get so dramatic!
I **should** be further along in my life by now.	"Shoulding"	I am disappointed and will work to progress.

Now it's your turn: Write some of your disturbing fictitious statements, identify the distortions, and then translate them into facts.

Fiction	Type of Cognitive Error	Fact
_____	_____	_____
_____	_____	_____
_____	_____	_____
_____	_____	_____
_____	_____	_____

Copyright © 2016 Judith Belmont. *150 More Group Therapy Activities & TIPS*, www.belmontwellness.com. All rights reserved.

Tip #72

Change that Distorted Thinking!

Notice the words in bold - They are inflexible, blown out of proportion, illogical, distorted thoughts that lead to anxiety and depression.

1. I **can't** stand it!
2. It is **terrible** that things go **wrong!**
3. He **shouldn't** be that way!
4. I **hate** being criticized!
5. They **should** listen to me!
6. I **can't** change what I think!
7. It's **terrible** to be wrong!
8. I **should** be able to control my kid's behavior!
9. I **can't** forgive them/myself
10. He makes me **nuts!**

11. It **drives me crazy!**
12. He **ruined** my life!
13. Things are **hopeless!**
14. It's **awful!**
15. It's my **fault** she is like that!
16. My childhood **always** affect me!
17. She **made me** feel that way!
18. I **can't** control my feelings!
19. I **can't** help the way I act!
20. He **always** does that!

Do you notice any phrases relate to you? Write them or other problematic thoughts below and change them into healthier thoughts.

Distorted Thinking	Healthy Thinking
Example: "She made me feel that way!"	She cannot control my feelings. Rather, I felt that way when she said that.

 Copyright © 2016 Judith Belmont. *150 More Group Therapy Activities & TIPS*, www.belmontwellness.com. All rights reserved.

From Problems to Solutions - It's All in the Way We Think!

Our thoughts and perceptions color our world and determine our feelings and the ways we behave. Consider these truths:

- The healthier your thoughts, the healthier your feelings and behaviors.
- Unhealthy thinking habits lead to anxiety, depression and unhealthy behaviors.
- Solution-oriented thinking habits are more factual, more rational and lead to healthy self-esteem, self-empowerment and healthy life choices.
- We can help to control disturbing emotions by replacing problematic thoughts with solution - oriented thoughts.

For each of the problematic thoughts, write at least one type of cognitive distortion.

Problematic Thinking Habits	Type of Cognitive Distortion
I **can't** stand it!	Black and white inflexible thinking
He **shouldn't** be so disrespectful.	
It's **terrible** if I am wrong!	
I **HATE** when he acts that way.	
He's a **jerk**!	
I'm a **loser**!	
I'll **always** feel this way.	
He **makes me nuts**!	
He doesn't really **mean** the compliment	

Now using the same examples of problematic thinking habits, offer solution-oriented thoughts. Notice how the solution-oriented thought habits are more flexible and less catastrophic. In bold italics notice the shift from inflexible thoughts shift to healthier and more flexible habits of thinking.

Problematic Thinking Habits	*Solution-Oriented Thinking Habits*
I **can't** stand it!	I **can** stand even what I do not like.
He **shouldn't** be so disrespectful.	I **would like** it if he acted more respectfully.
It's **terrible** if I am wrong!	It would be **unfortunate** if I am wrong - and human!
I **HATE** when he acts that way.	I feel **annoyed** when he acts that way.
He's a **jerk**!	I find him **disrespectful** to me.
I'm a **loser**!	There are some ways I would like to **improve**.
I'll **always** feel this way.	I'll **try to change** my thoughts to change feelings
He **makes me nuts**!	I **become unstable** in response to his behavior.
He doesn't really **mean** the compliment	I **appreciate** he said something nice about me.

Copyright © 2016 Judith Belmont. *150 More Group Therapy Activities & TIPS*, www.belmontwellness.com. All rights reserved.

What are some problematic thoughts that hold you back? Can you identify the types of distortion? How can you change those problematic thoughts to solution-oriented habits of thinking? Daily practice will help you improve your thinking habits!

Problematic Thoughts

_____

_____

_____

Type of Cognitive Distortions

_____

_____

_____

Solution-Oriented Thoughts

_____

_____

_____

REMEMBER: Change your thoughts — Change your life!

Copyright © 2016 Judith Belmont. *150 More Group Therapy Activities & TIPS*, www.belmontwellness.com. All rights reserved.

Trade in Your Words

Our thoughts often create our feelings. It is our thoughts and perceptions about events, not the events themselves, that determine our feelings and behaviors. Changing the way that we think can change feelings, and this worksheet helps you think about alternate word choices for your own self-talk. If you trade your unhealthy words that you say to yourself, you will change your thoughts to change your life.

Words and sentences to trade:

Trade *"can't stand"* with *"do not care for."*

Trade *"have to"* with *"choose to."*

Trade *"always"* with *"usually."*

Trade *"should"* with *"could."*

Trade *"must"* with *"will."*

Trade *"terrible"* with *"unfortunate."*

Trade *"never"* with *"infrequently."*

Your turn:

In the space below, write a few sentences or phrases with these words above and then trade those words for healthier word choices, which are more flexible and reasonable.

Unhealthy Phrase: _____

Alternative Phrase: _____

Unhealthy Phrase: _____

Alternative Phrase: _____

When you trade your words, you are trading negative emotions to more manageable ones.

You are trading *"devastated"* for *"unsettled."*

You are trading *"depression"* for *"sadness."*

You are trading *"shame"* for *"regret."*

You are trading *"rage"* for *"upset."*

You are trading *"worried"* for *"concerned."*

Can you think of others?

Trade _____ with _____

Trade _____ with _____

Copyright © 2016 Judith Belmont. *150 More Group Therapy Activities & TIPS*, www.belmontwellness.com. All rights reserved.

Having Clients Keep a Daily Thought Log

THEORY

Providing thought logs for journaling on a daily, weekly or somewhat regular basis will be very helpful outside of the session and also aid in processing during the group session. **Thought logs reinforce CBT skills and help group members identify their irrational thoughts and types of distortions.** Have members bring their logs to the next session to review progress with the group.

IMPLEMENTATION

Suggest to the group members that they use Daily Thought Logs to help them challenge faulty beliefs.

Thought logs help clients identify and track their:

- Triggering event
- Positive emotions
- Negative emotions
- Strength of emotions
- Anxious beliefs
- Challenging beliefs

- Degree of certainty of their beliefs
- Types of cognitive distortions
- Healthy behaviors
- Unhealthy behaviors
- Cost/Benefit analysis
- Conclusions and goals

Educate group members that rating the degree of certainty will help them think more rationally, as it will limit all or nothing, extreme, black and white thinking, and encourage them to see things in less extreme shades of gray. The goal of the following exercise is to step back and examine the certainty of their thoughts and gain objectivity. Encourage group members to have a plan of action and set goals based on healthier ways of thinking. Instead of automatically believing negative self-talk 100%, this TIP will help clients question the certainty of their beliefs and learn to think more critically.

The following example can be used to show the group how to fill out the logs:

Example:

Triggering Event: Marital breakup

Irrational thoughts: *I'll never love anyone again - I'll be alone the rest of my life.*

Certainty of belief: 40%

Type of cognitive distortion: Fortune telling, black and white thinking, jumping to conclusions

 Copyright © 2016 Judith Belmont. *150 More Group Therapy Activities & TIPS*, www.belmontwellness.com. All rights reserved.

Rational Thoughts: *I am in pain now but if I loved her, I will have the capacity to love someone else, and this time I'll be wiser in how I treat her.*

Certainty of belief: 85 %

Action Plan and Goals: In the short term, *I will work on getting my confidence back up in socializing and going on dates, without expectation of meeting anyone serious until I feel more confident and balanced.*

Have group members fill out at least one example outside of the session and bring them in for sharing and discussion at the beginning of the next session.

PROCESSING

The following thought log variations will offer structure between sessions to help your clients to practice improving the ways they think. Leave enough time at the beginning of the group to go over important homework assignments such as the thought logs. The group environment is ideal for processing these logs, as members receive and give feedback and support. Thought logs do not have to be used daily to be effective, but I use the term daily to encourage clients to incorporate this type of activity on a regular basis in order to practice healthier life skills.

Copyright © 2016 Judith Belmont. *150 More Group Therapy Activities & TIPS*, www.belmontwellness.com. All rights reserved.

Sample *Analyzing Anxiety: Daily Log Completed*

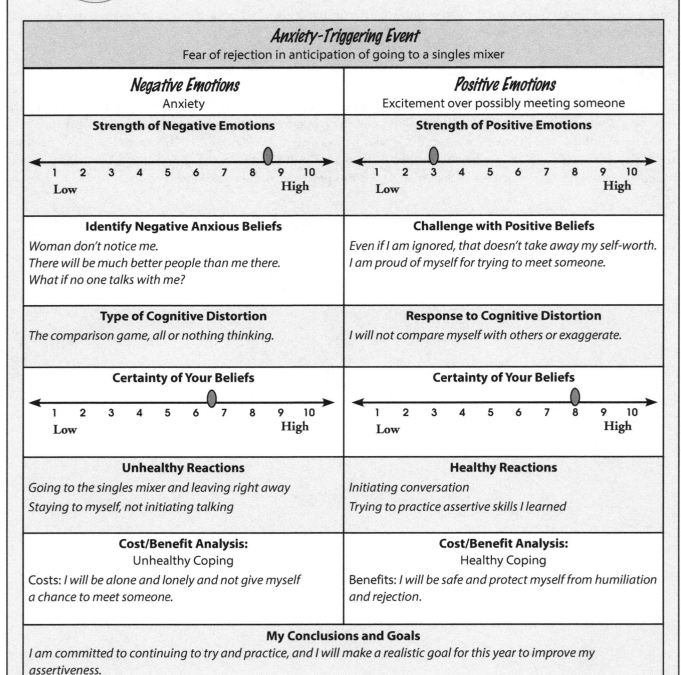

Anxiety-Triggering Event	
Fear of rejection in anticipation of going to a singles mixer	

Negative Emotions	**Positive Emotions**
Anxiety	Excitement over possibly meeting someone

Strength of Negative Emotions	**Strength of Positive Emotions**
1 2 3 4 5 6 7 8 9 10 Low　　　　　　　　　　　　High	1 2 3 4 5 6 7 8 9 10 Low　　　　　　　　　　　　High

Identify Negative Anxious Beliefs	**Challenge with Positive Beliefs**
Woman don't notice me. *There will be much better people than me there.* *What if no one talks with me?*	*Even if I am ignored, that doesn't take away my self-worth.* *I am proud of myself for trying to meet someone.*

Type of Cognitive Distortion	**Response to Cognitive Distortion**
The comparison game, all or nothing thinking.	*I will not compare myself with others or exaggerate.*

Certainty of Your Beliefs	**Certainty of Your Beliefs**
1 2 3 4 5 6 7 8 9 10 Low　　　　　　　　　　　　High	1 2 3 4 5 6 7 8 9 10 Low　　　　　　　　　　　　High

Unhealthy Reactions	**Healthy Reactions**
Going to the singles mixer and leaving right away *Staying to myself, not initiating talking*	*Initiating conversation* *Trying to practice assertive skills I learned*

Cost/Benefit Analysis: Unhealthy Coping	**Cost/Benefit Analysis:** Healthy Coping
Costs: *I will be alone and lonely and not give myself a chance to meet someone.*	Benefits: *I will be safe and protect myself from humiliation and rejection.*

My Conclusions and Goals	
I am committed to continuing to try and practice, and I will make a realistic goal for this year to improve my assertiveness.	

From *The Therapist's Ultimate Solution Book: Essential Strategies, Tips and Tools To Empower Your Clients* by Judith Belmont.
Copyright © 2015 by Judith Belmont. Used by permission of W.W. Norton & Company

Copyright © 2016 Judith Belmont. *150 More Group Therapy Activities & TIPS*, www.belmontwellness.com. All rights reserved.

Activity

Daily Thought Log

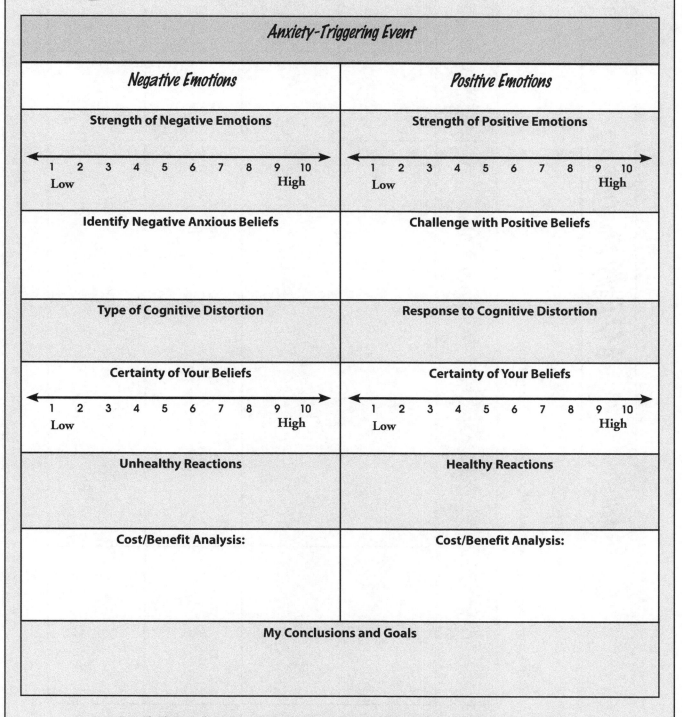

Anxiety-Triggering Event	
Negative Emotions	**Positive Emotions**
Strength of Negative Emotions 1 2 3 4 5 6 7 8 9 10 Low High	**Strength of Positive Emotions** 1 2 3 4 5 6 7 8 9 10 Low High
Identify Negative Anxious Beliefs	**Challenge with Positive Beliefs**
Type of Cognitive Distortion	**Response to Cognitive Distortion**
Certainty of Your Beliefs 1 2 3 4 5 6 7 8 9 10 Low High	**Certainty of Your Beliefs** 1 2 3 4 5 6 7 8 9 10 Low High
Unhealthy Reactions	**Healthy Reactions**
Cost/Benefit Analysis:	**Cost/Benefit Analysis:**
My Conclusions and Goals	

From *The Therapist's Ultimate Solution Book: Essential Strategies, Tips and Tools To Empower Your Clients* by Judith Belmont.
Copyright © 2015 by Judith Belmont. Used by permission of W.W. Norton & Company

My Daily Thought Log

Activity

Keep track of your cognitive distortions with this thought log!

Irrational Thoughts	Certainty of Beliefs (%)	Types of Cognitive Distortion	Alternative Rational Thoughts	Certainty of Beliefs (%)	Action Plan and Goals

From *The Therapist's Ultimate Solution Book: Essential Strategies, Tips and Tools To Empower Your Clients* by Judith Belmont. Copyright © 2015 by Judith Belmont. Used by permission of W.W. Norton & Company

 Copyright © 2016 Judith Belmont. *150 More Group Therapy Activities & TIPS*, www.belmontwellness.com. All rights reserved.

Turning TICS into TOCS

In his TIC-TOC technique, David Burns demonstrates CBT skills in a novel way. He identifies Task-Interfering Cognition (TICs) and demonstrates how to change those to TOCs (Task-Oriented Cognitions). This action oriented approach helps people defeat procrastination and increase proactivity.

TICS (Task-Interfering Cognitions)	Types of Cognitive Distortion	TOCS (Task-Oriented Cognitions)
"I'll never feel better"	Fortune telling, all-or-nothing thinking, sense of futility	*"I will feel better once I become more active in my healing and work on challenging my unhealthy ways of thinking."*

From *The Therapist's Ultimate Solution Book: Essential Strategies, Tips and Tools To Empower Your Clients* by Judith Belmont.
Copyright © 2015 by Judith Belmont. Used by permission of W.W. Norton & Company

Create Coping Cards

THEORY

Coping cards are a cornerstone of CBT. **Coping cards offer clients important reminders written on notecards that they can keep with them to improve coping skills.** Carrying coping cards in a pocket, wallet or purse can help individuals improve how they regulate their emotions when they experience instability with the emotional support and written reminders.

IMPLEMENTATION

Introduce the concept of coping cards to the group.

Coping cards can be easily made up using small 3 by 5 inch notecards, small enough to be portable even in a back pocket. They are carried around to serve as a reference when needed at the spur of the moment or in preparation for situations that cause anxiety and distress, such as in preparation for a social occasion or a workplace meeting.

Have group members choose from a variety of writing tools: crayons, pens, colored pencils, markers, pencils. I like using colored index cards to make them more attractive. For an interesting variation, supply magazines, scissors and glue so they can find words and pictures to decorate their cards.

Depending on the lesson of the group, or the type of group it is, you can tailor the coping card activity to it. The following are examples that you can do in your group:

For drug and alcohol groups, coping cards might address healthy self-statements, alternative behaviors and reminders when an individual has an urge to relapse.

For those with borderline and highly impulsive behavior, or anger management issues, the coping cards might offer a menu of calming behaviors the person can do when emotionally distressed. Some ideas include deep breathing, counting to 100 before reacting, calling a friend or family member, a reminder to reach for their "survival kit" to self-soothe, etc.

For those with low self-esteem and anxiety, coping cards which challenge negative self-talk or provide affirmations to refer to in times of high anxiety.

For those who get irrational and self-critical, depressed and filled with shame and regret, coping cards that show self-compassion and acceptance can be invaluable to help stop the self-bullying.

For emotionally volatile relationships, coping cards with reminders of how to express anger assertively instead of aggressively will be helpful. Perhaps having a mantra to remind group members of how to be assertive will be helpful such as "*make sure my goal is to express, not impress!*"

 Copyright © 2016 Judith Belmont. *150 More Group Therapy Activities & TIPS*, www.belmontwellness.com. All rights reserved.

Create **group coping cards** that include the ground rules for the group, to ensure the safe atmosphere for group members. These coping cards could serve as reminders for the group members to be nonjudgmental and accepting, and grateful for the safe and valuable experience.

You might want to use certain colors for certain type of cards. For example, the affirmation cards could be blue and the 2-sided irrational thought cards could be yellow. This makes them easier to locate in times of distress.

2-sided Card Variations – Write an irrational thought on one side and on the other side write the type of cognitive distortion. *"I will never love again!"* on one side can be offset by writing the type of cognitive distortion, such as Fortune Telling, All or Nothing Thinking.

Another 2-sided card could weigh the pros and cons of taking action in a situation.

A variation is to replace an unhealthy thought on one side with a healthier alternative on the other side.

Have a paper puncher to punch a hole in the corner of the cards on the corner, and have yarn or ring binders to hold them together. Supply clear contact paper to laminate the cards for extra durability.

PROCESSING

To make this a fun and social activity, encourage participants to talk and share while they are creating their cards, and have each person share one of their cards once they are completed. Processing with others in the group will help each individual get new ideas of how to manage emotions in times of distress.

Copyright © 2016 Judith Belmont. *150 More Group Therapy Activities & TIPS*, www.belmontwellness.com. All rights reserved.

Making Coping Cards for Each Other

THEORY

This activity in which group members make coping cards for one another unleashes the power of the group milieu. Sometimes getting the perspective of others is a much-needed relief from unhealthy ruts of thinking and behaving. After the idea of coping cards has been introduced and you have group members make up their own cards, now they can help others by making cards for one another. This activity taps into the power of the group camaraderie.

IMPLEMENTATION

Give each member in the group 3 by 5 inch cards so they have enough to create a coping card for each member of the group.

Have group members take turns briefly describing a challenging type of situation they commonly experience. Ask them to think of a specific common issue without going into a long story about one situation.

Examples might be:

- *When my boyfriend brings up the past, I "lose it" and we start arguing.*

- *I get so nervous in social situations that I tend to leave places early, and I want to be able to stick it out.*

- *I have trouble containing my anger when my parent criticizes me.*

- *When preparing to speak in front of a class or group of people, I get panicky and forget what I want to say.*

After the individual gives a brief explanation and everyone has time to ask questions, each group member writes on a notecard a coping tip for the person who describes their upsetting situation. Have them put their name on top and the name of the person they are making it out for.

Go around and have each person read his or her coping tip suggestion.

Repeat this activity for everyone in the group.

Each person will now have a set of coping cards written by group members!

PROCESSING

A set of coping cards made by others can be very powerful and gives some objectivity to group members' subjective distress. Having all read their cards and explain their suggestion will be very helpful for individual learning as well as group support and cohesiveness.

 Copyright © 2016 Judith Belmont. *150 More Group Therapy Activities & TIPS*, www.belmontwellness.com. All rights reserved.

Tip #79

Creating Metaphorical Coping Cards and Coping Boxes

THEORY

Coping cards are notecards that are popular in CBT and DBT, which remind individuals of healthy ways of thinking and coping in times of emotional distress. They usually contain coping statements, such as "These feelings will not last forever" and "I can get through this." Some coping cards are two sided – one side has an irrational thought, and the other has the type of cognitive distortion accompanied with a solution oriented thought. This TIP uses the power of metaphor for use with coping cards.

IMPLEMENTATION

Use of metaphors in counseling has always been quite powerful, and using them with coping cards will combine two effective therapeutic vehicles together.

Have the group brainstorm some metaphors or visualizations that help them stay calm amidst upsetting situations.

A fun group activity can be to think of other metaphors that represent images that are calming.

Actual items that they use for a metaphorical toolkit can be added to their box of coping cards. For instance, a stress ball will serve as a reminder to be flexible and resilient, as it is flexible, bounces back, and is able to float and roll with the punches.

You might also bring some familiar things around your house to use metaphorical demonstrations. For example, a sifter would represent sifting out your negative and erroneous thoughts.

Using metaphorical pictures drawn on notecards or cut out from a magazine - without even needing to use words - will be an interesting way to fill up and even decorate a coping card box.

PROCESSING

Have all members take turns showing a metaphorical coping card and explain why that can be useful in times of distress. This activity promotes group sharing and cohesiveness. Learning from other group members can also help develop creative and improved coping skills.

Copyright © 2016 Judith Belmont. *150 More Group Therapy Activities & TIPS*, www.belmontwellness.com. All rights reserved.

Tip #80

Making a Group Coping Card Basket

THEORY

In this activity, group members make one joint group basket to use in subsequent sessions. This adds a new dimension to creating coping cards, as **group members are working with one another to figure out joint solutions to their common problems**, and taps the power of the sense of universality that groups offer.

IMPLEMENTATION

Bring in a box or basket for the group activity.

As a group, go around and have each member talk about an issue they want to work on, and a few coping card suggestions that would address that issue. Each member gets help from the others to start off and then they each make up two or three cards to contribute to the group coping card basket.

Use this coping card basket for each group session to model the use of coping cards regularly at home, and practicing consistent use of them. Set aside 5 to 10 minutes at the start or end of each group to pick out a few of the coping cards and go over how using these skills could have helped them in the previous week or to prepare for the week ahead.

PROCESSING

This joint coping card basket will help develop comfort in sharing, improve group camaraderie, and tap the power of universality in groups. A group coping card basket will help group members feel connected to others and increase group support. As in almost all group activities, the effectiveness is determined by the quality of the group processing.

 Copyright © 2016 Judith Belmont. *150 More Group Therapy Activities & TIPS*, www.belmontwellness.com. All rights reserved.

Identify your Internal Core Beliefs

Tip #81

We all have ways we see ourselves and the world. Our core beliefs are the basic ways we see ourselves and the world, and serves as the filter for our view of ourselves and the world outside of us.

EXAMPLE: In the situation of a friend who no longer seems to have time for you, a person with a strong negative core belief (i.e. *I am not a likable person, I am a failure*) will process this event differently than a person with more positive core belief about themselves (*I am still a worthy and likable person.*).

This is how a core belief will cause you to make sense (or nonsense!) of yourself:

On the other hand, those individuals who have a positive core belief about themselves interpret and react quite differently to the same event.

Copyright © 2016 Judith Belmont. *150 More Group Therapy Activities & TIPS*, www.belmontwellness.com. All rights reserved.

Quiz | ## How Healthy are My Core Beliefs?

The following are examples of common positive and negative core beliefs. Make a check next to the alternative which best describes you. At the end, tally up your checks to find the strength of your core beliefs - do they tend to be more positive or negative?

<u>**Negative Core Beliefs**</u>	<u>**Positive Core Beliefs**</u>
Put a check on which alternative describes you best	

_____ I am unlikable	_____ I am likable
_____ I am unlovable	_____ I am lovable
_____ I am a bad person	_____ I am a good person
_____ I am not smart enough	_____ I am smart
_____ I am a loser	_____ I am special
_____ I am not pretty	_____ I am attractive
_____ I am a failure	_____ I am successful
_____ I am ashamed of who I am	_____ I am proud of who I am
_____ I am inferior to others	_____ I'm just as worthy as others
_____ I'm not "good enough"	_____ I am awesome

Negative Core Beliefs
Total score: _____

Positive Core Beliefs
Total score: _____

What Is Your Core Belief Quotient?

To find your Core Belief Quotient: Put a minus before your Negative Core Belief score and subtract your negative score from your positive one. (Example: A score of 2 on Your Negative Core Beliefs becomes -2) and add it to your Positive Belief Quotient.)

Total Score: _____

Then graph your score on this scale to find out how healthy is your Core Belief Quotient. The higher the number, the better!

Unhealthy Core Beliefs
(Needs help)

Healthy Core Beliefs
(Awesome!)

-10   -9   -8   -7   -6   -5   -4   -3   -2   -1   0   1   2   3   4   5   6   7   8   9   10

 Copyright © 2016 Judith Belmont. *150 More Group Therapy Activities & TIPS,* www.belmontwellness.com. All rights reserved.

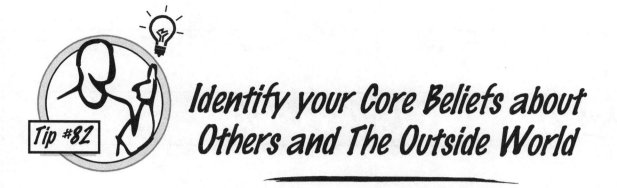

Identify your Core Beliefs about Others and The Outside World

Tip #82

Our negative core beliefs about ourselves will influence the way we see other people and the way we see the world. If we see ourselves with a negative filter, our world view will be smudged like we are wearing dirty glasses, and this filmy haze will be tainted with our negative perceptions. **Our view of the world and our place in it results from our core internal beliefs about ourselves**.

Those who tend to harbor negative core beliefs about themselves see others and the world as unsafe and menacing.

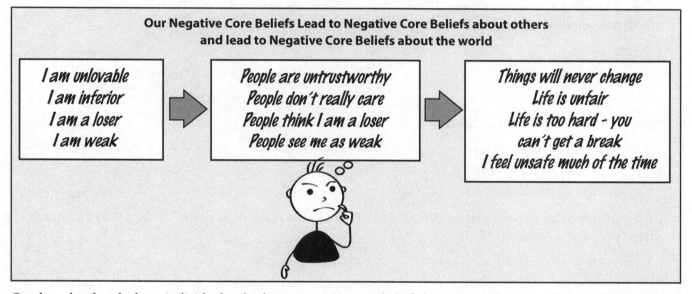

Our Negative Core Beliefs Lead to Negative Core Beliefs about others and lead to Negative Core Beliefs about the world

| I am unlovable
I am inferior
I am a loser
I am weak | People are untrustworthy
People don't really care
People think I am a loser
People see me as weak | Things will never change
Life is unfair
Life is too hard - you
can't get a break
I feel unsafe much of the time |

On the other hand, those individuals who have a positive core belief about themselves see others and the world as offering support, positivity and safety.

Our Positive Core Beliefs lead to Positive Core Beliefs about others and lead to Positive Core Beliefs about the world

| I am loveable
I am special
I am competent
I am strong | People are trustworthy
Many people care about me
People think highly of me
People see me as strong | Life offers many opportunities
Life might not always be fair,
but I make the best of it
Life is challenging but I make
my own breaks
I feel safe and have
gratitude to be alive |

Copyright © 2016 Judith Belmont. *150 More Group Therapy Activities & TIPS*, www.belmontwellness.com. All rights reserved.

My Core Beliefs

List 3 core beliefs about yourself:

    1. _____

    2. _____

    3. _____

Do they tend to be negative or positive? If any of them are unhealthy negative core beliefs, change them to be more positive.

    1. _____

    2. _____

    3. _____

Now list 3 core beliefs about others:

    1. _____

    2. _____

    3. _____

Do they tend to be negative or positive? If any of them are unhealthy negative core beliefs, change them to be more positive.

    1. _____

    2. _____

    3. _____

Now list 3 core beliefs about the world:

    1. _____

    2. _____

    3. _____

Do they tend to be negative or positive? If any of them are unhealthy negative core beliefs, change them to be more positive.

    1. _____

    2. _____

    3. _____

With practice, you can alter your negative
core beliefs to kinder, healthier and more positive ones.

 Copyright © 2016 Judith Belmont. *150 More Group Therapy Activities & TIPS*, www.belmontwellness.com. All rights reserved.

Weighing the Costs and Benefits

THEORY

One of the most widely used practices in both Cognitive Behavior Therapy and Dialectical Behavior Therapy is **performing the cost/benefit analysis**. This practice can be adapted quite well to both individual and group settings. Performing a cost/benefit analysis is like having two lists weighing the pros and cons for having certain beliefs or behaviors, helping to make a reasonable decision.

IMPLEMENTATION

Use a flip chart or white board to identify a behavior and then compare pros and cons to help group members make thoughtful decisions about a chosen behavior. On one side will be the benefits, or advantages, and the other side, the costs, or disadvantages, of a decision. See the example below.

Continuing to Drink Excessively

Benefits	Costs
Helps me "chill"	I end up feeling less "chilled" in the long run and actually get more anxious.
I am more relaxed around people	I am not developing the skills to be confident socially without using alcohol.
I am more fun to be around	I end up alienating the people I love the most.
I "deserve it"	I am making myself physically unhealthy and more prone to medical issues.

PROCESSING

Hearing and sharing the responses of others helps members appreciate and share how hard it can be to make healthy choices. They often learn as much from listening to others and gaining insights into the struggles of others in making decisions as they do from sharing their own. Learning skills together such as weighing the pros and cons will increase group trust and camaraderie, while helping group members learn valuable life skills.

Copyright © 2016 Judith Belmont. *150 More Group Therapy Activities & TIPS*, www.belmontwellness.com. All rights reserved.

Tip #84

Cut It Out!

Cognitive Behavior Therapy is based on the notion that **by changing our thoughts we can change our emotions**. This acronym will remind you to cut out those disturbing thoughts that cause problems! How do you do this? By cutting it out!

Correct

Unhelpful

Thoughts

Identify

Toxic

Over-catastrophizing

Unhealthy

Thinking habits

What thoughts do you need to *CUT OUT*?

_____

_____

_____

_____

_____

_____

For each unhelpful thought, write a healthier alternative thought.

_____

_____

_____

_____

_____

_____

Copyright © 2016 Judith Belmont. *150 More Group Therapy Activities & TIPS*, www.belmontwellness.com. All rights reserved.

Correcting My Unhelpful Thoughts

This worksheet will help you reflect upon and gain insight into unhealthy thought habits. Recognizing and increasing awareness will help you make progress to change!

1. What thoughts do I need to challenge?

_____

_____

2. What is not helpful about my unhelpful thoughts?

_____

_____

3. What type of thinking errors do these thoughts reflect?

_____

_____

4. What feelings do these thoughts cause in me?

_____

_____

5. How have these thoughts held me back from feeling better?

_____

_____

6. What proof do I have that those thoughts are true? Where's the evidence?

_____

_____

7. How would my life be different if I let go of those unhelpful thoughts?

_____

_____

Copyright © 2016 Judith Belmont. *150 More Group Therapy Activities & TIPS*, www.belmontwellness.com. All rights reserved.

Tip #86

Turning Judgements into Acceptance

When we "judge" others and ourselves, we are using "stinking thinking." Here are examples of how to be more accepting and kinder to yourself and others - and stop being a "judge." Leave judging to the ones in the courtroom! Acceptance based thoughts focus on reality, whereas judgmental thoughts are focused on the "shoulds."

Judgmental Thoughts	Acceptance Based Thoughts
He should not be that way	I wish he were not that way, but I can handle it.
I am a loser.	I am going through a hard time, but I am still worthy.
My sister is an idiot!	I do not like some of my sister's behaviors
He's acting like a big baby!	I do not like the way he is acting.

Your turn: Transform your judgments into accepting and compassionate thoughts.

Judgmental Thoughts	Compassionate Thoughts
_____	_____
_____	_____
_____	_____
_____	_____

BE A "SHOULD" BUSTER!

Copyright © 2016 Judith Belmont. *150 More Group Therapy Activities & TIPS*, www.belmontwellness.com. All rights reserved.

Stick Figures That Teach How to Change Thoughts

THEORY

Everyone can make stick figures, regardless of the level of artistic ability. They are quick, easy to make, and universally understood. Using stick figures can offer a vehicle to express thoughts and feelings in a nonthreatening way. The cartoon quality of stick figures give a little bit of lightness to this activity, injecting important lessons with a little bit of humor and perspective.

IMPLEMENTATION

Introduce or review the major concept underlying CBT, which is that your thoughts create your feelings, and distorted thinking is often the basis of hopelessness, depression and anxiety.

Suggest that one technique to use when they are upset is to write a stick figure with a callout over the head, and write the thoughts that are causing the emotional upset. This thought explains why the stick figure is unhappy.

Then draw next to it a stick figure with a smile and another callout with a more rational and positive thought than the disturbing thought.

To structure the activity further, pass out the attached worksheet so group members can fill in their own responses after the examples given.

Ask for volunteers in the group to show their stick figure cartoons and briefly explain their situation.

PROCESSING

Review with group members how replacing distorted thoughts with more rational alternatives will help keep them more positive. Using stick figures with captions to make the learning interesting and easily accessible will be a creative and fun activity for the group – and makes serious concepts fun!

Copyright © 2016 Judith Belmont. *150 More Group Therapy Activities & TIPS*, www.belmontwellness.com. All rights reserved.

You Can Change How You Think!

The examples below show how you can change your feelings by changing your thoughts!

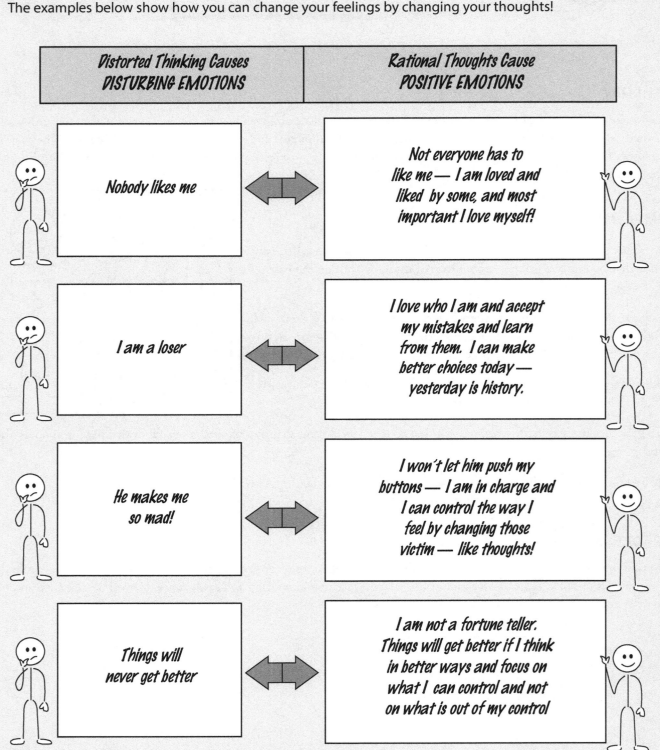

Distorted Thinking Causes DISTURBING EMOTIONS	Rational Thoughts Cause POSITIVE EMOTIONS
Nobody likes me	Not everyone has to like me — I am loved and liked by some, and most important I love myself!
I am a loser	I love who I am and accept my mistakes and learn from them. I can make better choices today — yesterday is history.
He makes me so mad!	I won't let him push my buttons — I am in charge and I can control the way I feel by changing those victim — like thoughts!
Things will never get better	I am not a fortune teller. Things will get better if I think in better ways and focus on what I can control and not on what is out of my control

Copyright © 2016 Judith Belmont. *150 More Group Therapy Activities & TIPS*, www.belmontwellness.com. All rights reserved.

You Can Change How You Think!

Now it's your turn to change how you think! Think of 4 of your irrational thoughts that cause problems, and think of more rational and positive self-talk in response to them.

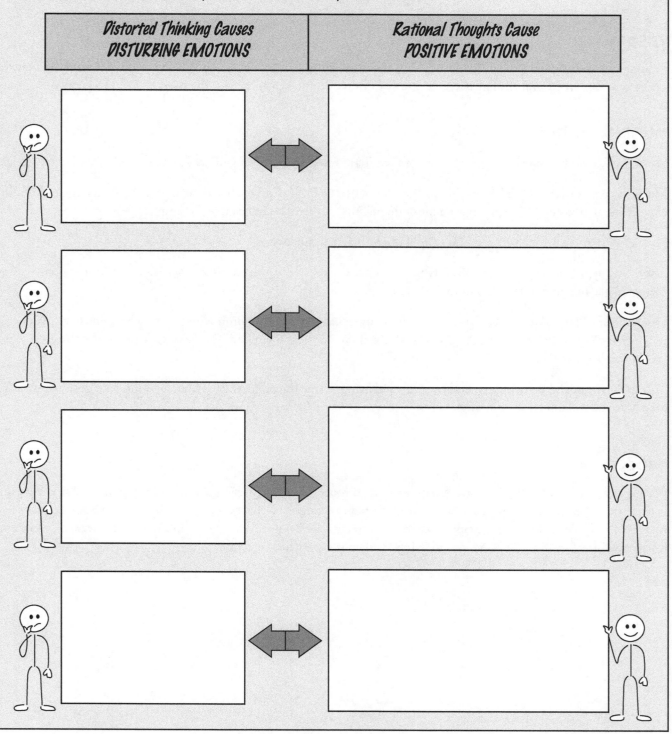

Distorted Thinking Causes DISTURBING EMOTIONS	*Rational Thoughts Cause* POSITIVE EMOTIONS

Copyright © 2016 Judith Belmont. *150 More Group Therapy Activities & TIPS*, www.belmontwellness.com. All rights reserved.

Using A Flair for the Dramatic

THEORY

Finding creative ways to teach CBT principles is always welcome in a group setting. **This activity effectively makes the point that our irrational thoughts create a lot of drama in our heads and in our lives.**

IMPLEMENTATION

Start this activity by asking the group if any of them have experience in being on stage or thinks they would like to act.

Make the point that although choosing to act as an amateur or professionally can be a growth producing and healthy choice, we often unintentionally inject a lot of drama into our lives by unhealthy thinking.

Have each participant identify an unhealthy thought they tell themselves.

Then have members take turns sharing their irrational thought with the group and act it out with one or two group members playing other characters in their drama.

Using the example, "I'm a loser," have the group member exaggerate by hamming it up as to what a lowly human being they are, etc. and encourage the other "actors" in the drama to help them with their exaggeration to the absurd, such as "yes, a flea has more self-worth!"

This exercise can end up being fun and comical, and brings home the point to keep drama on the stage and stop creating drama by irrational ways of thinking!

PROCESSING

Having people act out their flair for dramatics and then process how it felt can prove very enlightening. Ask the group what lessons they can learn from acting out their dramatic thoughts. Reflect on this activity at the next session to see if they were more conscious of the drama they inflict into their lives. Group members can share if they were able to inject less drama into their lives with the insight gained with this experiential activity.

Copyright © 2016 Judith Belmont. *150 More Group Therapy Activities & TIPS*, www.belmontwellness.com. All rights reserved.

5

Improve Coping Skills with Mindfulness and Stress Resiliency

Tips 89-119

Tip #89

Focusing on Mindfulness

THEORY

The *Third Wave* of psychotherapeutic orientations grew out of the awareness of the difficulty to reach some clients who lacked sufficient life skills and coping skills to deal with everyday life issues. **Mindfulness and acceptance strategies, which are at the core of the Third Wave orientations, emerged as a necessary addition to traditional CBT and supportive treatment.** Originally used for hard-to-reach populations, such as those with Borderline Personality Disorder, these practices have now become integrated into mainstream treatments.

IMPLEMENTATION

These are some ideas to include in your psycho-educational presentation to the group:

- One of the four modules of Dialectical Behavioral Therapy is acceptance, which includes various mindfulness practices, that helps to be "in the moment" with nonjudgmental awareness.

- *Mental Noting* and *Witnessing* are the terms often used to describe mindfulness practice. Mindfulness can be generally described as the process of staying present, focused, and mentally noting without getting distracted by judgments and fears.

- Mindfulness helps people observe, describe, and note their experience without being reactive to it.

- Accepting reality does not mean that you tolerate abuse or disrespect, but rather set limits accordingly without letting the reality ruin your life, increasing your ability to be stable and cope.

- Mindfulness does not eliminate anxiety and depression, but it changes your relationship to it and how you react to it.

The following are some mindfulness practices:

- **Body Scanning** - Used in Mindfulness-Based Cognitive Theory (MBCT) in which each part of the body is focused on one area at a time and "scanned" while focusing on the present sensations.

- **Progressive Relaxation** - Different parts of the body are tensed up and then released to contrast the feeling of tension with the sensation of progressive relaxation.

- **Being Mindful in Everyday Life Routines** - Activities such as driving, eating, setting the table, cleaning the house, are all opportunities to be mindful and present focused.

PROCESSING

Although mindfulness exercises seem to be a solitary exercise, processing with the group how the experience felt, what they observed about their ability to bring themselves back after being distracted, etc. can be very helpful in developing mindfulness practices as well as group support.

 Copyright © 2016 Judith Belmont. *150 More Group Therapy Activities & TIPS*, www.belmontwellness.com. All rights reserved.

Leaves Floating on a Stream

THEORY

A group setting provides an ideal forum for mindfulness and relaxation exercises, including guided imagery. **Sharing a group meditative experience and then being able to process with others in the group provides a rich experience** for members, and sets the stage to practice these exercises at home between sessions.

Stephen Hayes, the creator of Acceptance and Commitment Therapy, calls this guided imagery an example of a *cognitive defusion* technique.

IMPLEMENTATION

Have group members close their eyes and imagine leaves are floating on a slow moving stream. With any thought that goes into their heads, positive or negative, instruct them to imagine each thought is put on a floating leaf. Guide them to visualize watching those thoughts on leaves float down the stream and go out of sight. Have them try to detach from these thoughts – and *defuse* their habitual ways of thinking to observe thoughts – rather than look *from* them.

Guide the group not to try to stop or change the flow of the water - just observe. Accept that the thoughts on the leaves are not in their control.

Explain to the group that *cognitive defusion* helps people look *at* their thoughts in a new way. They are no longer fused to an old way of thinking, and they can detach from habitual irrational thoughts that cause pain and disturbance. By distancing from their thoughts, as in imagining watching their thoughts on leaves on the stream, they become witnesses to disturbing thoughts rather than identifying with them.

PROCESSING

Using this practice can help individuals be more objective about their thoughts and develop what can be termed as an "observing head." Reinforce that the more they practice this visualization, the more they will be able to separate and detach from their disturbing thoughts. The act of *cognitive defusion* is a cornerstone of ACT, and can be a compelling mindfulness practice to help group members learn ways to distance themselves from disturbing thoughts that interfere with healthy coping in everyday life.

Copyright © 2016 Judith Belmont. *150 More Group Therapy Activities & TIPS*, www.belmontwellness.com. All rights reserved.

Acceptance and Mindfulness Strategies

THEORY

Here are some quick tips from various experts in the field of mindfulness and acceptance practices. The following are **ideas of how to structure acceptance and mindfulness practice in your groups**.

IMPLEMENTATION

Marsha Linehan (*Cognitive-Behavioral Treatment of Borderline Personality Disorder*)

- Mindfulness practice entails learning the art of *observing* and *describing*. Linehan makes the point that mindfully observing is non-judgmental without interpretations.
- A mindfulness practice is merely looking at your hand, and asking yourself, "What do I see?"
- Mindfully observing *without judgment* would be thinking "five fingers, ring on one finger."
- Observing *judgmentally* would be: My fingers are "wrinkly, old and have ugly age spots."
- Practice observing without judgment - being descriptive without evaluation.

Terry Fralich (*The Five Core Skills of Mindfulness: A Direct Path to More Confidence, Joy and Love*)

Shifting into present awareness is like being a *witness* to your thoughts. Instead of believing your inner critic, witness the critic, therefore limiting the power of critical self-judgments. Focus on witnessing the critic, transform automatic negative thoughts about self and others into compassion and loving-kindness.

Use some sample self-affirming phrases to focus on while practicing the art of nonjudgmental mindfulness:

> *"I am glad I noticed my inner critic."*
>
> *"It gives me a chance to be kind and gentle to myself."*
>
> *"May I feel kind to myself."*
>
> *"May I feel the warmth of my being."*
>
> *"May I feel the love that connects everyone and everything."*

Lane Pederson (*Dialectical Behavior Therapy: A Contemporary Guide for Practitioners*)

- Using a piano or a musical instrument, play a note as you breathe in and breathe out as the note fades into silence. Pedersen encourages you to contemplate the importance of the rests - silences - between the notes.
- Begin each meal with five small mindful bites, chewing slowly. Allow your senses to notice the smell, taste, warmth or coolness of each bite.
- Mindfully eat a slice of fruit, engaging all the senses of touch, smell, sight, feel and taste, noting all the sensations while feeling totally immersed in the experience.
- Walk mindfully, being observant of your surroundings, while paying attention to the movement of your body and its connection to the ground.

- Use a "Beginner's Mind" in which you observe things like a child seeing it for the first time. Experience the here and now without being clouded by past experience.
- Using a 3-5-7 breathing technique, start by exhaling completely, and then inhale through your nose on a count of 3, hold it for 5 counts, and exhale slowly to the count of 7.

Debra Burdick (*Mindfulness Skills for Kids & Teens: A Workbook for Clinicians & Clients with 154 Tools, Techniques, Activities & Worksheets*)

To help in mastering slow, deliberate and deep breathing, exhaling through the mouth, Burdick uses the following:

- **A pinwheel** - watch how your breath makes it spin. Notice the difference when you breathe hard or slowly.
- **Bubbles** - Using a bubble wand with bubbles or even soapy water, gently blow bubbles to get the hang of exhaling gently while being present focused.
- **Kleenex** - Lifting a Kleenex, let it go and watch your breath make it dance in the air. Notice by blowing harder, you can lift it up.
- **Candles** - Blow gently to make the flame dance. Notice how hard you can blow until the flame goes out.

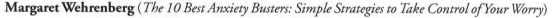

Margaret Wehrenberg (*The 10 Best Anxiety Busters: Simple Strategies to Take Control of Your Worry*)

Imagine a sphere of light above your head, and imagine it is a color that you associate with peace and calmness. With each inhalation and exhalation, imagine this light going in and out of you above your head. Imagine this color growing through your body. You might add a word you associate with calmness, such as "calm" or "peace." Use this imagery regularly to revive yourself during the day.

Thomas Marra (*Depressed and Anxious: The Dialectical Behavior Therapy Workbook for Overcoming Depression & Anxiety*)

One of the most fundamental acronyms for mindfulness in DBT is ONE MIND. This mindfulness skill is focused on helping people to live in the moment, in the HERE and NOW.

Using the mnemonic of ONE MIND, practice focusing on:

O — **O**ne thing at a time

N — Being in the here and **n**ow

E — Attend to the **e**nvironment

M — Be attentive to the **m**oment

I — **I**ncrease your five senses

N — Take a **n**on-judgmental stance

D — **D**escribe what you experience without interpretation

If you practice ONE MIND, you are working on taking an objective, non-judgmental stance in which you observe and describe what is going on around you without interpretations of yourself or others. You are taking in everything with all five senses, and you are feeling fully engaged in the experience.

PROCESSING

The acceptance and mindfulness practices in this tip will give you various strategies for incorporating mindfulness practices in your groups. Of course, processing the reaction of group members and sharing experiences from the activities will make the learning more impactful and memorable. These practices will help your group members look AT their disturbing thoughts more objectively than look FROM them.

Copyright © 2016 Judith Belmont. *150 More Group Therapy Activities & TIPS*, www.belmontwellness.com. All rights reserved.

Mindfulness Exercise

THEORY

Guided imagery is a very effective mindfulness exercise to help people be present in the moment, focusing on imagery that is calming and healing. **Guided imagery can help create new neural pathways**. People use imagery in their everyday lives, such as before a performance, speaking at a meeting or playing in an athletic event. Having members experience the power of visualization offers yet another life skill to enhance their sense of personal effectiveness.

IMPLEMENTATION

Take a few minutes and help members focus their imagination on healing images and thoughts. Some people refer to this as guided meditation or visualization.

There is no shortage of guided imagery and the type of imagery to use will arise from the group topic and the type of group you are leading. The following visualization is a shortened adaptation taken from *Guided Imagery For Healing Children and Teens* by Ellen Curran:

> *In this visualization, you can have the group imagine themselves on a beautiful beach, lake, park or their ideal setting. After you describe the warmth of the sun on them and the soothing fresh warm air, have them visualize picking up a shell, stone, or a stick and seeing the word "peace" or "acceptance" written there. Or have them imagine a that shell or stone be magical, and can take away all their worries and problems. Have them imagine talking to their shell or stone, carrying it with them to serve as a protection from worries that come along in their lives. Encourage them in their everyday life, whether in a garden, their back yard, a park or a beach, to find their magic stones, sticks or shells. It is up to each of us to unleash the magic with the help of this visualization!*

You can have group members take turns each session leading their own guided imagery that they think of themselves or that they find in books or on the internet.

A particularly great internet resource for guided imagery is: *Staying Well with Guided Imagery* by Belleruth Naparstek.

Playing soft music in the background can increase the relaxation experience. Have group members breathe deeply and become aware of their breaths.

One of my favorite guided-imageries is borrowed from both ACT founder, Stephen Hayes, and MBCT founder Jon Kabat-Zinn:

> *Have your clients imagine leaves floating on a stream. Then have them imagine that each disturbing thought is placed on a leaf, outside their head, and encourage them to watch those thoughts float away in all different directions and disappear. (For a terrific detailed description of this technique, see the reference by Russ Harris in his book, ACT Made Simple.)*

PROCESSING

Ask your group how it felt to use guided imagery. What images did they conjure in their minds? Encourage them stay present-focused.

Copyright © 2016 Judith Belmont. *150 More Group Therapy Activities & TIPS*, www.belmontwellness.com. All rights reserved.

The 4 Steps to Mindfulness Practice

Mindfulness practice is a core component of contemporary psychological theories such as DBT and ACT. The idea behind mindfulness is that the more we are present focused and "mindful" of the present, the less we listen to our internal unhealthy messages from the past. **The focus on today limits what is called the "monkey mind"** which is our racing thoughts, judgments, etc. which distracts us from totally experiencing the present. Exposing your group to the practices of mindfulness offers improved coping strategies to deal with the ups and downs of everyday life. Suggest that with regular mindfulness practice, they will likely be more effective at using the strategies – especially during emotional upset - when coping skills are needed the most!

1. **Choose An Activity to Practice Mindfulness.** *Choose an activity that interests you to practice mindfulness - petting a dog or cat, playing a sport, walking, knitting, playing an instrument, etc.*

2. **Focus On the Present Moment While Engaged In This Activity** *With your given activity, focus on the present moment - notice the sensations you have, the way it feels, smells, sounds. Focus on your breathing, slowly and deeply inhaling and exhaling. Slow down!*

3. **Be Aware Of When Your Attention Drifts From The Present Moment** – *Become aware when your attention gets distracted from the present moment. Mindfulness is not about staying in the present moment, but rather it is about bringing yourself back to it.*

4. **Gently Bring Yourself Back To The Present Moment Without Judgement** - *Without judgment and being negative about the wandering attention, gently bring your focus back to the present moment.*

Based on *Don't Let Your Emotions Run Your Life for Teens: Dialectical Behavior Therapy Skills for Helping You Manage Mood* by Sheri Van Dijk

Tip #94

Making a Mindfulness Glitter Calming Jar

THEORY

A very popular activity with children's groups (which can also be fun for adults) is making a Mindfulness or Calming Jar. With just the basic ingredients of water, glue and glitter your **group can enjoy a very powerful activity that they can use at home to keep their anger, stress and anxiety in check**. It helps clients practice mindfulness by shaking up a jar and then watching as the glitter calms and settles. It can also serve to calm emotions like anger and anxiety by waiting to react until the glitter is settled at the bottom of the jar. The glitter represents thoughts and feelings that need time to settle. When a jar is shaken, thoughts and feelings swirl around randomly and can seem rather uncontrollable, and letting the "dust" settle will having a calming effect.

IMPLEMENTATION

Mindfulness glitter jars can be found all over the internet, with various recipes including some basic ingredients such as water, glitter and glue, as well as extra ingredients such as small Lego men or small objects, food coloring, glycerin and dish soap. One of my favorites is by Akane Everitt, from the site: http://www.jugglingwithkids.com. She suggests using the calming jars as an alternative to a time out punishment in helping children refocus.

These are her basic ingredients:

small jar	food coloring
glitter glue	warm water

Directions: The ratio of glue to warm water is one cup warm water to one tablespoon glitter glue. The amount will depend on the size of the jar. Add food coloring. She notes warm water helps dissolve the glue so she heats water in a microwave for about 30-60 seconds.

Another favorite is from Momma Owls Lab (http://mommaowlslab.blogspot.com). Here is an example that takes only about 2 minutes to make up:

1/4 cup glycerine	2 tsp salt
3/4 cup hot water	3-4 drops dish soap
1 tsp silver glitter	

Debra Burdick (*Mindfulness Skills for Kids & Teens: A Workbook for Clinicians & Clients with 154 Tools, Techniques, Activities & Worksheets*) has some great recipes for mindfulness calming jars in her book and has excellent processing questions to use with this activity.

 Copyright © 2016 Judith Belmont. *150 More Group Therapy Activities & TIPS*, www.belmontwellness.com. All rights reserved.

Burdick states that the success of most therapeutic activities, result from how you process the activity - this is what makes the activity a therapeutic activity rather than merely a craft activity. The following are some of her suggestions on how to process the activity to make it meaningful:

- Ask the client to shake the bottle and have them visualize how it feels when their mind is revved up, wired, angry, worried or busy.

- Explain that just as the glitter settles, our disturbing thoughts in our minds become more settled and clear once we are still.

- Have the client jump up and down with the bottle, shaking it, and then stand still and watch it settle.

By calming the body with this mindfulness activity, their mind becomes more calm and their thoughts settle like the glitter in the bottle.

PROCESSING

The suggested activities above that include making and using a Mindfulness Calming Jar will appeal to all ages. Adding a little sparkle to your lessons will be sure to add a bit pizzazz to your group!

Copyright © 2016 Judith Belmont. *150 More Group Therapy Activities & TIPS*, www.belmontwellness.com. All rights reserved.

Tip #95

Taking a Mindfulness Moment

THEORY

DBT has become increasingly popular in part because of its **focus on mindfulness and acceptance practices**. Mindfulness is one of the 4 basic modules of DBT. The following TIP is a sample of DBT inspired quick mindfulness exercises and ideas from a few noted practitioners.

IMPLEMENTATION

These TIPs can provide a basis to conduct a "Mindfulness Moment" as part of every group session.

- A Mindfulness Moment will remind members about the importance of mindfulness practice and reinforce the use of using mindfulness in everyday life.

- This Mindfulness Moment can be different each week, using quick activities that you find in this section that will encourage members how to incorporate mindfulness in their everyday lives.

- You might ask your group members if they have their own mindfulness exercises and have them guide the group through one. For example, each week, have a person volunteer to lead a Mindfulness Moment.

- There are many exercises in the public domain that are easily searchable on the internet.

PROCESSING

Even though the mindfulness exercises are usually individually experienced, the power of the group is unleashed when members can process their unique experiences and reactions to the exercises with the group as a whole or in smaller groups. Having each member take turns leading a Mindfulness Moment will be good reinforcement for the importance of mindfulness.

 Copyright © 2016 Judith Belmont. *150 More Group Therapy Activities & TIPS*, www.belmontwellness.com. All rights reserved.

Tip #96

My Observing Head

THEORY

My Observing Head is another *cognitive defusion* resource to teach clients **how to use mindfulness techniques to develop more objectivity**. Having clients remind themselves to use their observing head will help to develop more objectivity and be less emotionally distraught, leading to better life choices and coping skills. Have clients learn to be a witness to their thoughts, which helps them detach from their emotional upset.

IMPLEMENTATION

With an observing head, clients will learn to be more objective and become an observer to the drama in their lives rather than being the key protagonist in the grips of emotional distress.

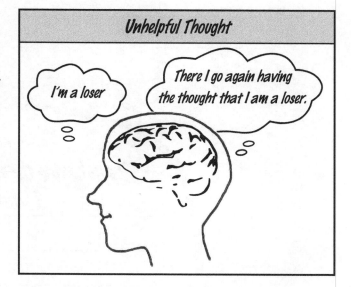

Objectify your thoughts

Using an observing head, replace thoughts such as "I am a loser" to the thought that "I am having the thought that I am a loser." This type of thinking will help clients be more objective and identify less with their disturbing thoughts.

Imagine thoughts in a balloon and then letting them drift away

This is another example of using imagery to distance yourself from upsetting thoughts. Watch your disturbing thoughts disappear.

Watch your thoughts like a movie

My clients have found this visualization very helpful in distancing themselves from emotional crises. I instruct them to watch the drama objectively as if they were watching it on a movie screen, and then keep on going back in the rows to develop even more objectivity, finally reaching the back of the theater. This visualization helps your clients look *AT* their thoughts and behaviors instead of *FROM* them, gaining mental objectivity.

PROCESSING

After sharing some of these visualizations with the group, have them work on changing disturbing thoughts by using the accompanying worksheet. Allow a short period of time for group members to fill out their sheets and then process answers with one another. This worksheet can help your group members learn to distance from their disturbing thoughts as they visualize their "observing head." Using these mindfulness and acceptance practices can help individuals be more objective about the drama of their lives. Reinforce that the more they practice these types of visualizations, and work on increasing their "observing head," the more they will be able to detach from their disturbing thoughts and thus deal with them more rationally.

Copyright © 2016 Judith Belmont. *150 More Group Therapy Activities & TIPS*, www.belmontwellness.com. All rights reserved. **161**

Activity

My Observing Head Worksheet

In the spaces below, write up to 5 disturbing thoughts. Then, write in the observing head another way to think about those disturbing thoughts that will allow you to be a witness to those thoughts rather than identify and be upset by them.

Disturbing thoughts I would like to change:

1. _____

2. _____

3. _____

4. _____

5. _____

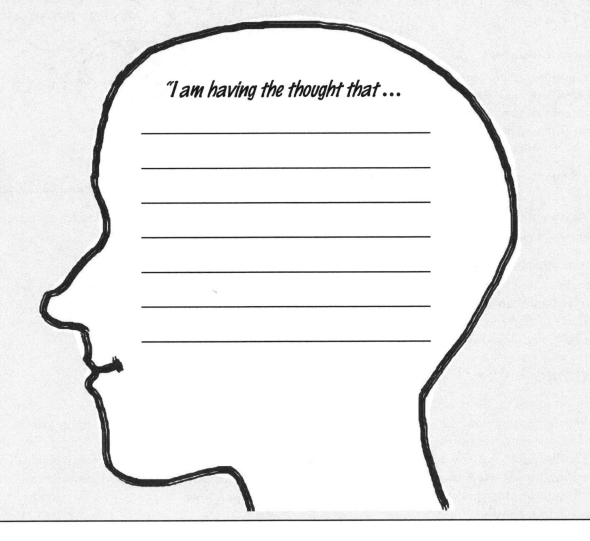

"I am having the thought that ...

Copyright © 2016 Judith Belmont. *150 More Group Therapy Activities & TIPS*, www.belmontwellness.com. All rights reserved.

Tip #97

Teaching Acceptance Strategies through Visualization

THEORY

The Third Wave of psychotherapeutic orientation, in which acceptance strategies are the cornerstone, grew out of a difficulty in reaching some clients who lacked sufficient life skills and coping skills to deal with everyday life challenges. The *Third Wave* orientations include DBT, MBCT and ACT. **All *Third Wave* orientations rely heavily on CBT concepts softened with the Eastern approaches of acceptance and mindfulness.** Even CBT, which is considered the Second Wave of psychological orientations (The First Wave includes the psychoanalytic and classic behavioral approaches), has also expanded to include acceptance and mindfulness practice.

IMPLEMENTATION

These TIPs offer some effective visualization strategies for teaching your group members acceptance and mindfulness practices. Acceptance practices help us make peace with reality and what cannot be changed. This orientation helps to decrease upsetting thoughts and rumination based on the past.

The following are some other powerful visualizations and demonstrations to teach acceptance strategies:

- **Quicksand Visualization** - Hayes uses the metaphor of being stuck in quicksand as being like a person who fights reality and ends up getting deeper and deeper in the quicksand. Only by acceptance of the quicksand by lying spread eagle-like - and not resisting- can we keep ourselves from sinking deeper.

- **Beach Ball Visualization**- If you put a beach ball in a tub of water and push it down it will keep popping back up. This demonstrates the impossibility of resisting reality and pushing thoughts away. If we persist in denying or fighting reality, it will keep coming back stronger, just as the beach ball in water will keep popping back up. As the saying goes, "what you resist will persist."

- **Helicopter or Airplane Visualization** - To gain a more objective perspective, imagine you are in a helicopter or an airplane. From the air, you can get a larger perspective on the world, with a bit more objectivity and detachment.

- **A Mountain** - Regardless of the weather, rain, snow, sleet, hail and sunshine, the mountain still stands and is unwavering. It does not react to inclement weather.

- **A Train** - Imagine standing on a bridge and watching a train go by, with each boxcar having a negative thought, word or phrase written on it. As you watch it go by, you are detaching yourself from those thoughts.

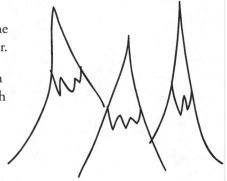

Copyright © 2016 Judith Belmont. *150 More Group Therapy Activities & TIPS*, www.belmontwellness.com. All rights reserved.

- **Balloons Drifting** - Imagine balloons drifting away. Have your clients imagine holding a whole cluster of balloons, each written with a memory, thought or disturbing situation. Then suggest that they imagine themselves letting go and watching the balloons fly away and disappear.

- **Computer or Movie Screen Visualization** - Imagine watching your thoughts on a computer screen. You can imagine these thoughts going by as if they are stock market quotes on a ticker tape at the bottom of the financial channels.

  Just like the stocks, whether they go up or down, just watch them dispassionately and distance yourself from the panic. Think of a stock market analyst on TV. They are reporting dispassionately; they are not freaking out when the market plummets.

- **Teflon Mind** - Lane Pedersen uses the image of *Teflon mind* in describing how to let go of your thoughts instead of getting attached to them. With Teflon - things don't get stuck!

PROCESSING

Ask group members how they felt using these visualizations. Suggest that they practice these visualizations and demonstrations at home. The success of the activities depends on the processing as a group. Ask your group members if they can share some of their own visualizations that have helped them become more mindful and accepting.

Copyright © 2016 Judith Belmont. *150 More Group Therapy Activities & TIPS*, www.belmontwellness.com. All rights reserved.

Embracing Life's Dialectics

THEORY

The term dialectic refers to things that appear to be opposite. This therapeutic approach, just like our lives, is filled with premises that are contradictory. It combines the outwardly differing approaches of both Eastern and Western therapeutic orientations. The Eastern focus on mindfulness and acceptance is integrated with Western strategies of cognitive therapy and other behavioral training such as assertiveness training. The models of B.F. Skinner and Buddha cross paths in this East meets West model of treatment. **A cognitive behavioral focus is softened with the practices of mindfulness and acceptance.**

IMPLEMENTATION

Dialectical behavior therapy integrates the seemingly opposite approaches of Eastern and Western practices, which together comprises one overall mode of psycho-educational treatment.

Use some of the following examples of commonly held opposing needs, wishes and thoughts that many of us experience, supporting the concept of dialectics in everyday life:

- Feeling hurt by a loved one, so you end up acting hurtful.

- Loving someone so much that it hurts.

- The more you cling to someone, the more you push them away.

- We often need to loosen our grip to hold on to important relationships.

- You want to lose weight, but end up eating more.

- Loving someone and treating them badly.

- Loving your spouse and having an affair.

- Loving your children but getting into conflicts and being critical of them.

- Feeling depressed so you drink alcohol excessively—also a depressant!

- You want to feel better so you self-medicate with drugs and alcohol.

Make up a list with the group members of their own dialectics.

Copyright © 2016 Judith Belmont. *150 More Group Therapy Activities & TIPS*, www.belmontwellness.com. All rights reserved.

For a fun side activity, introduce the concept of oxymoron, which are dialectical, paradoxical phrases.

- Jumbo shrimp

- Bittersweet

- Deafening silence

- Definite maybe

Can you and your group members think of more examples?

Ask the group to pick a dialectical example in their life to share with the group.

Ask how they can take steps to make peace with this conflict. This allows for individuals to see that their emotional conflicts are not something to be avoided, but they are normal and to be expected, and making peace and reconciling them is just part of a healthy life.

Use the accompanying worksheet to help group members personalize this lesson using the dialectics they struggle with in their own lives.

PROCESSING

Exploring dialectics of everyday life is especially powerful in a group setting because participants can learn from each other's examples and often this normalizes our universal human struggles. The relief of realizing "I'm not the only one" is a very reassuring concept for group members.

The group situation reminds us that we are not alone and we all struggle with similar issues. Finding life's oxymorons is a fun activity to do as part of a group brainstorming session, and expect lots of smiles and laughter!

Copyright © 2016 Judith Belmont. *150 More Group Therapy Activities & TIPS*, www.belmontwellness.com. All rights reserved.

The Dialectics of Everyday Life

These are some common dialectics (opposing wants and needs) of everyday life.

Check if any apply to you and explain in the spaces provided below.

_____ The more we try to control others, the more we lose our own control!

_____ Loving someone and wanting to be so close that I end up pushing others away.

_____ Having the most conflicts and fights with the people I love the most!

_____ Preventing myself from getting hurt by putting up walls and ending up feeling more isolated.

_____ Hanging on too tightly to someone so that I end up alienating them.

_____ Being so angry at and even hating those I love the most.

_____ Being a loving parent while being very judgmental.

_____ Feeling depressed and reaching for alcohol, which is a depressant.

_____ Saying "I don't care," when I really care so much that it hurts.

_____ Feeling so intensely that I end up feeling numb.

Explain your answers:

_____

_____

_____

Now write your own dialectics that cause conflict for you:

_____

_____

_____

To further keep in mind life's dialectics, write some more familiar oxymorons, which are contradictory word pairs.

Pretty ugly • Growing smaller • Big baby

Copyright © 2016 Judith Belmont. *150 More Group Therapy Activities & TIPS*, www.belmontwellness.com. All rights reserved.

How To Be A Stress Manager...
and Not A Stress Carrier

Tip #99

THEORY

Helping group members learn the difference between managing their stress and carrying it will be very eye-opening. Most people think that stress is bad, but in presenting to them that stress just "is" will help them **embrace stress and learn ways to handle it rather than avoid it.**

IMPLEMENTATION

Educate the group about what stress is by asking them how they would define it. Write the responses on a white board or flip chart and put a plus or a minus sign depending on whether the responses are positive or negative.

Most responses you get will be negative, as stress is generally thought of as negative, but it is actually not either positive or negative - it just "is." Add some positive examples of stress to the list, such as having a baby, going on vacation, family gatherings, new job, etc.

Make the point that stress is a fact of life. We need stress to be vibrant and adaptive, involved and charged. However, if stress is in our control we can manage it, but if our stress feels out of our control we feel "distressed."

A stress manager is one who handles their stress and balances it. They have enough stress to feel involved and committed but not too much that they feel they will snap like a rubber band.

I like to get oversized rubber bands for each person so they can share with the group visually how stressed they feel in various situations. I also demonstrate that a rubber band that is stretched too much will snap, but if it is not stretched at all, it is limp and not engaged.

Instead of trying to avoid stress, embrace it, as long as it is in balance – not too tight and not too limp. Just like a string instrument, if a string is too loose it will drone, and a string that is too tight will snap – but, a string that has just the right amount of tension will make beautiful music!

As a show of hands, ask if they are more like a stress carrier? Or a stress manager?

Stress managers are generally positive, well adjusted, assertive and respectful to themselves and others. Stress carriers, on the other hand, tend to be anxious, fearful, resentful, aggressive or non-assertive and are often disrespectful to themselves or others.

Ask them to think of an example in their lives of someone who is a stress manager and share with the group why they chose that person. Use the following quiz help them differentiate between a stress manager and a stress carrier.

PROCESSING

This psycho-educational lesson on stress will be very enlightening for many who regard stress as something to be avoided at all costs. Once group members learn to embrace stress and thrive with stress, they will be more likely to avoid being "distressed." Using the following handout will help reinforce the point that they can use stress positively to be a stress manager, or can be gripped negatively by it and be a stress carrier.

 Copyright © 2016 Judith Belmont. *150 More Group Therapy Activities & TIPS*, www.belmontwellness.com. All rights reserved.

Quiz

Are You A Stress Manager...
Or a Stress Carrier?

Stress managers do not wish stress away, but rather thrive under stress. The following are characteristics of a stress manager and a stress carrier. For each numbered item, circle one in each column which describes you best. At the end, total up your scores. In which column did you score highest in? Are you more like a stress carrier or a stress manager? This quick quiz will help you identify areas to focus on if you want to improve your stress resiliency skills!

Characteristics of a Stress Carrier	*Characteristics of a Stress Manager*
1. Anxious about change	Embraces change and growth
2. Unforgiving	Forgiving
3. Opinionated, controlling	Respectful of differences
4. Is non-assertive or aggressive	Communicates assertively
5. Tends to think in irrational ways	Thinks rationally
6. Inadequate self-care	Good self- care
7. Feels like a victim	Feels like a victor
8. Needs to be "right"	Does not need to be right
9. Low self–esteem	High self-esteem
10. Hates being wrong	Accepts failures and mistakes as part of life
11. Feels pressured	Feels relaxed
12. Rushes around continuously	Is able to slow down
13. Pressured speech	Relaxed speech
14. Feels tense	Feels calm
15. Fault finding	Grateful

Total _____

Total _____

Copyright © 2016 Judith Belmont. *150 More Group Therapy Activities & TIPS*, www.belmontwellness.com. All rights reserved.

Tip #100

Stress: Are You Positively or Negatively Charged?

THEORY

Stress is often thought of as detrimental to our health, although this is far from the truth. **Stress is a vital part of life**, and by managing stress rather than carrying it, we can make stress work for us. It is important to bust the myth that stress is negative in our lives.

IMPLEMENTATION

Keeping in mind the effectiveness of using analogies and visuals in teaching important life skill points, batteries are a great metaphor for stress. Having an object to take home with the daily lesson is ideal for a psycho-educational group.

When giving out the battery, point out that batteries work because they have a positive and negative charge. Use this as an analogy to stress: Stress can also charge us positivity or negatively, and most of the time we are in fact "in charge" of whether stress positively or negatively charges us.

Start with asking the group how they would describe stress and write the responses on a white board or flip chart.

Notice with the group that most of the answers are negative, such as "exhausting, tiring, and overwhelming." Some other types of responses might include "job" "boss" "kids" "money." A small amount of the responses will be positive, such as stress is "motivating, healthy."

For each item, decide which word is a positive or a negative charge. Put a plus next to the items that are desirable, a minus next to the ones that are not, and both a plus and a minus for a mixed bag. For instance, a job, kids, spouse brings positive as well as negative stress - money is positive as well as negatively stressful if you don't have enough of it, and even if a job is challenging, having a job is positive!

To enhance this lesson on stress, the following are visualizations that help to demonstrate the continuum of stress.

1. **Using a rubber band**, show that too much stress will make the band snap by being pulled too much. If there is too little tightness, it will make it limp. However, the right amount of stress is somewhere in the middle, in which the band is pulled slightly, showing a life balance. A balloon demonstration can work the same way. Giving group members a rubber band (or a balloon) and asking them to show the group how stressed they were this week by pulling the band out in front of them for the group to see will often get some chuckles as people show how stressed they are! Use oversized jumbo rubber bands for a real impact!

2. Using the example of a **stringed instrument**, make the point that a string is just like stress. If the strings are tightened too much they will break, and if the key is not tightened enough it will snap. Only by the right balance will the strings be able to play beautiful music!

3. Educate them that **"stressed" spelled backwards is "desserts."** It shows how sweet stress can be!

 Copyright © 2016 Judith Belmont. *150 More Group Therapy Activities & TIPS*, www.belmontwellness.com. All rights reserved.

PROCESSING

The lesson on the positive and negative charges of stress, demonstrated by the example of the battery, will help group members regard stress in a healthier way. Group members will start to identify the ways that stress is positive in their lives. For example, those who play competitive sports, or have children who play on sports teams, will agree that participating in sports is indeed nail biting and stressful, but also can be exhilarating and exciting. Not knowing the outcome of the game is much more exciting, although stressful, than knowing in advance what the score will be. Having participants share with the group the positive stresses in their own lives will help make the lesson even more meaningful.

Copyright © 2016 Judith Belmont. *150 More Group Therapy Activities & TIPS*, www.belmontwellness.com. All rights reserved.

Keeping a Stress Log

THEORY

Changing life skills takes practice, practice, and practice, and this log offers help to practice managing stress. After learning what stress is and is not, and learning the difference between being a stress manager and a stress carrier, now the group members are ready to fill out a stress log. This log helps them track their progress and practice stress management techniques.

IMPLEMENTATION

Group members gain insight on how to identify the main areas to focus on to change their behaviors. This outline of issues to address should be a summary of what they have learned in group about stress and their ability to manage it.

The logs help clients identify and track their:

- Positive emotions

- Negative emotions

- Strength of emotions

- Negative beliefs

- Positive beliefs

- Degree of certainty of their beliefs

- Healthy behaviors

- Unhealthy behaviors

- Conclusions and goals

Use the example on the next page to show clients how to fill out a stress log.

PROCESSING

Have group members fill out the log between sessions, so that they can review them with the group at the next session. Sharing their unique situation with the group will help reinforce major topics to address when working on managing stress. Also, hearing the situations and struggles of others will help to increase personal insight as well as group camaraderie.

 Copyright © 2016 Judith Belmont. *150 More Group Therapy Activities & TIPS*, www.belmontwellness.com. All rights reserved.

Sample

Stress Log

Stressful Event Description
Making a presentation for a meeting at work

Negative Emotions	Positive Emotions
Anxiety, Fear	Excited for the opportunity, energized

Strength of Negative Emotions	Strength of Positive Emotions
1 2 3 4 5 6 7 8 9 10 Low High	1 2 3 4 5 6 7 8 9 10 Low High

Identify Negative Beliefs	Challenge with Positive Beliefs
They might not agree with me *It would be awful if I got tongue-tied* *I wish I was as smart as Nancy*	*Even if they don't, it wouldn't be terrible* *It would be frustrating, but not a tragedy* *Nancy's intelligence doesn't diminish my own; we are different*

Type of Cognitive Distortion	Healthy Alternative
Catastrophizing; making comparisons	*Sticking to the facts, not interpretations*

Certainty of Your Beliefs	Certainty of Your Beliefs
1 2 3 4 5 6 7 8 9 10 Low High	1 2 3 4 5 6 7 8 9 10 Low High

Unhealthy Behaviors	Healthy Behaviors
Avoiding eye contact and relying on reading my presentation	*Expressing my thoughts in a meeting* *Trying to practice assertive skills I learned*

Cost/Benefit Analysis: Unhealthy Coping	Cost/Benefit Analysis: Healthy Coping
Costs: *Alienates others; isolates myself* Benefits: *Keeps people away; protects me*	Costs: *Takes time to plan and practice what I will say* Benefits: *Helps me feel empowered, organized, and prepared. Feel part of the team.*

My Conclusions and Goals
By challenging my irrational beliefs and replacing them with more rational thoughts, I will use this presentation as an opportunity to grow healthier

From *The Therapist's Ultimate Solution Book: Essential Strategies, Tips and Tools To Empower Your Clients* by Judith Belmont.
Copyright © 2015 by Judith Belmont. Used by permission of W.W. Norton & Company

Copyright © 2016 Judith Belmont. *150 More Group Therapy Activities & TIPS*, www.belmontwellness.com. All rights reserved.

Activity

Stress Log

Stressful Event Description	
Negative Emotions	**Positive Emotions**
Strength of Negative Emotions ← 1 2 3 4 5 6 7 8 9 10 → Low · · · · · · · · · High	**Strength of Positive Emotions** ← 1 2 3 4 5 6 7 8 9 10 → Low · · · · · · · · · High
Identify Negative Beliefs	**Challenge with Positive Beliefs**
Type of Cognitive Distortion	**Healthy Alternative**
Certainty of Your Beliefs ← 1 2 3 4 5 6 7 8 9 10 → Low · · · · · · · · · High	**Certainty of Your Beliefs** ← 1 2 3 4 5 6 7 8 9 10 → Low · · · · · · · · · High
Unhealthy Behaviors	**Healthy Behaviors**
Cost/Benefit Analysis:	**Cost/Benefit Analysis:**
My Conclusions and Goals	

From *The Therapist's Ultimate Solution Book: Essential Strategies, Tips and Tools To Empower Your Clients* by Judith Belmont.
Copyright © 2015 by Judith Belmont. Used by permission of W.W. Norton & Company

Copyright © 2016 Judith Belmont. *150 More Group Therapy Activities & TIPS*, www.belmontwellness.com. All rights reserved.

Keep Your Anger in Check

Is my anger in my control or does it make me "out of control?"
Anger can be an adaptive reaction to what is unfair and unjust. However, all too often we let anger control us rather than us being in control of our anger.

Is my anger due to intolerance and narrow mindedness, thinking people should be more like me?
At times our anger arises not from healthy reasons, but from intolerance, disgust, narrow-mindedness, and the refusal to let go of unrealistic expectations of self and others.

Is my thinking too "all or nothing" and extreme?
The ability to keep our thoughts in perspective in order to combat irrational thinking is of prime importance to control anger. Thinking in black and white and extreme ways will, for sure, make you see red!

Am I holding onto self-righteous judgments and unrealistic "shoulds?"
Getting rid of unrealistic "shoulds" of how you think others "should" be, as well as combating one's own need to be perfect, will provide the foundation for healthy thinking.

Do I keep in mind the long term consequences of what I say?
Once the words come out you can never get them back! Just like a feather pillow that is torn, once the feathers fly away you can never get them back.

Is my anger causing me to act aggressively?
Resist the temptation to express anger in an aggressive way. A lot of people think anger and aggression are the same thing but they are not. Anger is a feeling, while aggression is a behavior. Feeling angry is fine, but acting aggressively is not!

Do I acknowledge that anger expressed aggressively leads to shame?
Once you are no longer seeing red, most healthy people regret behaviors done and words said in anger. This leads to shame, which will then turn the anger inward towards yourself!

Am I more interested in being right or being kind?
Arguments happen because people want to be right, ignoring the importance of building relationships and being kind.

What do you need to remember to keep your anger in check?

_____

_____

_____

REMEMBER: Don't lose control by trying to control others!

"Whatever is begun in anger ends in shame." – Benjamin Franklin

Copyright © 2016 Judith Belmont. *150 More Group Therapy Activities & TIPS*, www.belmontwellness.com. All rights reserved.

Taking Control of Your Anger Triggers!

No one can make us angry! We are in charge of our emotions and our behaviors. Whatever triggers you is in your control!

This is an example of a child's anger at a sibling, and how the usual aggressive response can be changed to a healthier reaction.

Example: *I am so angry when my brother tells me I'm fat.*

My Usual Response: *Tell him to shut up, stomp off or punch him.*

Changed Response: Tell him assertively *I do not appreciate him saying that and ask for an apology. This requires no yelling or childish behavior. If he does not stop, walk away and seek the help of a parent or adult.*

Can you think of your own examples and how you can change your response?

Your Example: _____

Usual Response: _____

Changed Response: _____

Your Example: _____

Usual Response: _____

Changed Response: _____

Your Example: _____

Usual Response: _____

Changed Response: _____

**REMEMBER: You deserve to be treated respectfully. But when you are treated
with disrespect, it does not mean you act disrespectfully back - just be assertive
and set limits - even if you need to walk away!**

 Copyright © 2016 Judith Belmont. *150 More Group Therapy Activities & TIPS*, www.belmontwellness.com. All rights reserved.

Controlling Anger- for Kids

When you are angry ask yourself these questions. Keep in mind that **we are in charge of our anger - don't give anyone else the power!**

- *Is my anger in my control or does it make me "out of control?"*

- *Am I thinking in all or nothing extreme ways, using words like "I can't stand it!" "I hate him!"*

- *Do I expect people should to be more like me or how I think they should be?*

- *Is my thinking too "all or nothing" and extreme?*

- *Am I too critical of others?*

- *Do I keep in mind the long-term consequences of what I say? Remember once things are said or done, you can't take them back.*

- *Is my anger causing me to behave aggressively?*

- *Am I more interested in being right or being kind?*

- *How can I turn my anger into a goal?*

Copyright © 2016 Judith Belmont. *150 More Group Therapy Activities & TIPS*, www.belmontwellness.com. All rights reserved.

Reducing My Anger Producing Thoughts

Anger arises not from another person but from what we tell ourselves about that other person.
No one can make you angry - that happens between your own ears! **People can trigger our anger, but it is up to us to develop rational coping statements so that our anger does not get out of control.**

When we are angry, our self-talk is often inflexible, judgmental, extreme, black or white, and characterized by "shoulding" on others and ourselves. By recognizing our extreme habits of thinking and developing healthier coping statements, we can reduce our anger.

Anger Producing Thoughts	Anger Reducing Thoughts
He makes me so mad!	He does not have the ability to make me feel anything. My feelings are inside job. Rather, I am mad at him.
I HATE her!	I really do not like her.
He ruined my life!	I am very upset with her.
She has NO RIGHT to say that!	I am disappointed that she said that.
I won't let him get away with this!	I will tell him I am very offended about what he said.

Now it's your turn!
Fill in below some of your own anger producing and anger-reducing thoughts.

Anger Producing Thoughts

_____

_____

_____

_____

_____

Anger Reducing Thoughts

_____

_____

_____

_____

_____

 Copyright © 2016 Judith Belmont. *150 More Group Therapy Activities & TIPS*, www.belmontwellness.com. All rights reserved.

STOP- and Pause!

Feeling Angry?

Don't know what to do? How about imagining a STOP sign?

Remember to **_Spot Thoughts Over a Pause_**

When you feel angry, you don't need to be aggressive, which is taking out your anger on others, even if they are not acting nicely to you.

Imagine a stop sign and **STOP** and **PAUSE!** Think about what you are thinking - are they helpful thoughts?

An unhelpful thought would be, "He's an idiot."

A helpful thought you can replace it with is "I don't like his behavior but that does not mean he is worthless or an idiot. Rather, he is a person who is acting badly, but it does not mean he is a bad person."

What are some unhelpful thoughts that you might think when you are angry and can you think of a more helpful thought when you and **STOP** and **PAUSE**?

1. Unhelpful thought: _____

2. Helpful thought: _____

1. Unhelpful thought: _____

2. Helpful thought: _____

Copyright © 2016 Judith Belmont. *150 More Group Therapy Activities & TIPS*, www.belmontwellness.com. All rights reserved.

My Anger Checklist

Below, check off any items that apply and explain.

_____ I can identify my "anger triggers"

_____ I can describe how it feels

_____ I identify my irrational self-talk

_____ I can replace it with more rational self-talk

_____ I have thought of healthy ways to handle anger

What to do when I am angry:

Check off ideas that can help me to manage my anger:

_____ Count to ten before responding

_____ Keep calm with healthy self-talk

_____ Write feelings in a journal

_____ Remember "I" statements

_____ Talk it out with a friend

_____ Take a walk to cool down

_____ Forgive others for being unhealthy

_____ Remove myself from the situation

_____ Role-play ways to handle anger

_____ Write a letter (I don't have to send it)

_____ Remind myself to only change myself - not others!

_____ Confront someone assertively

_____ Draw what I am feeling

_____ Look behind the difficult behavior

_____ Identify my "shoulds"

_____ Breathe very slowly

_____ Exercise, discharge energy

_____ Ask for help

Ask Yourself: How will my life be different if I am able to put these ideas into practice?

_____

_____

_____

Ask Yourself: Are there other strategies that work for me?

_____

_____

_____

   Copyright © 2016 Judith Belmont. *150 More Group Therapy Activities & TIPS*, www.belmontwellness.com. All rights reserved.

Tip #107

Using Acronyms for Tolerating Distress

THEORY

To understand the DBT model is to familiarize yourself with its acronyms in the four content areas: **Emotional Regulation**, **Interpersonal Effectiveness**, **Distress Tolerance** and **Mindfulness**. DBT uses acronyms for all 4 modules. Using an acronym makes learning efficient.

IMPLEMENTATION

You can introduce the concept of acronyms using familiar ones in everyday life - these are a few examples:

ATM: Automated Teller Machine

ADD: Attention Deficit Disorder

AA: Alcoholics Anonymous

One of the DBT acronyms for Distress Tolerance is **IMPROVE** - which offers a "cliff note" version of skills to use when coping with distressing situations. With enough practice with acronyms, group members can develop better coping strategies. You can encourage group members to use IMPROVE as part of an everyday routine!

Imagery: Use imagery to visualize a peaceful scene. Use guided imagery, relaxation CDs, and make it a part of your everyday routine.

Meaning: Find meaning in each experience you have. Everything can help you grow if you let it! Find a purpose to your life.

Prayer: Ask help from a higher spiritual power, or even others. There is hope!

Relaxation: Take a breath! Doing slow breathing will calm you down and increase oxygen!

One-Mindfully: Focus on taking one step at a time, one thing at a time.

Vacation: Take time for yourself by taking a walk or calling a friend, even for a couple of minutes.

Encouragement: Be your own cheerleader. Say nice things to yourself!

For each of the 7 points, you can brainstorm with the group how they can personalize the acronym IMPROVE for themselves.

Copyright © 2016 Judith Belmont. *150 More Group Therapy Activities & TIPS*, www.belmontwellness.com. All rights reserved.

Another acronym in the distress tolerance module is wise mind ACCEPTS, offering ideas and reminders of how to replace unpleasant activities with pleasant ones.

Activities - *Find outlets that are pleasurable.*

Contribute - *Do things to help others.*

Compare – Compare yourself to others less fortunate to find reasons to be grateful.

Emotion - Use an opposite emotion to lift spirits (ex: singing when sad).

Push away – Mentally leave the disturbing situation and disturbing thoughts.

Thoughts - Distract with the thoughts like focusing on a puzzle, or counting to 10.

Sensations - Distract yourself with sensations of taste, feel, or smell - like holding an ice cube, enjoying a hot bath, lighting a scented candle.

Have the group make up their own acronyms and share how they can tolerate distressing situations easier.

PROCESSING

Process with the group how they can use acronyms to remember soothing skills in times of upset. Sharing and learning from others in the group how they use these and other acronyms will underscore the importance of using practical techniques to structure how they tolerate distress.

Copyright © 2016 Judith Belmont. *150 More Group Therapy Activities & TIPS*, www.belmontwellness.com. All rights reserved.

Breaking Old Habits with a Piece of Paper

THEORY

We all know that old habits are hard to break. Well-ingrained habits are so automatic that clients are often highly resistant to change in terms of reworking their well-worn habits of thinking. Making this point with simple demonstrations can help individuals develop insight into the need to change their well-worn habits of thinking.

IMPLEMENTATION

Mindfulness author Debra Burdick offers this very simple exercise that helps group members gain insight into how automatic ways of thinking is a result of our brain working through old brain pathways that take effort to change.

The following are her instructions from her book *Mindfulness Skills for Kids & Teens.*

- Take a heavy piece of paper.

- Crease it in half, and fold it in half again and then again. Then have group members flatten the creases.

- Now open the paper.

- Have them follow the procedure again, noticing how much easier it is this time to fold the paper on the creases that are already there, just as our neural pathways in our brain are worn with habits of thinking.

They will find that in the process of folding and unfolding a few times, it becomes even easier and easier to fold over the worn creases.

PROCESSING

Make the point that sometimes we need to make it harder for ourselves in the short term by making new creases (developing new habits) to form new habits and coping strategies. Burdick also points out that this demonstration shows that it is harder to think flexibly in new ways once we already have ingrained thinking habits. With this point in mind, encourage your group members to be aware of how it might be hard to learn something new when we are used to doing things in a certain way. Using this example of the well-worn creased paper, you can stress that just like there are many ways to fold a paper, there are many other ways to perceive the same thing in a situation, reminding that their attitude and perspective is within their control.

Copyright © 2016 Judith Belmont. *150 More Group Therapy Activities & TIPS*, www.belmontwellness.com. All rights reserved.

Tip #109

Letting GO

THEORY

This TIP further supports the premise that in order to make therapeutic points, **visualizations are often more effective than simply using words alone**. Using commonly known visualizations make learning memorable.

IMPLEMENTATION

- Start the discussion by asking group members if there are things in their lives that hinder their personal growth and happiness. Examples could include unhealthy thought habits, unhealthy behaviors, and relationships that do not support their growth.

- Using the image of a hot air balloon in the accompanying worksheet, have them write or draw in the weights of the balloon the negative and irrational thoughts that prevent the balloon from flying away. In the hot air balloon itself they can put their positive thoughts, goals, hopes, values that can help them soar!

- Supply colored pencils or crayons to allow group members to express themselves creatively.

- Alternatively, or to follow up the first activity, they can also write or draw positive thoughts that can set them free as the balloon rises.

- Some therapists use actual balloons to represent the hot air balloon, and have clients put little slips of paper in the balloon and then release the balloon. For practical as well as for environmental reasons, I prefer using the visualization.

PROCESSING

Make sure you leave time to allow group members to take turns sharing their creations. What did they choose to let go of? What is holding them back? What are their goals and aspirations that they have which can make their spirits and hope soar? As in all group activities, the processing and sharing promotes individual as well as group growth in a creative and non-threatening way.

 Copyright © 2016 Judith Belmont. *150 More Group Therapy Activities & TIPS*, www.belmontwellness.com. All rights reserved.

Activity

Letting GO

On the weights of the balloon, write or draw the things in your life that weigh you down and limit your growth. These could include unhealthy thoughts, behaviors, relationships or anything that you think holds you back. In the hot air balloon itself, write or draw your positive thoughts, goals, hopes, positive thoughts and feelings that can help you feel like you are not only growing but soaring!

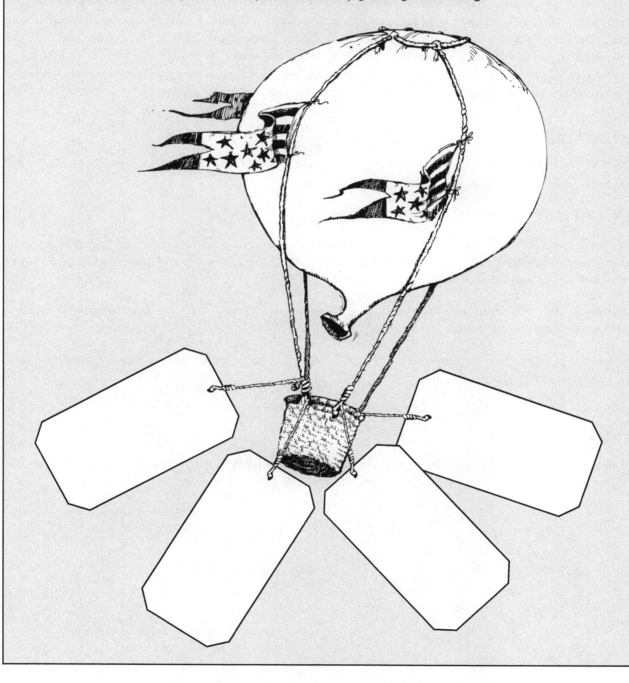

Copyright © 2016 Judith Belmont. *150 More Group Therapy Activities & TIPS*, www.belmontwellness.com. All rights reserved.

Accepting Regrets

Tip #110

THEORY

It has been clear in my practice that one of the hardest things for clients to do is to be accepting of past mistakes and forgiving themselves for not having the foresight to know what is now so obvious in hindsight. Clients who keep beating themselves up for past mistakes and even failures are closing the door on living TODAY. The problem with regrets is that they keep us anchored and defined by our past - and as we all know, the past never changes. Neil Roese in this book, *If Only: How to Turn Regret Into Opportunity* suggests **turning unproductive regrets into productive regrets**. Instead of focusing on yesterday, focus on how you can be a better person now based on lessons learned and new choices you make.

IMPLEMENTATION

Have your group members list 2 or 3 major regrets they have in their lives. Have them share how these regrets have held them back from accepting their lives in the present.

It might help to start off with the phrase "If only. . ." and continue with "then. . ..."?

Have your group close their eyes and take a few minutes to imagine how life could be if they could be more accepting of their past errors and their regrets. What would life be like if they forgave themselves and others and focused only on moving forward with lessons learned?

Suggest to them that they can turn unproductive regrets into productive regrets if they have learned from choices gone wrong and have become wiser and more empathic.

This focus on accepting the past and growing from it, replacing a past focus with a present focus, will help members incorporate acceptance strategies into their lives.

PROCESSING

Focusing on how you can turn unproductive regrets into productive regrets, and even into goals, can be quite therapeutic. It is helpful processing as a group for the purpose of self-disclosure and group bonding.

 Copyright © 2016 Judith Belmont. *150 More Group Therapy Activities & TIPS*, www.belmontwellness.com. All rights reserved.

Tip #111

Accepting Life's Changes

THEORY

There is one thing that is constant in life, and that is change. All too often people say they do not like change, and many of our clients resist change, but the truth is that change is an important part of life. Opening a discussion about change with some of the following demonstrations and activities can **help group members learn to embrace change as necessary and desirable** instead of repeating the all too common refrain, "I don't like change!"

IMPLEMENTATION

Start a discussion about change by asking them to complete the rest of the sentence,

"Change is. . .. . ."

Write the responses on a flip chart or board. Make sure in the conversation you brainstorm the positive aspects of change: meeting a new friend, getting married, or going on vacation. Put a plus or a minus, or both, next to each item on the list. I do this activity exchanging the word *'change'* with *'stress.'*

Group members will be surprised at how change (like stress) can be good, despite the fact that many people think "I don't like change."

Brainstorm with the group some changes that are so common that we take them for granted:

- A young child growing into a young lady or young man.

- A baby learning to crawl, walk and talk.

- Learning new skills at school, work and in life.

- Caterpillars transform into colorful butterflies.

- A slab of clay on the potters wheel transforms into a centered bowl.

- Cooking in the oven or stove transforms ingredients into edible food - after all, you would not want to eat flour and water raw instead of real bread - though you might want to eat cookie dough instead of waiting for it to bake!

- People who sail need the winds of change to propel their boat - no wind, no movement!

Copyright © 2016 Judith Belmont. *150 More Group Therapy Activities & TIPS*, www.belmontwellness.com. All rights reserved.

Demonstrate to the group change before their eyes:

- Use an ice cube or some snow in a clear cup and watch it melt.

- Put food coloring in water and watch the dye color the water.

- Put baking soda in water and watch the water get cloudy.

- Shake a bottle of soda and watch it fizz.

- Use a piece of paper and put a match to it and watch it flame (of course only if it is safe in your setting) and making sure you have something like a metal can to put the fire out.

- A fun one is putting a Mentos into a bottle of diet cola and watch it erupt!

"My How You've Changed" Activity: A tried and true activity on change is to pair up with a partner, have the partner turn away, and give the other partner a minute to change 3 things about themselves. Then, the person with the back turned turns around and tries to see if they can recognize what has changed. Take turns with this activity so both partners get a chance to be the changer and also the observer of change.

Change as A Metaphor: Using actual money as a metaphor for change, you might suggest to your group that every time they handle coins for their purchases throughout the day, use those moments as a reminder of the important role change has in our lives!

PROCESSING

This potpourri of change metaphors, activities and demonstrations can help spur discussions about how change can be positive in our lives. Make the point that the more we resist change, the more we will fight inevitable transitions in our lives that can help us grow. These ideas are just a few to help your group members see the desirability of change, and learn to embrace it.

Copyright © 2016 Judith Belmont. *150 More Group Therapy Activities & TIPS*, www.belmontwellness.com. All rights reserved.

Reaction to Life Changes Log

THEORY

This log will help group members track their thoughts and feelings. By identifying them, **they can then replace unhealthy thoughts with healthier thoughts**. The completed log is offered as an example and will help clients familiarize themselves with some tried and true CBT techniques.

IMPLEMENTATION

Give out both the completed form and the blank one to fill in. Look it over with the group to introduce how to use the logs. Have your group fill in the log at home and bring it in the next week to go over with the group.

This log will ideally be given out after the group already had basic CBT lessons including understanding cognitive distortions. It serves a good summary for the major techniques used in CBT to tackle unhealthy thinking. The log includes:

- Problematic situation
- Positive emotions
- Negative emotions
- Strength of both emotions
- Identifying negative beliefs
- Challenging with a more positive belief

- Types of cognitive distortions
- Degree of certainty of their beliefs
- Healthy reactions to change
- Unhealthy reactions to change
- Cost/Benefit analysis
- Conclusions and Goals

PROCESSING

Going over the logs at the beginning of the session will offer valuable opportunities to build group support through sharing and learning from others. This log will ideally be a staple in the homework review portion of subsequent group sessions. Homework review with the help of handouts including these logs can help group members apply CBT principles to their lives, and provides a springboard for sharing and learning.

Copyright © 2016 Judith Belmont. *150 More Group Therapy Activities & TIPS*, www.belmontwellness.com. All rights reserved.

Sample

Reaction to Life Changes Log

Stressful Event Description
Difficulty adjusting to new job right after graduation from college

Negative Emotions	Positive Emotions
Afraid, intimidated	Excited, hopeful

Strength of Negative Emotions	**Strength of Positive Emotions**
1 2 3 4 5 6 7 8 9 10 Low High	1 2 3 4 5 6 7 8 9 10 Low High

Identify Negative Beliefs	**Challenge with Positive Beliefs**
They might regret hiring me - I'm not smart like alot of the others. It would be TERRIBLE to make a mistake.	*I need to stop comparing myself with others. They know I have little experience and just graduated. It's OK to make mistakes.*

Type of Cognitive Error	**Response to Cognitive Error**
Over-catastrophizing, all or nothing thinking, making comparisons	*I will stick to the facts. I will only compare myself to myself before today - not others.*

Certainty of Your Beliefs	**Certainty of Your Beliefs**
1 2 3 4 5 6 7 8 9 10 Low High	1 2 3 4 5 6 7 8 9 10 Low High

Unhealthy Reactions to Change	**Healthy Reactions to Change**
Withdraw after work, isolate myself	*Will try to make new friends at work, ask them to lunch for example*

Cost/Benefit Analysis:	**Cost/Benefit Analysis:**
Will feel stressed and depressed	Will meet new people and be open to new experiences

My Conclusions and Goals
I will get nothing out of isolating myself and being intimidated. I will use this new job as a chance to embrace change and grow from it professionally and personally.

From *The Therapist's Ultimate Solution Book: Essential Strategies, Tips and Tools To Empower Your Clients* by Judith Belmont.
Copyright © 2015 by Judith Belmont. Used by permission of W.W. Norton & Company

 Copyright © 2016 Judith Belmont. *150 More Group Therapy Activities & TIPS*, www.belmontwellness.com. All rights reserved.

Activity

Reaction to Life Changes Log

Stressful Event Description	
Negative Emotions	**Positive Emotions**
Strength of Negative Emotions 1 2 3 4 5 6 7 8 9 10 Low High	**Strength of Positive Emotions** 1 2 3 4 5 6 7 8 9 10 Low High
Identify Negative Beliefs	**Challenge with Positive Beliefs**
Type of Cognitive Error	**Response to Cognitive Error**
Certainty of Your Beliefs 1 2 3 4 5 6 7 8 9 10 Low High	**Certainty of Your Beliefs** 1 2 3 4 5 6 7 8 9 10 Low High
Unhealthy Reactions to Change	**Healthy Reactions to Change**
Cost/Benefit Analysis:	**Cost/Benefit Analysis:**
My Conclusions and Goals	

From *The Therapist's Ultimate Solution Book: Essential Strategies, Tips and Tools To Empower Your Clients* by Judith Belmont.
Copyright © 2015 by Judith Belmont. Used by permission of W.W. Norton & Company

Copyright © 2016 Judith Belmont. *150 More Group Therapy Activities & TIPS*, www.belmontwellness.com. All rights reserved.

Using Coping Cards for Stress Resilience

THEORY

As we saw in Chapter 4, *Changing Thoughts to Change Your Life*, the use of coping cards is an integral part of both CBT and DBT techniques.

Coping cards are among the effective treatment tools of major cognitive therapists used heavily by notables such as Judith Beck and David Burns. In individual therapy or group therapy, coping cards are a common CBT homework assignment in which a client writes important reminders that are highlighted in the session, helping them cope with extreme and upsetting emotions and thoughts.

IMPLEMENTATION

Making up coping cards is a great activity for groups. In individual treatment, coping cards are generally done for homework, so a group situation lends itself to an activity rich in social support and group cohesiveness, enhancing the learning – and the fun! Using note cards, clients write down improved skills, healthier thoughts and improved behavioral alternatives. Making up coping cards in the context of a group allows for interaction, feedback, learning from others, sharing with others, and solidifying new improved ideas for thinking and behaving.

A group situation creates a safe environment for members to share their struggles and solutions with others.

Having notecards and markers is all you need for making coping cards.

They can be simple affirmations to remind individuals of their basic self-esteem, self-worth and self-efficacy.

Other coping cards list an array of alternative behaviors to control impulsive behavior, while others offer rational thoughts to combat automatic irrational ones that lead to excessive anxiety, depression and unhealthy behaviors. For those with particularly destructive habits, such as substance abuse or eating disorders, alternative behaviors are written as a reminder since during times of heightened upset, effective coping skills are often forgotten or ignored.

Remind your group members that coping cards should be carried around in a wallet or purse, to serve as reminders to make healthy choices in times of emotional distress. A few of my clients have written up cards and laminated them with clear contact paper, keeping them together with a binder ring, so that the cards will be preserved well even if frequently used.

Coping cards can be two sided - one side for a common negative thought such as "I can't do anything right," with the healthier thought on the other side being "I am a person who tries her best but is human and makes mistakes. I will keep trying to improve."

   Copyright © 2016 Judith Belmont. *150 More Group Therapy Activities & TIPS*, www.belmontwellness.com. All rights reserved.

Side #1	**Side #2**
I am lazy.	I am having trouble getting motivated.
I can't deal with him.	I am having trouble communicating with him.
It's useless - I will never get this done!	I will break up this problem into smaller steps that are more manageable.
I am a loser.	I admire and love myself, and I deserve to have a good life.

PROCESSING

When group members take turns sharing, they will be encouraged by the examples and struggles of others. Sharing of these problems and solutions will help clients see the universality of their issues and offer alternative solutions to common struggles. They will also benefit with ideas from others that they might have not thought of, and help gain objectivity in their private struggles.

Copyright © 2016 Judith Belmont. *150 More Group Therapy Activities & TIPS*, www.belmontwellness.com. All rights reserved.

Coping Card Varieties

Coping cards are very powerful aids to help in times of emotional upset. The following are types of cards that can help cope with strong emotions, conflicts, depression and anxiety.

Affirmations

I am worthy and as good as everyone else.

Assertive Reminders

- Make sure my goal is focused on expressing myself, not changing others.
- Use "I" statements.
- Stay calm and not defensive.

Reminders to myself

These feelings will pass, even if it seems like they will last forever.

Quotes

"Holding on to anger is like grasping a hot coal with the intent of throwing it at someone else; you are the one who gets burned."

— Buddha

Things to do when I am upset

- Call a friend
- Count to 100 before responding
- Use my breathing techniques
- Write in my journal
- Write down my thoughts and challenge them

Beware of My Cognitive Errors

- All or nothing thinking
- Fortune telling
- Jumping to conclusions

Coping statement that help me deal with panic

- I know I can handle this.
- I will focus on one thing at a time. I will not die from a panic attack. I have been through this before and survived!
- I can learn and grow from this.

 Copyright © 2016 Judith Belmont. *150 More Group Therapy Activities & TIPS*, www.belmontwellness.com. All rights reserved.

Activity

Coping Cards

Now it's your turn to make up your coping cards. Use 3 by 5 index cards, or if you do not have any, use the cards below that you can cut out and put together in a plastic bag for protection.

Affirmations	Things To Do When I Am Upset

Assertive Reminders	Beware of My Cognitive Errors

Quotes	Reminders To Myself

Coping Statements For Anxiety	Coping Statements For Anger Management

Healthy Choices	Things To Do To Help Me Cope With Panic

Copyright © 2016 Judith Belmont. *150 More Group Therapy Activities & TIPS*, www.belmontwellness.com. All rights reserved.

Tip #115

Skills to Chill

THEORY

Offering practical strategies to help clients **improve their life by improving their coping skills is one of the main goals we have as therapists.** Life skills such as de-escalating anger, delaying impulsive actions, and being calm in times of stress and upset are some of the life skills we try to impart to our clients. This activity, "Chill Skills in a Jar," helps provide some great structure, particularly in group settings, for developing these important life skills. This particular jar from Free Spirit Publishing is geared to teens, but you can pick and choose many of the cards in the jar that are appropriate for any age population or add to them on your own.

IMPLEMENTATION

Chill Skills in a Jar provides four types of cards to help stimulate discussion and problem solving about how to improve coping skills.

The four categories, with an example for each, are:

> **TIPS** *Find a calming place. If you're feeling angry about something, find a quiet place you like where you feel peaceful. This might be your room, a local park, or any other place that helps you feel calm inside.*

> **What Would You Do?** *You're walking down your street when someone standing in a group yells an insult at you. You keep walking, but then the whole group starts to call you names.*

> **Act It Out!** *Use Deep Breathing: Someone threatens you and puts a finger in your face. To stay calm, you take five deep breaths (breathing in through your nose and breathing out through your mouth). Show the group how to do deep breathing.*

> **Share** *Talk about a time you responded to anger in a positive way and it made the situation better.*

You can either pick the skills in one category for each lesson, or use all the cards randomly in the same session.

Ask the group members to relate a real life situation that reading a card triggers, to make the examples and learning more relevant.

A meaningful group activity would be to have members make up their own cards and put them in a jar and all group members can choose.

PROCESSING

These cards serve as great discussion starters to learn from one another what coping skills work for them, and what does not work. Tailoring the four types of cards to the theme and purpose of the group session will further make the learning relevant - and fun too!

 Copyright © 2016 Judith Belmont. *150 More Group Therapy Activities & TIPS*, www.belmontwellness.com. All rights reserved.

Tip #116

Tips for Emotional Resilience

- **Stop trying to rework yesterday.** It happened. Take your licks, learn your lessons, and move on.

- **Use mistakes and failures as learning experiences.** The road to success is paved with failures. Build on your mistakes to gain wisdom and perspective.

- **Things don't usually have to change around you for your life to change** - In many cases, change in life requires only a change in attitude.

- **Focus on what you can control, not what's out of your control.** *Be solution-focused, not problem-focused.*

- **Alter your perceptions.** Don't blame others for making you feel a certain way! As Epictetus said in 1 A.D., "It is not events which disturb us, but our view of those events."

- **Stop being angry because of your unrealistic expectations.** Anger can be constructive in response to abuse or gross misconduct, but all too often we are angry because we simply expect life should be different. Give up the need to have things go your way.

- **Grieve what could have been, should have been, but wasn't.** It takes courage to mourn the loss of unrealized expectations - and move on from them.

- **Instead of asking "Why" move on to "What's Next?"** It is not "Wise" to ask too many "whys." We often will never know - shift forward to *"what's next?"*

- **Strive for goodness, not perfection!** Give up the need to be right. Limit defensiveness. Forgive – both yourself and others. Accept limitations. Let go of "shoulds" which make you bitter.

- **Develop compassion.** Choose kindness over being right. Resist the need to be critical and judgmental - to yourself or others.

- **Develop good self-care habits.** Allow yourself "mental health breaks" and "time outs" regularly. Take care of needs in mind, body, and spirit. Eat well, exercise, and get enough sleep. Pamper yourself. Set limits, prioritize, and delegate.

- **Don't isolate yourself – CONNECT!** Avoid self-absorption. Seek to understand – not to only be understood.

- **Look for the humor in things.** Lighten up! Life is too serious to be taken too seriously. Accept that life isn't fair!

- **Develop mindfulness.** Be present and focused.

- **Wherever you go, bring your sense of humor** - Never leave it at home!

Copyright © 2016 Judith Belmont. *150 More Group Therapy Activities & TIPS*, www.belmontwellness.com. All rights reserved.

Are You Emotionally Fit and Resilient?

THEORY

Quick quizzes can offer great opportunities for personal insight, identifying mastery and knowledge of the topic, and provide a basis for group sharing. **Quizzes provide a valuable basis for meaningful discussion and sharing.**

IMPLEMENTATION

Have all group members spend a few minutes taking the following quiz. This should take no more than 3-5 minutes. Since some particularly low scorers might not want to reveal their score, you might just ask how many scored 28 and above and how many scored below the mean. Have each member take one score that was the lowest and share which item they need to work on with the group's help.

PROCESSING

Having a tangible score and a quick inventory of some major factors that lead to emotional health, you can brainstorm traits of an emotionally healthy person. Topics for discussion from this quiz include some of the major facets of the emotionally resilient person such as forgiveness, gratitude, positive thinking, letting go of blame and regret, feeling a sense of empowerment and control, and having the ability to connect and self-disclose.

Copyright © 2016 Judith Belmont. *150 More Group Therapy Activities & TIPS*, www.belmontwellness.com. All rights reserved.

Quiz

Emotional Resiliency

Most of us know guidelines for physical fitness and the basics of healthy eating. Yet all too often people are unaware of the key elements of "Emotional Wellness." Below is a quick quiz to get your Emotional Wellness I.Q. Test yourself occasionally to gauge if you are boosting your Emotional Wellness!

Below are 8 items that you may agree with or disagree with. On a scale of 1 to 7, rate your level of agreement with each item, being honest and open with yourself.

7 — Strongly Agree

6 — Moderately Agree

5 — Slightly Agree

4 — Neither Agree or Disagree

3 — Slightly Disagree

2 — Moderately Disagree

1 — Strongly Disagree

_____ I feel satisfied with who I am and where I am in my life.

_____ I refuse to allow regrets and disappointments to cloud "today."

_____ I feel a strong sense of connection with others and don't feel isolated.

_____ I tend to think rationally and optimistically.

_____ I do not hold on to grudges and can forgive others for not living up to my expectations.

_____ I feel a great sense of control over my emotions, thoughts & feelings.

_____ I have a healthy sense of humor and can laugh at life's imperfections.

_____ I feel more gratitude for what I have rather than focus on what I lack.

Total your score here: _____

51-56 — Resiliency and Wellness is extraordinary!

47-50 — High level of Resiliency and Wellness

40-46 — Moderate level of Resiliency and Wellness

32-39 — Resiliency and Wellness needs some boosting!

24-31 — Resiliency and Wellness is low & needs attention.

16-23 — Resiliency and Wellness is dangerously low - seek help!

Below 15 — Danger Zone! Need help immediately!

Copyright © 2016 Judith Belmont. *150 More Group Therapy Activities & TIPS*, www.belmontwellness.com. All rights reserved.

Tip #118

Proactivity for Stress Resilience!

THEORY

In Stephen Covey's book, *The 7 Habits of Highly Effective People,* he sees proactivity as the foundation of all the other six habits, and therefore has proactivity as habit #1.

Covey regards **proactivity as the act of taking charge of your life, being responsible for it, and taking action to master your life.** Covey focuses on choice as a principle that underlies proactivity, as we ultimately have the choice of how we respond to what happens to us in our lives and it is our reactions that determine how things affect us. People who lack the proactivity habit tend to be reactive, seeing themselves as victims of circumstance, feeling disempowered.

IMPLEMENTATION

Teach the points made above to your group to emphasize the importance of being proactive. According to Covey, proactivity is:

1. The ability to set goals and work towards achieving them.
2. Creating opportunities, not waiting for them to come your way.
3. Taking conscious control of your life.
4. Understanding the choice you have in engineering your life.
5. Applying governing personal principles and core values to determine what is right in making decisions.
6. Having imagination and creativity to explore possible alternatives.
7. Realizing you are independent will allow you to choose your own unique response.

In his landmark book, Covey differentiates between the "have's" and the "be's." The latter focuses on your character and how you can take charge of your life. Instead of focusing on the thought "If I had a better job," a proactive person would focus on thoughts like "I can be more resourceful."

For today's activity, focus on what you can 'be' not on what you "have."

Have the group write down at least three "have or had" phrases and transform them into "be" phrases.

> For example: The thought "If I only had a better boss" can be changed to "I can 'be' stronger in dealing with her."

Remember the importance of being proactive and not reactive!

Suggest to the group that each participant devise a specific action plan based on your decisions to "be," whether it be a checklist, schedule, or chart in which you reward yourself for sticking to your goals.

PROCESSING

Have each person in the group go around and commit him or herself to one idea of how they can be proactive in the next week. Remind them in devising their goal to use the more proactive "be" thoughts rather than their "have" thoughts.

> *"If you're proactive, you don't have to wait for circumstances or other people to create perspective expanding experiences. You can consciously create your own."* – Stephen Covey

    Copyright © 2016 Judith Belmont. *150 More Group Therapy Activities & TIPS,* www.belmontwellness.com. All rights reserved.

Being an Emotional Translator

THEORY

In times of stress, we are all too often guided by our emotional reasoning rather than by logic and the facts. This emotional translation activity will help group members to learn to revise their emotional language with the help of the group's objectivity and support.

IMPLEMENTATION

Give group members a few minutes to write down a troublesome thought that causes their emotional upset.

You might offer examples such as:

> *"I just don't care about anything anymore - nothing works out for me."*
>
> *"People can't be trusted and will disappoint you."*
>
> *"I can't seem to get my life together and feel like a failure."*

Alternatively, you can have samples of these troublesome thoughts already written out on cards and have group members pick them out of a box or other container.

Have the first person read one of the items and the next person serve as their emotional translator.

> 1st group member: *"I just don't care about anything anymore - nothing works out for me."*
>
> 2nd group member: *"You are hurting too much to care - and feel hopeless that things will change."*
>
> 1st group member: *"People can't be trusted and will disappoint you."*
>
> 2nd group member: *"You are afraid of getting hurt and want to protect yourself from getting your feelings hurt yet again."*

Leave a couple minutes to process the statement and the translation, getting feedback from the group as well as the 1st group member. Be prepared to help the translator think of a healthy translation.

The idea of this activity is that it is often easier to develop the ability to be more objective and become an emotional translator when you can be objective about someone else's statements. By practicing with the examples of others, group members practice the skills of being an emotional translator that they can then apply to themselves.

Another version of this activity is to collect everyone's note cards after they have written down responses. Then you read each of the statements and ask group members to be the emotional translator, without anyone knowing who wrote the card. You can let the group know that they do not have to be identified as the writer of the card, so that members can feel more comfortable writing down their thoughts.

PROCESSING

This activity can be extremely helpful on a variety of levels including group sharing, enlisting group support, gaining practice to view upsetting statements in healthier ways, and gaining perspective. The responses of others can serve as objective reality checks for group members.

Copyright © 2016 Judith Belmont. *150 More Group Therapy Activities & TIPS*, www.belmontwellness.com. All rights reserved.

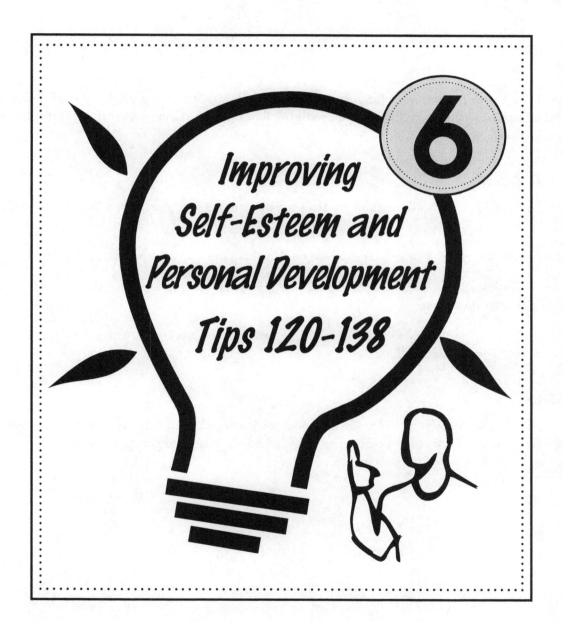

6

Improving Self-Esteem and Personal Development

Tips 120-138

Introduce Positive Psychology

THEORY

Positive psychology, with its focus on happiness and well-being, is a relatively new field, although the roots go back centuries. **The focus of positive psychology is on wellness**, life satisfaction, and emotional and spiritual health, rather than overcoming pathology.

IMPLEMENTATION

The following are handouts and worksheets on positive psychology topics such as happiness, forgiveness, self-esteem and gratitude.

Use the material as a springboard for group discussion on why these areas are so important to well-being.

Taking turns reading aloud one of the handouts and having group members pick a favorite TIP can set the stage for a productive and positive discussion.

Use the topics of positive psychology to tie in the following handouts and worksheets with metaphorical toolkits such as the "Positive Life Toolkit."

PROCESSING

Each of the following self-empowering and positive handouts and worksheets depict areas of wellness, such as gratefulness, forgiveness and happiness. They can be best used as self-help homework assignments to process in the next session.

 Copyright © 2016 Judith Belmont. *150 More Group Therapy Activities & TIPS*, www.belmontwellness.com. All rights reserved.

Tip #121

10 Tips to Being The Best YOU!

Here are 10 tips for living a life of emotional wellness and positivity, so you can be the BEST YOU!

1. **Stop looking on the outside for happiness that you can only get within.**

    Although things on the outside can help considerably - Nothing on the outside makes us truly happy – It's all in how we look at things – so only WE can!

2. **Like yourself and others will too!**

    When you like yourself and think positively about yourself, it will attract others!

    Don't look for approval from others any more than seeking your own approval.

3. **Be flexible and resilient in the face of challenge.**

    Staying flexible and changing your perceptions will enhance your ability to overcome obstacles.

4. **Be a stress manager . . . and not a stress carrier!**

    Stress for success - use stress to motivate, not debilitate.

5. **Communicate assertively.**

    Use "I" Statements instead of "You" statements.

    Avoid rhetorical questions.

6. **Use positive self – talk.**

    Our feelings are caused by our thoughts - think rationally!

    No one makes us feel a certain way - we do!

    Think straight to feel great!

7. **Have an attitude of gratitude.**

    Choose kindness over being right.

8. **Forgive others and forgive yourself!**

    Misery starts when being able to forgive ends. We all are human, we make mistakes, we don't always know what we are doing. Learn from what happened and improve today!

9. **Anchor yourself in today - not yesterday or tomorrow.**

    All too often people live in the past rather than learn from it, and are also caught up in the "what ifs" or the unknowns of the future. Remember the famous saying, "Yesterday is history. Tomorrow is a mystery. Today is a gift. That's why it is called the present." (Alice Morse Earle)

10. **Connect with others!**

    Many times people protect themselves by shutting down when they really need to open up. Isolating ourselves only breeds unhappiness - seeking support will open up channels for a happier life!

Copyright © 2016 Judith Belmont. *150 More Group Therapy Activities & TIPS*, www.belmontwellness.com. All rights reserved.

Activity

Being the Best ME!

Using TIP# 121 as a reference, personalize each of the 10 items to you.

1. **Ways I create my own happiness:**_____
_____

2. **Ways that I increase my self-esteem:**_____
_____

3. **How I can be more flexible and resilient in face of challenge?**_____
_____

4. **How I can manage stress . . . instead of carry it?**_____
_____

5. **Ways to communicate more assertively:**_____
_____

6. **What are some positive phrases I can use to remind myself?**_____
_____

7. **What am I grateful for?**_____
_____

8. **What do I need to do to be more forgiving of others? Of myself?**_____
_____

9. **How can I be more mindful and immersed in TODAY?**_____
_____

10. **How can I improve relationships with family and friends?**_____
_____

 Copyright © 2016 Judith Belmont. *150 More Group Therapy Activities & TIPS*, www.belmontwellness.com. All rights reserved.

10 Simple Tips To Be Happy

10 simple tips to being happy:

1. **Happy people like themselves!**

   It's not what you have - it's who you are!

2. **Happy people don't compare themselves to others.**

   The only person they compare themselves to is themselves, and how they have grown since yesterday. They don't need to be better than others - as they know that will only make them bitter.

3. **Happy people have a strong sense of social support.**

   Happy people love to love - and be loved.

4. **Happy people are forgiving of themselves and others.**

   Those who do not hold grudges against themselves and others tend to be happier people.

5. **Happy people spend little time looking over their shoulders.**

   They live life picking themselves up and moving forward. Looking back is useful only to learn from, not to live in.

6. **Happy people fully realize that there are some things they will never get over.**

   Happy people realize that some things are never really healed, but you can be happy despite the thorns in life. They don't deny the thorns, they just don't dwell on them.

7. **Happy people are trusting and don't spend much time being self-protective.**

   Happy people are trusting, mostly because at base they trust and like themselves.

8. **Happy people are optimistic.**

   Optimism is not pretending things are okay when they are not, but rather making the best out of things.

9. **Happy people are proactive - not reactive.**

   Happy people don't wait for things to happen - they MAKE them happen!

10. **Happy people are filled with self-compassion and compassion towards others.**

    Happy people focus on acceptance rather than living steeped in judgment about themselves and others.

In looking at this list, are there some areas that are more challenging for you than others? Choose one or two tips that you would like to work on, and make an action plan to develop your happiness habit!

_____

_____

_____

Copyright © 2016 Judith Belmont. *150 More Group Therapy Activities & TIPS*, www.belmontwellness.com. All rights reserved.

Quiz

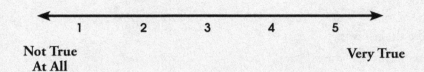

How Happy Are You?

This quick quiz highlights some of the important ingredients to happiness. Rate each of the items on what best characterizes you.

1   2   3   4   5

Not True
At All   **Very True**

_____ I don't look for my inner happiness in outside things.

_____ I really love and value myself, and see this as a foundation for really loving others.

_____ I regard challenges as opportunities to grow and deepen, and develop resiliency.

_____ I stay positive and optimistic, and try to make the best out of even the most troubling situations.

_____ I seek and give support to others, and widen my social network as I grow.

_____ I am able to forgive and don't hold grudges, while setting limits on those who treat me poorly.

_____ I live life mindfully now, learning from yesterday with an eye towards moving forward into tomorrow.

_____ I am self-compassionate and compassionate toward others.

Score: _____

Use this quiz often as a way of measuring your happiness quotient, comparing your score only to your previous scores. The higher you score, the happier you are! Any score below 3 needs some work! If you score on the lower side, be easy on yourself. The idea is to keep moving forward and increasing your happiness!

 Copyright © 2016 Judith Belmont. *150 More Group Therapy Activities & TIPS*, www.belmontwellness.com. All rights reserved.

10 Tips to Being Highly Happy

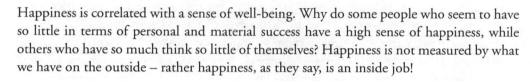

Happiness is correlated with a sense of well-being. Why do some people who seem to have so little in terms of personal and material success have a high sense of happiness, while others who have so much think so little of themselves? Happiness is not measured by what we have on the outside – rather happiness, as they say, is an inside job!

These are characteristics of highly happy people:

1. **Highly happy people measure their worth in terms of personal success.**

   Those with high self-esteem are not fooled with material possessions such as fancy cars, expensive clothes and posh vacations as the places where true happiness is found. They know all too well that no matter how many things you have, you can still feel empty within.

2. **Highly happy people have high self-esteem.**

   Happy people have a foundation of self-love. Unhappy people spend futile time comparing themselves to others. The happy person compares themselves only to themselves and who they were yesterday - they just want to grow and improve.

3. **Highly happy people have a strong sense of social support.**

   Happy people are connectors and have a strong sense of love and being loved. They engage others with kindness and an open heart, instead of distrust, protectiveness and bitterness. They will agree with the saying "We might not have it all together, but together we have it all!"

4. **Highly happy people are forgiving of themselves and others.**

   Those who do not hold grudges against themselves and others tend to be lighter and less bogged down emotionally than those who carry a backpack of regrets and grudges.

5. **Highly happy people spend little time looking over their shoulders.**

   They live life looking and moving forward, not backwards. Those who are steeped in regret and their "*woulda, coulda, shouldas*" imprison themselves in the past and surrender their power to the past. Rather, highly happy people focus on learning from the past and doing something about it NOW!

☺ 6. **Highly happy people fully realize that there are some things they will never get over.**

People who are highly happy don't expect life to always go smoothly, and realize that life's happiness does not go on without interruptions; in fact, a full life has times of great sadness. Rather than rail against life's injustices, they accept difficult times as opportunities for growth.

☺ 7. **Highly happy people are trusting and have faith that there can be beauty and happiness after loss.**

The one thing that highly happy people do not do is to spend energy trying to protect themselves from being hurt. Rather, they have enough confidence in themselves that looking to others for warmth, comfort and support has more potential to make them stronger, not weaker. They trust others, but realize the foundation for trusting others is trusting themselves. A great analogy is imagining yourself in a rowboat in the middle of a lake - you will be more likely to trust the person rowing if you can swim!

☺ 8. **Highly happy people are optimistic.**

Those who are optimistic do not expect for things to always turn out okay. They have the belief that no matter what, *they* still can turnout okay. They have confidence in themselves that they can make a positive spin on almost anything that happens, without pretending to feel something they don't. Rather than shrugging their feelings off, or pretending that they don't care, they address their feelings and thoughts head on. They have faith in themselves to work through difficult feelings and find a lesson or silver lining.

☺ 9. **Highly happy people are proactive - not reactive.**

Instead of waiting for someone else to set the stage for their actions, they have priorities, direction and values that drive them. They know how to conduct their lives, driven by their sense of priorities, direction and values rather than passively waiting for things to happen.

☺ 10. **Highly happy people are filled with self-compassion, without self-loathing, hate or bitterness.**

People who have the secret to happiness know that it's all about love: self-love, love for others with an attitude of acceptance instead of criticalness and judgmentalness. Lessons given in anger never work, but lessons in love often do. Kindness and compassion trump everything, even the need for being right.

Copyright © 2016 Judith Belmont. *150 More Group Therapy Activities & TIPS*, www.belmontwellness.com. All rights reserved.

Are You Highly Happy?

Here is a quiz to find out your "happiness quotient!"

For each of the 10 items below, rate your response on the continuum of highly untrue to highly true. Add them up and divide by 10 to get your happiness quotient!

| 1 | 2 | 3 | 4 | 5 | 6 | 7 | 8 | 9 | 10 |

Highly Untrue   **Not Sure**   **Highly True**

_____ I measure my worth on what's inside and intangible, not the "things" I have.

_____ I like who I am and have high self esteem.

_____ I have a strong degree of social support.

_____ I am forgiving of myself and others.

_____ I tend to focus on now instead of being steeped in past regrets.

_____ I do not expect to "get over" everything, but I am resilient enough to "get through" everything.

_____ I am open and trusting with others and spend little energy feeling like I need to be self-protective.

_____ I tend to be optimistic and positive about my life.

_____ I tend to make things happen and feel empowered to be proactive.

_____ I tend to feel love and share love, filled with compassion towards self and others.

Total _____

Divide total by 10 to get your happiness quotient _____

8-10 — Happiness Master

6-7 — Happiness Novice

4-5 — Happiness Seeker

1-3 — Danger Zone - Need a happiness infusion!

Copyright © 2016 Judith Belmont. *150 More Group Therapy Activities & TIPS*, www.belmontwellness.com. All rights reserved.

What Is Your Forgiveness IQ?

THEORY

The importance of forgiveness has become apparent in modern day psychological theory, and **positive psychology in particular focuses on the importance of forgiveness**. Letting our clients know that forgiveness is a choice and a conscious act - despite pulls of anger, negativity and hurt - will help them be more in control of their resentful feelings.

IMPLEMENTATION

The following is a quick quiz to survey the main characteristics of forgiveness.

After having group members complete the quiz in the session, have them share their lowest and highest scores in small groups or pairs.

Ask them to discuss a situation which they had a hard time forgiving and how they can learn to forgive now.

Have them imagine how life would be if they were able to forgive others - as well as themselves.

PROCESSING

As in all other quizzes, the more group members process with one another, the more they will get out of it. Remind them that forgiveness is not about condoning behavior, but rather the ability to let go. Letting go of expectations does not mean that people should not set limits and consequences, and have standards of how they will accept others to treat them. However, it does help people get away from the "shoulds" they impose on others and themselves.

Quiz *What is Your Forgiveness IQ?*

It's not easy to forgive when you feel slighted or wronged, yet we know that the inability to forgive causes us to hold on to bitterness and negativity. For some, forgiving oneself for past actions and choices proves to be the most challenging of all. It is important to keep in mind that forgiveness is a choice and reflects a conscious decision. The first step is to identify the essential elements of forgiveness, which provides a basis to focus on the areas that need the most attention.

For the following 10 questions, rate each item from 1 to 10 to find your "forgiveness IQ."

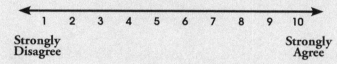

1 2 3 4 5 6 7 8 9 10
Strongly   **Strongly**
Disagree   **Agree**

_____ I will not forgive people if they are not sorry and admit what they've done.

_____ Those who have wronged or slighted me but take no responsibility for hurting me do not deserve to be forgiven.

_____ I find that my inability to forgive leaves me stuck thinking about what happened in the past.

_____ I can't forgive because I don't want to condone bad behavior.

_____ A difficulty in forgiving makes it hard for me to trust others.

_____ It's hard to forgive, because forgiving means letting people off the hook and makes them no longer accountable.

_____ Forgiveness is something that you just feel, not a trainable skill.

_____ Since there is nothing I can do about things now, I tend to keep things in and don't share my hurt with others.

_____ If I forgive, that means I will be vulnerable again, and I need to protect myself.

_____ I can't forgive myself for past mistakes, choices and failures.

Total _____

How did you do? The lower the score, the better your forgiveness IQ.

15 or lower — You are a forgiveness genius! Congratulations!

16–29 — Strong forgiveness competency. You have given yourself the gift of forgiveness and stay positive.

30–49 — Moderate forgiveness competency. You have some work to do on becoming less negative and stuck in past resentments.

50–69 — Moderate forgiveness impairment. A difficulty with forgiveness has limited your ability to stay positive and live fully in the present.

70–84 — Severe forgiveness impairment. Consider seeking professional help to give yourself the gift of forgiveness.

85–100 — Danger Zone! A lack of forgiveness impairs your mental health. Consider seeking psychological help.

From *The Therapist's Ultimate Solution Book: Essential Strategies, Tips and Tools To Empower Your Clients* by Judith Belmont. Copyright © 2015 by Judith Belmont. Used by permission of W.W. Norton & Company

Tip #125

My Positive Day Log

THEORY

This simple journal worksheet can be a prototype for group members to use **to remind themselves of things each day that are positive**. Sometimes it is hard to keep positive, but this activity emphasizes that positivity is a conscious choice.

IMPLEMENTATION

- Give this worksheet out for homework and ask them to complete for the next group.

- Tell members that they will be asked to share their responses with the group, so only include answers they are willing to talk about.

- Encourage them to fill it out a few items each day so they can stay focused on positivity and gratefulness.

- When they come back with completed logs, ask them how it felt to focus on the positives in their lives, and how that focus can change their life situation in general.

- Break into small groups of 3 or 4 to share their responses.

- Make the point that to be positive and proud of yourself is not selfish, conceited or bragging - rather, it's expressing appreciation for who you are and this appreciation will help you spread cheer and goodwill to others.

- **Positivity is contagious**!

PROCESSING

This worksheet establishes a positive forum to share with group members, increasing social cohesiveness with others, while enhancing self-esteem. Process with the group as a whole how it felt to focus on positive things daily - did they recognize more positives in themselves and in their day because of this assignment? Suggest to the group that they use this log frequently to keep staying positive. This will help them to be more aware of their day-to-day victories and accomplishments that they might otherwise disregard. This is a great activity for children as well as adults.

 Copyright © 2016 Judith Belmont. *150 More Group Therapy Activities & TIPS*, www.belmontwellness.com. All rights reserved.

My Positive Day Log

My Thoughts	My Responses
SUNDAY	
Something positive about what I accomplished today:	
My most positive moment today was:	
I felt proud today because:	
MONDAY	
I felt the best about myself today when :	
Something I tried differently today:	
Something nice I did for others because:	
TUESDAY	
The best thing that happened to today was:	
I'm most grateful today because:	
The most courageous thing I did today was:	
WEDNESDAY	
I was kind today when I:	
I felt happy about myself today because:	
I feel special today because :	
THURSDAY	
The thing I admired most about myself today:	
I feel unique today because:	
I felt I was very good at this today:	
FRIDAY	
The best choice I made today:	
I felt successful today because:	
This is the best thing I learned today:	
SATURDAY	
I'm most awesome today because:	
I admire myself today because:	
What I love most about myself today:	

Copyright © 2016 Judith Belmont. *150 More Group Therapy Activities & TIPS*, www.belmontwellness.com. All rights reserved.

Making a DBT House

THEORY

Tying a universally known image to a life skills lesson can make it relevant and memorable. Using the image of a house to facilitate self-discovery can help children, as well as adults, **identify important issues about themselves**, such as values, coping skills, their strengths, and the quality of their support systems. This is an activity used in Dialectical Behavior Therapy (DBT) as a life skills exercise.

IMPLEMENTATION

Have group members fill out the house on the different parts and various levels. These are some suggested ideas to fill in for the various parts of a house, but you can choose your own ideas based on what you are trying to elicit from the group.

House Floors:

- Level 1: List behaviors you want to change.

- Level 2: List emotions you want to increase.

- Level 3: List things in your life you are happy about.

- Level 4: List values that govern your life.

House Parts:

- Foundation: List or draw the values that govern your life.

- Door: What doors do you need to open in your life?

- Windows: List or draw your dreams and hope.

- Walls: List or draw those people that support you.

- Roof: List or draw who protects you.

- Chimney: List or draw how you let off steam.

PROCESSING

Have each member show the group their house and explain their answers. This is a creative way to identify things to change in oneself, improve coping skills, as well as to help identify core values and support systems.

 Copyright © 2016 Judith Belmont. *150 More Group Therapy Activities & TIPS*, www.belmontwellness.com. All rights reserved.

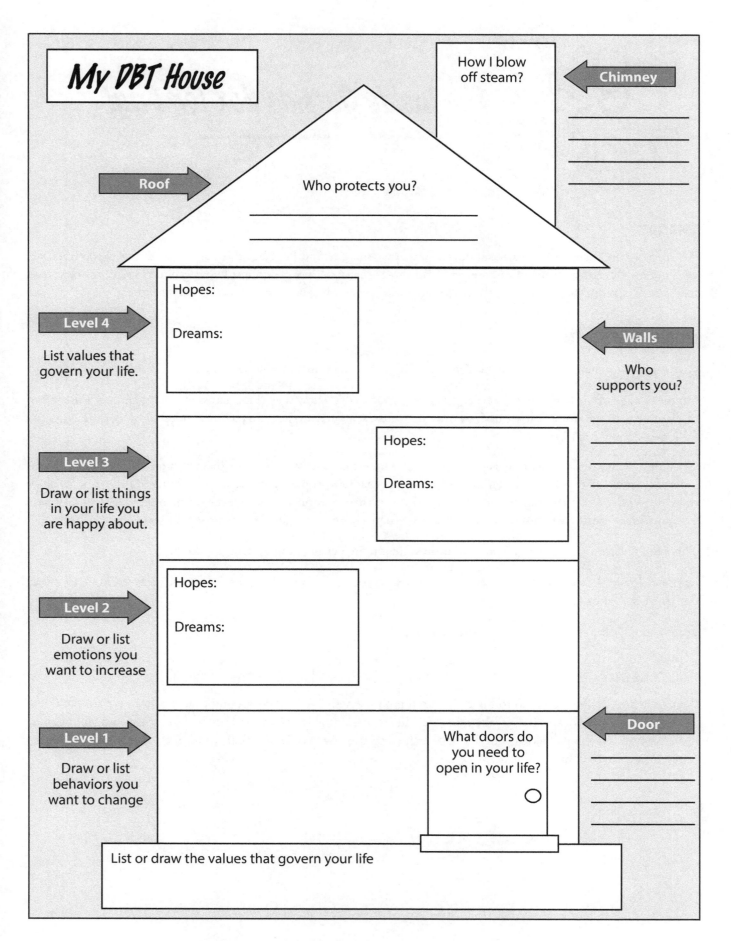

My DBT House

How I blow
off steam?

Chimney

_____
_____
_____
_____

Roof

Who protects you?

_____
_____

Level 4

List values that
govern your life.

Hopes:

Dreams:

Walls

Who
supports you?

_____
_____
_____
_____

Level 3

Draw or list things
in your life you
are happy about.

Hopes:

Dreams:

Level 2

Draw or list
emotions you
want to increase

Hopes:

Dreams:

Level 1

Draw or list
behaviors you
want to change

What doors do
you need to
open in your life?

Door

_____
_____
_____
_____

List or draw the values that govern your life

Copyright © 2016 Judith Belmont. *150 More Group Therapy Activities & TIPS*, www.belmontwellness.com. All rights reserved.

The Inside Outside Box (or Bag)

THEORY

We are all aware there are things about ourselves that we share with others, but there are other things we do not share with others. By sharing some of our "secrets" and things that most people do not know, group cohesiveness and trust increases. **Activities that promote self-disclosure** make the group experience personally therapeutic.

IMPLEMENTATION

Give each group member a small lunch size paper bag or box, and provide colored pencils or crayons.

On the outside of the bag or box, instruct group members to draw how they come across to others, and what they show of themselves to the world. They can draw or write words, sentences, or just use pictures to depict various thoughts and feelings.

Once they write, draw or paste what they present to others on the outside, have them put inside of the bag or box notecards on which they have written some of the things that few people know about them, things they do not generally show the world. If the bag can be turned inside out or if there is enough room on the inside of the box, you can have group members write there instead of notecards. Alternatively, they can glue or tape images or words on the inside.

This activity encourages group members to express their more personal thoughts and feelings.

Let the members know that they do not have to share everything they put in the inside, but are expected to share at least one thing with the group.

Leave enough time in the session to process and share.

PROCESSING

Processing and sharing will help to build trust and group cohesiveness. Make a point that the more we feel confident about ourselves and trust ourselves, the more we will feel comfortable expressing ourselves to others, and will be more likely to have less things hidden. Emphasize that finding trusting people to talk to will limit the isolation of keeping things inside the box (bag).

 Copyright © 2016 Judith Belmont. *150 More Group Therapy Activities & TIPS*, www.belmontwellness.com. All rights reserved.

Tip #128

Finding Significance in Everyday Life

THEORY

This TIP was adapted from Bernie Siegel, MD in his book, *101 Exercises for the Soul,* and **reminds us that nothing is insignificant**, and we can find meaning in everything if we stop a moment to be mindful and aware.

IMPLEMENTATION

Tell the group that this will be an awareness exercise to remind them to be mindful of even the most seemingly insignificant things in everyday life. A great example to use is a penny.

Pass out pennies for everyone to examine.

Point out that a penny has these things on it:

> **Lincoln's Face** - One of the most popular presidents in history, known for his honesty, dedication and making the nation whole.

> **Lincoln Memorial or Union shield** - In 2010 the pennies changed from the memorial to the symbol of the unified union of 13 states.

> **The word** *Liberty*

> **The words** *In God We Trust*

> **The Latin phrase E PLURIBUS UNUM** - "One out of many" or "One from many"

When they exchange money at stores, ask them to be aware of passing around these sentiments to those around us and reminding themselves of what the penny represents.

PROCESSING

The penny represents that you can find significance in even seemingly insignificant things. Encourage them to take a moment every time they use money to be mindful and aware. This exercise underscores the importance of how increasing mindfulness in everyday life will help to improve their own personal development and life satisfaction.

Copyright © 2016 Judith Belmont. *150 More Group Therapy Activities & TIPS*, www.belmontwellness.com. All rights reserved.

50 Life Lessons

THEORY

The following inspirational handout developed by *The New York Times* bestselling author Regina Brett will provide some positive structure to discuss **important life lessons**.

IMPLEMENTATION

Introduce the idea that the group collectively has many life lessons, and you would like to tap into the wealth of knowledge the group has experienced.

Pass out Regina Brett's *45 Life Lessons and 5 to Grow On* handout.

Give them a few moments to look it over and circle the five items that resonate the most, and think about why these items mean something to them.

Break up into pairs or triads to share answers in small groups. After about 10 to 15 minutes, bring the group back to together and have each person share the life lesson they identified most with and why.

Have them imagine how their life would be different if they would be able to incorporate that lesson 100% in their lives.

Ask for thoughts about other life lessons they have learned that are not on this sheet.

PROCESSING

The success of this activity is in allowing time to process meaningful answers as a group. You can even narrow the focus into what you have learned in the past year, or even the past week or month. We are all works in progress and always learning, and it is never too late to learn lessons no matter what age you are!

 Copyright © 2016 Judith Belmont. *150 More Group Therapy Activities & TIPS*, www.belmontwellness.com. All rights reserved.

Regina Brett's 45
Life Lessons and 5 To Grow on

I have written the 50 lessons life has taught me:

1. Life isn't fair, but it's still good.

2. When in doubt, just take the next small step.

3. Life is too short to waste time hating anyone.

4. Don't take yourself so seriously. No one else does.

5. Pay off your credit cards every month.

6. You don't have to win every argument. Agree to disagree.

7. Cry with someone. It's more healing than crying alone.

8. It's OK to get angry with God. He can take it.

9. Save for retirement starting with your first paycheck.

10. When it comes to chocolate, resistance is futile.

11. Make peace with your past so it won't screw up the present.

12. It's OK to let your children see you cry.

13. Don't compare your life to others'. You have no idea what their journey is all about.

14. If a relationship has to be a secret, you shouldn't be in it.

15. Everything can change in the blink of an eye. But don't worry; God never blinks.

16. Life is too short for long pity parties. Get busy living, or get busy dying.

17. You can get through anything if you stay put in today.

18. A writer writes. If you want to be a writer, write.

19. It's never too late to have a happy childhood. But the second one is up to you and no one else.

20. When it comes to going after what you love in life, don't take no for an answer.

21. Burn the candles, use the nice sheets, wear the fancy lingerie. Don't save it for a special occasion. Today is special.

22. Over prepare, then go with the flow.

23. Be eccentric now. Don't wait for old age to wear purple.

Copyright © 2016 Judith Belmont. *150 More Group Therapy Activities & TIPS*, www.belmontwellness.com. All rights reserved.

24. The most important sex organ is the brain.

25. No one is in charge of your happiness except you.

26. Frame every so-called disaster with these words: "In five years, will this matter?"

27. Always choose life.

28. Forgive everyone everything.

29. What other people think of you is none of your business.

30. Time heals almost everything. Give time.

31. However good or bad a situation is, it will change.

32. Your job won't take care of you when you are sick. Your friends will. Stay in touch.

33. Believe in miracles.

34. God loves you because of who God is, not because of anything you did or didn't do.

35. Whatever doesn't kill you really does make you stronger.

36. Growing old beats the alternative - dying young.

37. Your children get only one childhood. Make it memorable.

38. Read the Psalms. They cover every human emotion.

39. Get outside every day. Miracles are waiting everywhere.

40. If we all threw our problems in a pile and saw everyone else's, we'd grab ours back.

41. Don't audit life. Show up and make the most of it now.

42. Get rid of anything that isn't useful, beautiful or joyful.

43. All that truly matters in the end is that you loved.

44. Envy is a waste of time. You already have all you need.

45. The best is yet to come.

46. No matter how you feel, get up, dress up and show up.

47. Take a deep breath. It calms the mind.

48. If you don't ask, you don't get.

49. Yield.

50. Life isn't tied with a bow, but it's still a gift.

Reprinted with the permission of Regina Brett

 Copyright © 2016 Judith Belmont. *150 More Group Therapy Activities & TIPS*, www.belmontwellness.com. All rights reserved.

There's Something Special About Me

THEORY

Giving group members the forum to offer something special about each person helps each individual long after the group is over, **drawing strength by the positive perceptions of others**. This is a great activity for any age.

IMPLEMENTATION

In this activity, start by telling the group that everyone is special in their own way. We are all worthy, even if when we compare ourselves to others we find ourselves falling short. For this activity, tell the group that you want to help them to appreciate their uniqueness by getting feedback from others in the group. Sometimes others can be more objective and less critical than we are about ourselves.

- Each group member should write their name on the top of a blank sheet of paper.

- Then pass all the papers to the right and everyone write one or two lines about something special about the person whose name is at the top of the page.

- Pass the papers around until the circle is complete and everyone has a turn to write something nice.

- You might ask that person to also write something special about him or herself.

- When all the papers have gone around, each person gets their own and looks at all the responses of why they are special.

- Now have all group members take turns sharing how it feels to be so special!

- Emphasize that this activity underscores the importance of treating yourself with self-compassion and leaving their inner critic behind (with the help of the group feedback and non-judgmental support).

- Kristin Neff's breakthrough book, *Self-Compassion: The Proven Power of Being Kind to Yourself*, is an excellent resource to guide self-compassion.

This is an ideal activity once a group is established. The more they have the chance to get to know one another, the more meaningful the feedback. This is a great team building activity which also improves self-esteem and self-compassion.

PROCESSING

This is a fun activity to process with the group. Ask group members after completing the activity if there were any surprises. Were they surprised about what others wrote about them? Do they agree with what was written? How can they develop healthier views of themselves with the feedback from the group and increase their acceptance of themselves by being more self-compassionate? The best part of this activity is that group members have something tangible to remind them of their specialness!

My Self-Compassion Log

High self-compassion is correlated with happiness and even longevity. It serves as a cornerstone to an emotionally healthy life and healthy relationships. Below are some truths about self-compassion, with space to write your thoughts and examples. Use this log regularly to help stay positive and remind yourself of how special you are!

Truth #1: The more you give to yourself, the more you can give to others.

Ways I can nurture and support myself: _____
_____

How can that help me nurture others: _____
_____

Truth #2: I am as worthy and special as everyone else.

I am special in many ways such as: _____
_____

Truth #3: I am a beautiful person and deserve to be happy and forgive myself.

The following are examples of why I am a beautiful person and what is forgivable:
_____
_____

Truth #4: I do not deserve to be down on myself.

Critical thoughts that I will stop listening to and more positive thoughts I will listen to instead:

Critical Thoughts _____
_____

Positive Thoughts _____
_____

Truth #5: I can use my past challenges as a way to learn, grow and deepen instead of weaken.

What I have learned from my life challenges: _____
_____

 Copyright © 2016 Judith Belmont. *150 More Group Therapy Activities & TIPS*, www.belmontwellness.com. All rights reserved.

Tip #131

You Can't Get a Hamburger at a Hardware Store

All too often we expect unrealistic things of ourselves, other people and even life that are not realistic.

For example, **no one can give you what he or she does not have himself or herself**.

Some examples of things that you cannot expect:

- You can't expect to get a hamburger at a hardware store.

- You can't expect to get milk at a furniture store.

- You can't expect to get things from people that they do not have to give.

- You can't expect people with limited insight to understand you.

If people are self-absorbed and lack empathy, you can't expect them to have empathy for you.

Can you add to this list? _____
_____
_____
_____
_____
_____

Are you in relationships that you expect others to be something that they are not? Do you find yourself expecting others to give you what they do not have to give?

_____
_____
_____
_____

Mature vs. Immature Love - Which is it?

THEORY

Perry Como's song, *"Love Makes the World Go 'Round"* underscores the importance of love in living a healthy life. Unfortunately, in the name of love, all too often relationships are unhealthy and destructive, hindering personal growth instead of increasing it. What better forum to focus on love and relationships than in the context of a group setting? Group members have the opportunity to evaluate their own relationships and discriminate between healthy/mature and unhealthy/immature love.

IMPLEMENTATION

Ask group members to each think of an important love relationship in their lives, either past or present, or how they envision one in the future (if they are presently not in a relationship). Make the point that the healthier the love is, the more an individual can grow.

Stress that some of our best self-discoveries are made through relationships with others, not in isolation. Mature love can help you grow, but love that is unhealthy will cause endless heartache and conflict.

Unfortunately, it is not uncommon for relationships to erode self-esteem in the name of love. All too often in unhealthy relationships people lose themselves trying to find someone else. The accompanying handout can be a springboard for conversation on healthy vs. unhealthy love.

Relationships that are very one sided are less healthy than those that have a better balance of give and take. Have group members visualize a love relationship of their choice using the metaphor of a see-saw. Is there some degree of balance or is it very lop-sided? Do they rely on the other person to hold them up or do they sacrifice their own needs too much to accommodate the other person?

After a discussion of the characteristics of mature vs immature love, have the group members spend a few minutes taking the following quiz to rate their own love relationship either past or present, or how they would imagine one to be in the future. Do allow time to share their scores with the group.

PROCESSING

Encourage group members to reflect on the health of their love relationships past and present. Make the point that no relationship is worth sacrificing your own self-respect if you're not treated well. Process with group members if their love relationships help them grow or are stifling their growth.

 Copyright © 2016 Judith Belmont. *150 More Group Therapy Activities & TIPS*, www.belmontwellness.com. All rights reserved.

Relationship IQ

Below are the continuums of healthy vs. unhealthy relationships. Think of the most important relationship in your life and rate each item on the scale of 1 to 10. The higher the score, the healthier is your relationship.

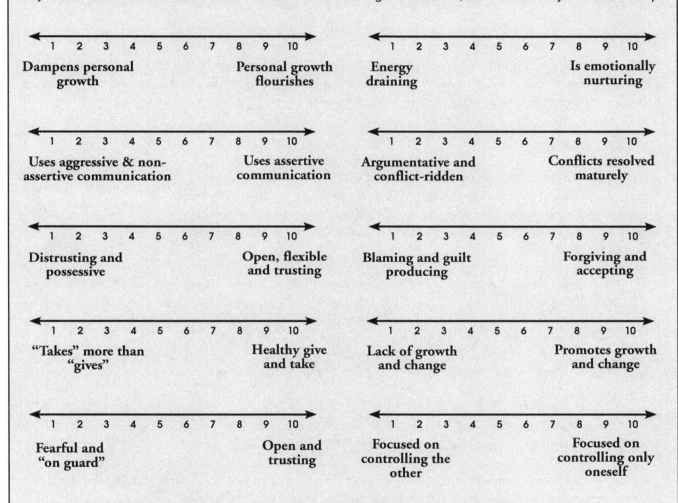

1 2 3 4 5 6 7 8 9 10	1 2 3 4 5 6 7 8 9 10
Dampens personal growth / Personal growth flourishes	Energy draining / Is emotionally nurturing
Uses aggressive & non-assertive communication / Uses assertive communication	Argumentative and conflict-ridden / Conflicts resolved maturely
Distrusting and possessive / Open, flexible and trusting	Blaming and guilt producing / Forgiving and accepting
"Takes" more than "gives" / Healthy give and take	Lack of growth and change / Promotes growth and change
Fearful and "on guard" / Open and trusting	Focused on controlling the other / Focused on controlling only oneself

Add up the numbers and divide by 10 to get your "Relationship IQ!"

9-10 — Congratulations! Your relationship is mature and thriving! You are a relationship pro!

7-8 — Your relationship has many healthy qualities, but needs some attention to growth

5-6 — The relationship has some signs of immaturity and trouble - needy of healthy growth and change

3-4 — Relationship is in jeopardy and individual growth is being compromised. SOS warning!

1-2 — Relationship is emotional abusive and toxic - seek help or considering distancing from the relationship

Copyright © 2016 Judith Belmont. *150 More Group Therapy Activities & TIPS*, www.belmontwellness.com. All rights reserved.

What's Your Positive Intention for the Day?

Tip #133

THEORY

Having a positive intention for the day helps people think positively. **Starting the day with a positive intention** can be a great way to start the day - as well as a start to each group. The Law of Attraction focuses on the importance of having positive intentions to make positive things happen.

IMPLEMENTATION

Ask group members: How do you wake up each day? Do you start your day already feeling pressured and rushed? Do you go through the morning routine without much thought at all, doing what you "have to do" to start your day? How about starting each new day with a moment to stop, breathe and think of a positive intention for the day?

- Make the point that each day is a new beginning and a blank canvas. How would you like to create your day? Think of it as a blank canvas – What would you like to paint on it? What can you create? If you wake up in a negative mindset, you are more likely to paint a dark picture throughout the day, and your canvas will not reflect hope, happiness and joy.

- Having a positive intention will set the tone for the day: What positive outcome can reflect your positive intention?

- Recommend that they write down a positive intention each morning - or look at themselves in the mirror and say it aloud. Suggest that every evening they can reflect on how they did!

- Have the group members write on notecards a positive intention for the rest of the day that they can bring home. Go around and have them read their positive intention to the group.

Here are examples of positive intentions:

- Today I would like to replace my feelings of annoyance towards my co-worker with feelings of acceptance.

- Today I will focus on what I am grateful for in my life, rather than what is missing, and express gratefulness to others.

- Today I want to slow my life down and take time to savor the moment, especially with my children.

 Copyright © 2016 Judith Belmont. *150 More Group Therapy Activities & TIPS*, www.belmontwellness.com. All rights reserved.

Suggest a Positive Intention Box in which they can keep their notecards and pick a card each day.

Following are some points you can make to the group to show how daily positive intentions can help them:

- Each day you will give yourself the gift of an "attitude of gratitude."

- Visualizing how you would like your day to be like will help release positive energy from within you and you will attract more positive energy from those around you.

- Instead of spinning your wheels in an old way of thinking, each day is a chance to reframe and re-look at things in a different way.

- You can experience a feeling of appreciation for the beauty of the world each day.

- You will shift from an "I can't" to an "I can" mindset.

- With a focus on positive intentions, you will feel more empowered and feel more like a "victor" than a "victim."

- When you are more mindful of the present, you will be more likely to live fully in the present each moment of each day. After all, the past is a great place to visit, but you don't want to live there.

PROCESSING

Using each day to recommit yourself to positive thinking and intention will help you create the life you want and that you deserve.

Copyright © 2016 Judith Belmont. *150 More Group Therapy Activities & TIPS*, www.belmontwellness.com. All rights reserved.

We're All Stars!

THEORY

A group situation is a great place to get feedback from one another about how we are valuable and how we shine. From children to adults, **we all need to feel important and worthy**, and are like the stars, shedding light around us.

IMPLEMENTATION

Start by reminding the group that the universe has infinite stars, shedding light and sparkling in the sky. Even when you cannot see them, they are there, and only when it is dark can we see them shine and sparkle.

Brainstorm with the group how all of us are like the stars in the sky. Some points to make are:

☆ We all have the capacity to shine and sparkle.

☆ We are all points of light.

☆ Just as the darkness reveals the stars, it is our greatest times of challenge that allows us to reveal our specialness.

☆ Sometimes we need be in darkness to allow us to shine our best light.

☆ We do not compare stars to one another - they all have beauty and light.

☆ Even if we feel invisible and unimportant, we can still shine brightly and possess light and beauty.

☆ We are all worthy and have our own ability to shine.

☆ Everyone can be a STAR!

Share this acronym to help remind the group that they are all **STARS**:

Special, **T**errific, **A**wesome, **R**adiant, **S**uper!

Break into pairs and give group members a few minutes to take turns telling each other how they think that they are special, i.e. how they are like a star - how they are special, terrific, awesome, radiant and super.

Then pass out the following star handout. For each ray, have them write how they shed light on the world around them, and how they are special. What are their good qualities?

PROCESSING

A group situation is ideal for giving and receiving feedback to boost self-esteem and appreciate individual uniqueness. This is a great team-building exercise and is ideal for children and adults to boost self-esteem by uncovering how each person is special and able to shine and sparkle. **WE ARE ALL STARS!**

 Copyright © 2016 Judith Belmont. *150 More Group Therapy Activities & TIPS*, www.belmontwellness.com. All rights reserved.

We Are All Stars!

You are a star! For each "point" in the star, write how you are special!

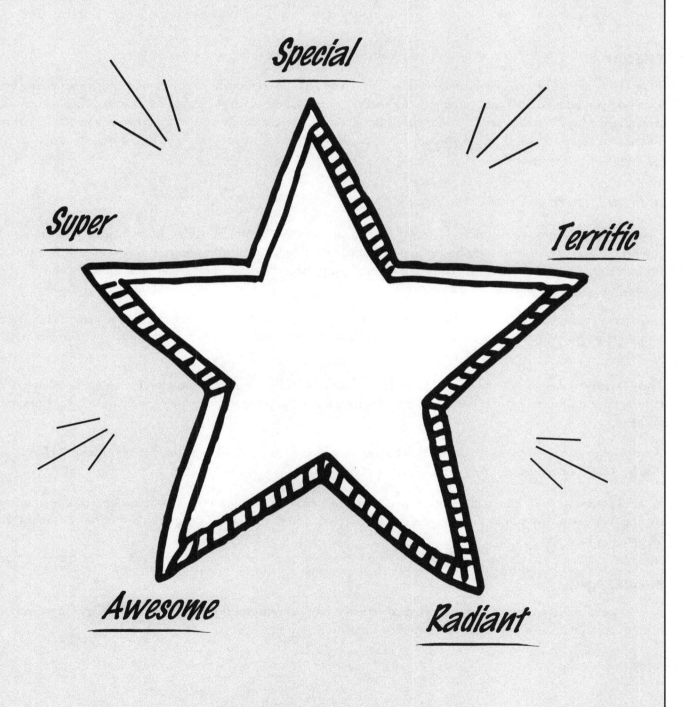

Special

Super

Terrific

Awesome

Radiant

Copyright © 2016 Judith Belmont. *150 More Group Therapy Activities & TIPS*, www.belmontwellness.com. All rights reserved.

How Do You Want To Be?

THEORY

This activity involves a type of behavioral rehearsal, which is called covert modeling. Covert modeling is **visualizing how someone you admire acts**, and learning from them vicariously. Some clients have told me that in difficult situations, they imagine how I would handle it and what I would say. If you can conjure up your healthy role models any time you are not dependent on them always being there to help you - you have some internal mechanism for modeling the behavior that you visualize.

IMPLEMENTATION

First, start with a group relaxation. Have members focus on their breath, breathing from their diaphragm, slowly and deeply. Have them relax their bodies by intentional relaxation or progressive muscle relaxation, which is tensing systematically various parts of their body and then relaxing them. Noticing the tension with muscles contrasting of relaxing can help people feel more relaxed overall.

Have them envision someone from their own lives whom they admire, and who they regard as assertive. This can be someone they know well, a teacher, mentor, friend, family member, or can be even a public figure they admire, present or deceased.

Then have them imagine a situation that is challenging for them. Have them imagine who they would be talking to or in front of, and then instead of imagining themselves, have them think of that person they choose handling the situation for them.

What do they say? How composed are they? What can they learn from watching their role models in action? How could they use some of their visualization in their life?

In small groups or pairs, you might want to have group members act out each other's visualization, with their partner playing the person they admire. Or you can do a role reversal and have them be the person they most admire and the partner playing them!

PROCESSING

As in all communication skills scenarios, even covert ones, processing with the group provides sharing of ideas and can be very cathartic to those who generally keep their thoughts and feelings in.

 Copyright © 2016 Judith Belmont. *150 More Group Therapy Activities & TIPS*, www.belmontwellness.com. All rights reserved.

Tip #136

Reflecting on Feelings

THEORY

Identifying feelings is not always easy for people, regardless of their age. This exercise brings home the point that there is no shame in feelings and **all feelings are to be accepted and learned from**. All too often our clients judge their feelings and regard them as wrong and embarrassing. This activity helps group members embrace and accept their feelings as merely part of being human. In addition, often our clients confuse thoughts and feelings, and this activity helps them to differentiate them. This is a great activity for all ages, being particularly helpful with children who need to learn skills to identify and manage feelings.

IMPLEMENTATION

Write on various notecards different feelings, with clip art showing the emotions or just the words themselves:

- Angry
- Confused
- Sad
- Delighted
- Overjoyed
- Afraid
- Anxious
- Worried

Put the notecards in a box.

Go around the room and have each group member pull out a card, read the emotion, and share with the group a time that they felt this emotion very strongly. This helps individuals accept their emotions without judgment, and also gives structure to group sharing and support.

PROCESSING

The fact that we all have the right to feel all sorts of ways, and need not deny them or be ashamed of them, is a novel concept to some individuals. This activity can help embrace feelings in a more accepting way and learn that feelings are not wrong - only behaviors are. In processing the activity, emphasize that thoughts and feelings are not the same although they are often confused.

Copyright © 2016 Judith Belmont. *150 More Group Therapy Activities & TIPS*, www.belmontwellness.com. All rights reserved.

You've Come a Long Way Baby!

THEORY

The slogan "You've come a long way baby!" has been around for decades, stemming from the commercial campaign developed in 1968 for cigarette maker Virginia Slims. Bringing in baby pictures will give a forum to identify and share with the group how far they have come from infancy, what they have learned, and also remind themselves that the precious child has not gone away. Although as children get older and become adults, their sense of preciousness is often lost, this activity will be a **reminder they are indeed still precious**, just like when they were babies.

IMPLEMENTATION

Have group members bring in baby pictures if they have them, or bring in a drawing or simply think of a mental image of himself or herself as a baby.

Ask what they think of this young child. Remind them that they are no less worthy now than they were as a baby. Nothing has changed - they are still this same person, although they might have lost that sense of preciousness.

Complementary Activity: Take a twenty dollar bill. Pass it around the room. Let people crumble it, step on it, take turns folding and unfolding – going around the room. When it gets back to you, unfold it and ask how much it is worth. Of course the answer is twenty dollars!

This demonstration represents that no matter what happens to us, how crumbled our life becomes, how many creases we have, we still maintain the same precious worth.

You might also want to give each a shiny gemstone bought at a hobby store, to help the group members carry with them a reminder of how special they are!

PROCESSING

These activities emphasize this point to be processed with the group: Self-worth remains the same no matter how many times they fail or how many times they feel down on themselves. We are all precious inside, no matter how many mistakes we have made or how creased we might feel!

234 Copyright © 2016 Judith Belmont. *150 More Group Therapy Activities & TIPS*, www.belmontwellness.com. All rights reserved.

Tip #138

Your Best Advice to Your Younger Self

THEORY

Sometimes the **simplest activities are the most compelling**. This question posed to the group is a simple one, but can reach into group members' inner complexities. Sometimes asking just the right questions can lead to a very productive opportunity for self-discovery and group sharing.

IMPLEMENTATION

Pose this question to the group: *What are the three things that you would tell your younger self?* Or - *What is the best advice you would give to your younger self?*

Depending on the time frame for this activity, have them write or even draw their responses and then share with the group, or split up into pairs and answer the question. Then process their answers with the group.

This is the type of question that members will likely think about outside of the group. Talking about their most important life lessons will often spur further discussion on past regrets. Encourage group members to give themselves a break for not always knowing everything. Hindsight is always 20-20.

This would be a good entry into talking about the difference between unproductive regret and productive regret. Unproductive regret keeps you stuck in the past and can't ever be changed. Productive regret builds on the lessons of your regrets to make changes in your life "today."

Encourage them to treat their younger selves not with blame and criticism, but forgiveness for being human and being a work in progress.

PROCESSING

Processing this lesson can be very meaningful as they are imagining themselves as younger and naive, and can help clients with developing self-compassion. This activity helps realize that we often think things are obvious in retrospect that are not so obvious without the benefit of hindsight.

7

Group
Endings
Tips 139-150

Questions to Ask Yourself in Reviewing Your Group

THEORY

Along with having a checklist for beginnings and endings, below are reminders for **important questions to ask yourself** in reviewing the week's group. Sessions that have most elements of this checklist will be solution-oriented, giving your group members countless tools to learn life skills.

IMPLEMENTATION

In devising strategies for your psycho-educational sessions, reviewing these questions will help ensure you are structuring the group effectively.

After the end of the session, ask yourself:

- How did the group go?
- Did I provide enough opportunity at the end for feedback and closure?
- Did I incorporate some psycho-educational tools in the learning?
- Did the participants stay engaged and involved?
- Did they have time to practice learned skills?
- Did I create a safe and supportive environment?
- Was my assignment for self-help practice between sessions relevant to the group learning?

In preparing for the next session, these are some things to think about:

- How will I structure the homework review based on the assignment of the week?
- What kind of mood check activity can I use?
- Based on what I learned and what came up in this session, what will be the next session's goals?
- What props and metaphors can help me bring home my points for the next session?
- What interactive exercises can I use to help reinforce the concepts we're discussing?
- How can I use role play and other experiential techniques that everyone can do next session?
- What self-help assignments would be a good follow-up from this session's assignment?

PROCESSING

Using the accompanying checklist, you can give yourself your own homework assignment to make sure your group is staying on track, in either reviewing the past session or preparing for the next.

 Copyright © 2016 Judith Belmont. *150 More Group Therapy Activities & TIPS*, www.belmontwellness.com. All rights reserved.

The Clinician's Psycho-Educational Group Checklist

Activity

_____ 1. **Use psycho-educational activities in almost every session.**

Strategy Note _____

_____ 2. **Start each session with a mood check.**

Strategy Note _____

_____ 3. **Clarify goals at the start of each session.**

Strategy Note _____

_____ 4. **Use props, metaphors, and creative visualizations and demonstrations to make the learning memorable and tangible.**

Strategy Note _____

_____ 5. **Use self-help assignments between sessions for encouraging practice.**

Strategy Note _____

_____ 6. **End each session with a feedback check.**

Strategy Note _____

_____ 7. **Use role-play variations often for skill building to improve communication and thinking skills.**

Strategy Note _____

_____ 8. **Use quizzes and handouts in and between sessions to practice skills learned.**

Strategy Note _____

_____ 9. **Above all, ensure a supportive, safe atmosphere for self-disclosure and team building.**

Strategy Note _____

_____ 10. **Have a mixture of individual, small group and large group activities to make the learning dynamic and experiential in a variety of ways.**

Strategy Note _____

Copyright © 2016 Judith Belmont. *150 More Group Therapy Activities & TIPS*, www.belmontwellness.com. All rights reserved.

Additional Checklist for Group Endings

THEORY

Since the elements of a successful group ending are so important to leading an effective group, this is yet another checklist tool which is in more detail for some particularly important elements for designing your group closures. Space is left at the end to write other strategies you would like to add.

A group should not end merely because you run out of time. Keeping these general guidelines will ensure effective group endings.

IMPLEMENTATION

For each session, check off the items you included at the end of your group, in no special order:

_____ **Provide a handout or worksheet from the topic of the week**, which will remind group members of the important life skill lessons and takeaways from the session.

_____ **Feedback check.**

Leave time at the end to share their reactions about the group experience, such as what they found helpful and or unhelpful in the session.

_____ **Assign homework.**

An effective psycho-educational group will have a homework assignment between each session, to be reviewed in the following session. This can be in the form of a handout to read, skill to practice, worksheet to fill out, activity to complete, etc.

_____ **Goal Setting for the week.**

Encourage each group member to set goals for the week to work on, sharing them with the group as a whole or in small groups or pairs. Setting goals can be simply accomplished by going around and asking each member to complete this sentence:

This week I would like to _____.

_____ **Have a positive intention for the week.**

Have each member think of a positive intention for the week, so they can remind themselves to stay focused on staying positive. You might have them write this down on notecards to serve as a reminder.

  Copyright © 2016 Judith Belmont. *150 More Group Therapy Activities & TIPS*, www.belmontwellness.com. All rights reserved.

_____ **Give out a metaphorical object to remind them of the lesson.**

Visual reminders from important group lessons will help reinforce the learning. They could be as simple as, for example, a rubber band, for the topic of stress management. The elastic band represents stress which is not to be avoided, but managed, and reminds the importance of optimal amount of stress in an involved and engaged life. By the final group session, they will have a metaphorical toolkit to remind them of each of the lessons.

Other ideas to close a successful group session:

_____ _____

        _____

        _____

_____ _____

        _____

        _____

_____ _____

        _____

        _____

PROCESSING

Although each group might not have all the elements suggested, ideally your endings will include most of them. Use this checklist as a way to ensure your group is structured for maximum effectiveness.

Copyright © 2016 Judith Belmont. *150 More Group Therapy Activities & TIPS*, www.belmontwellness.com. All rights reserved.

Ask for Feedback

THEORY

A feedback check ties the experience together, and it is a vital component of a successful psycho-educational group. Groups should not end because you run out of time. Careful attention to ending the group with a few important elements, one being a feedback check, will ensure the group's effectiveness.

IMPLEMENTATION

At the end of each group, ask for feedback from the session.

These are some questions to prompt feedback:

- Ask them to fill in the blank: Today I learned _____.

- What was the best takeaway from the group today?

- How can you apply your best takeaway to your life this week?

- What was the most valuable thing we did in the group today?

- What was the best thing about the group today and what did not work out as you would have liked?

- What do you think was the most interesting thing you learned today in the group?

When individuals give their view about the group and what they learned, they'll often discover others have that same thought, feeling or impression. This will tap into the power of universality that a group provides, realizing they are not alone in their struggles or thoughts.

PROCESSING

This feedback loop provides the best opportunity for group sharing, so allow time accordingly. Know your group. Sometimes at the end of the group, when you're asking for feedback, that's when people will start opening up the most!

   Copyright © 2016 Judith Belmont. *150 More Group Therapy Activities & TIPS*, www.belmontwellness.com. All rights reserved.

Making a Handout of Group Takeaways

THEORY

By the time of the final session, group members will have some valuable skills and takeaways that they would like to remember. To help keep these thoughts alive well after the end of the group, and to keep some connection to the group after it is over, **comprising a group handout on the last session** will be a nice way of providing some closure to the group.

IMPLEMENTATION

Go around and ask each group member to share one or two of the most important things they learned in the group. What was the most meaningful to them?

Record all feedback on a computer or flip chart. After the group is over, type them up into a group handout and send the handout to each member.

It might be helpful to do this activity actually at the end of each session, or at least many of them. If you do this each week, by group conclusion, you will have handouts from each week's topic and the major takeaways. If it is not the final group, just hand out the takeaways to review at the beginning of the next group. This will serve as a tie in from what they learned in the last session, and how this week's topics will build on those lessons.

You might have the names of who said what next to each item to give credit for each contribution.

PROCESSING

Making a group handout is a great way to summarize the important lessons. Handouts are very helpful in serving as a reminder of many life skills, and having a handout made by group members is even more meaningful.

A Group Thank-You Note

THEORY

A nice sentiment at the end of the group is to have an opportunity to **give thanks for what others contributed throughout the sessions**. This is personalized to each individual of the group, and can be quite meaningful for all members.

IMPLEMENTATION

Use the accompanying handout, and have one copied for each member with their name on top. With the one person's name on top who is being thanked, have the other group members' names below with a couple lines to fill out why they are thankful for that person.

Have members pass around the papers until each group member has given thanks to everyone in the group.

Example:

Thank you <u>Sara</u> for:

Name: Dan

> Your sense of humor and the way you were kind to everyone. Thank you for bringing laughter to the group. Thanks also for helping me in my role play situation.

Name: Jodi

> You always have such perceptive things to say that made me understand things in other ways. You also were very supportive of everyone in the group and were a very positive influence.

PROCESSING

When all the papers are finished, each person has a sheet of "thank you notes" to remind them of the impact they had on the other group members. Don't forget to include yourself as the leader in this activity; both in being the person thanked and writing why you are thankful for each person.

 Copyright © 2016 Judith Belmont. *150 More Group Therapy Activities & TIPS*, www.belmontwellness.com. All rights reserved.

Activity

A Group Thank-You Note

Thank-you _____ for:

Name: _____

_____

_____

Name: _____

_____

_____

Name: _____

_____

_____

Name: _____

_____

_____

Name: _____

_____

_____

Name: _____

_____

_____

Name: _____

_____

_____

Copyright © 2016 Judith Belmont. *150 More Group Therapy Activities & TIPS*, www.belmontwellness.com. All rights reserved.

Spreading Kindness With a Kiss and a Hug

THEORY

This short but meaningful activity brings home **the importance of kindness and showing appreciation to others**. This is an ideal group activity at closing, and a sweet one at that!

IMPLEMENTATION

Have Hershey® Kisses (or Hugs) and pass three to each person.

Tell them that we often do not think of expressing appreciation to others, but the act of expressing appreciation is a gift you give to others.

Tell the group members to keep one kiss for themselves since self-love underlies loving anyone else - and with the other 2 (or whatever number you wish) go up to different people in the group and give them a "kiss" - and express what you appreciate about them.

You might want to watch for those who are not chosen to give them a "kiss" and give them one of your own so they don't feel left out.

You can make these points:

- The more we can give and receive love, the happier we tend to be.
- Showing appreciation for others feels good for the giver and the receiver!
- Expressing positive feelings makes everyone feel good inside.
- Love and caring gives our life meaning.
- As the saying goes, love makes the world go round!
- Make a point to look at someone when you talk to them - it is easier to express positive feelings when you look them in the eye!
- Don't forget to give yourself a hug and a kiss too!
- Don't be shy about asking for a hug and a kiss!

PROCESSING

For an adult group, suggest to have a bowl of kisses at home or work to freely give to others in expressing appreciation. This is also a great team-building tool for any workplace or school. With the candy kisses or hugs, spreading love can be so sweet. You can use this activity at the groups' conclusion or every session ending. After all, appreciation and positivity is not something to be doled out sparingly!

 Copyright © 2016 Judith Belmont. *150 More Group Therapy Activities & TIPS*, www.belmontwellness.com. All rights reserved.

Tip #145

Assigning Homework and Following Up

THEORY

One of the crucial aspects of psycho-educational groups, as well as the popular orientations of CBT and DBT, is the **focus on between-session homework**. Just as a piano student will not really learn piano by just going to lessons, as much of the proficiency is developed between sessions, assigning homework at the end of each group session will ensure practice to incorporate learning life skills. This is not an optional part of a psycho-educational group – **it is an inherent part of it**.

IMPLEMENTATION

Often the homework assignment will be a logical outgrowth of the session topic.

Make sure you give either a handout or a worksheet, or both, for group members to refer to between sessions. A handout will be informational and offer the main points of the lessons, while a worksheet offers skill practice designed to be filled out by group members.

Some of the homework assignments will be more behavioral, such as being assertive with a family member after role-playing in the session. Practicing communication skills in-session will set the stage for implementing outside the group. The beauty of the group situation is that members can report what happened in the next session during the homework check portion of the following session. This group sharing and updating from one session to the next offers considerable support to group members, often giving them confidence to try new skills outside of the group.

To tie the idea of homework with the feedback loop, have members decide on a goal for the week to practice or incorporate a new concept that was especially meaningful.

Often homework will include monitoring automatic thoughts, trying out new behaviors, completing a behavioral daily log or thought record, or committing themselves to a behavioral goal.

It can be quite helpful for each group member to have the same book to provide structure for between session homework, such as David Burns' *Feeling Good: The New Mood Therapy*. Having Biblio-therapy resources and assigning certain pages and quizzes to be completed can be quite helpful and structure skill building between sessions.

PROCESSING

Make sure at the beginning of the session that you review the homework as a group, discussing how their behavioral practice went. This is very important part of the structure of the psycho-educational group, and will provide feedback to members as well as the leader, as all group members learn how to apply psycho-educational lessons to their everyday life.

Tip #146

Throwing a Party

THEORY

It is not unusual for people in therapy groups to have some degree of social anxiety. What better way to tackle this issue than to **use the group situation to enact a real life group gathering** to practice social skills? Having a party could be a fun way to end a group session.

IMPLEMENTATION

One of the best things about group therapy is to help people with developing their social and communication skills, and a party is a perfect time to hone skills.

First have each member of the group decide on a goal for coping more effectively in group situations. The more specific the goal, the better chance they have of achieving it. For example, instead of having a goal "To feel more comfortable" break it down into smaller goals such as "To go up to one person and start a conversation."

Other examples of goals are:
- Having a healthy alternative opinion to an idea someone expresses
- Developing skills to introduce themselves
- Shaking hands assertively
- Using good eye contact when addressing others
- Carrying on a conversation when you don't have anything to say

It might help to have the group pretend they do not know one another, so that they can introduce themselves and develop confidence in approaching others they do not know.

To make it more realistic and festive, you can bring drinks and food.

After the party scenario, leave enough to time to process with the entire group, giving and receiving feedback on how each other came across, suggesting skills to work on in the coming weeks.

PROCESSING

This activity can be a fun way to celebrate individual and group successes, as well as improve social skills in a supportive environment. If you are having a party at the end of a regular group session, you might ask for feedback of how they felt interacting, how anxious they felt, and what can help them feel more comfortable in social situations. If this is a party to celebrate the final group, you might not process individual goals or give and get feedback. Rather, you might have no structure other than offering food and drinks, and have fun celebrating the end of a successful group experience.

 Copyright © 2016 Judith Belmont. *150 More Group Therapy Activities & TIPS*, www.belmontwellness.com. All rights reserved.

A Metaphor to Remember Me By

THEORY

Throughout the group, you likely will have used some **metaphorical objects to help members remember and visualize important life skills lessons.** In the final session, have people bring in an object that acts as a metaphor to represent how they want to be remembered by the group. Having them distribute their object will help all group members have a meaningful collection of metaphorical objects to remember important life skills. It is a bonus that these objects were given to them by other group members.

IMPLEMENTATION

In the session prior to the final, ask for each member to bring in an inexpensive metaphorical object that represents them and how they want people to remember them by, and bring enough to distribute to each member of the group.

They can be inexpensive items such as paper clips, crayons, Hershey Kisses, etc. The idea is not to spend a lot of money but to think of a metaphor that is meaningful to them to share with group members. They could also use notecards and draw their metaphoric image, or find some printable images online.

Before each person shares their metaphor, pass a paper or plastic bag around for each person to collect all the metaphors they get from group members.

Have each person take turns explaining his/her metaphor and then pass out their metaphorical gift.

PROCESSING

Metaphorical objects from this activity will serve as handy reminders of the group experience and the personal relationships developed. These objects might be a great addition to each member's own life skills metaphorical toolkit or calming box.

Copyright © 2016 Judith Belmont. *150 More Group Therapy Activities & TIPS*, www.belmontwellness.com. All rights reserved.

Tip #148

Making a Friendship Bracelet

THEORY

Friendship bracelets are popular, and having a bracelet made with the group will **remind members of the friendships and support received**.

IMPLEMENTATION

Precut about 10-inch pieces of multicolored string.

You can provide inexpensive bags of beads of different colors, enough for each person in the group. For example, if there are 12 group members, have 12 beads in various bags, and in each bag are 12 of the same color beads.

It does not matter if 2 or 3 of the group members choose the same color, since this activity is not predicated on all different colors. If you want to be part of this activity, have a bead for yourself.

Have each person pick a color. Then, go around and say why you chose that color and the one thing about the group that was special. After sharing their answer, have each member pass out a bead to each person from their bag of similar colored beads. Do this until all members had a turn and everyone has beads from everyone.

Have them knot one end, or have them pre knotted if they are younger children, and string the beads on, representing the wisdom of all the people in the group.

Have them knot the other end (or knot it for them) and have them put it either around their wrist or as a key chain to add to their keys or backpack zippers.

PROCESSING

Make the point that this friendship bracelet represents the group support long after the group is over. It will also help them be mindful of lessons learned and provides a tangible reminder of the group experience.

 Copyright © 2016 Judith Belmont. *150 More Group Therapy Activities & TIPS*, www.belmontwellness.com. All rights reserved.

Sweet Endings

THEORY

Using candy as a way to make a "sweet ending" is a nice touch for the end of a session or the end of an entire group. It adds a fun and light touch to the ending of a group, and **gives some sweetness to take home**.

IMPLEMENTATION

One way to have a "sweet ending" is to have a bag or dish of Skittles or M&M's and have each group member take a few pieces. Having a larger bag of individual packaged M&M's to distribute would be ideal and very sanitary too!

Have a guide on a whiteboard or flip chart with the different colors of candy, with each representing a question to discuss. These questions can be good group closure questions.

Examples are:

Green – What was the most valuable thing you learned in the group?

Red – What is the one thing you will miss about this group?

Yellow – What is the one thing you will work on based on what you learned from the group?

Orange – What is one thing that someone said in the group that made an impression on you?

Blue – What is the best metaphor you learned in the group that can help you remember some important life skills?

PROCESSING

This activity can provide meaningful experiences using candy, and it as it adds a touch of lightness – and sweetness – to any group!

Tip #150

Sending a Wellness Note to Yourself

THEORY

At the final session, it is always helpful for members to think introspectively about what they have learned throughout the group. To make sure lessons will not fade over time, have them **write a memo to themselves** about the main points they want to remember.

IMPLEMENTATION

Distribute pens, a card, or piece of paper, envelope, and stamp to each group member.

Ask them to think of the few major points they want to remember about the group experience and suggestions of how they can continue working on their emotional wellness. It might be something that was said, a way that they felt, a lesson that they learned, an activity that they enjoyed, or some way that they grew from the experience. They might want to write reminders of their goals and hopes, or their commitment to working on continuing the skills learned in the group.

Have them seal the memo or note in the envelope, address it to themselves, and put on the stamp. Let them know that in two months these memos/notes will be sent to them to remind them of important thoughts from the group experience.

Ask for volunteers to share one thing that they wrote.

PROCESSING

This activity provides an opportunity for self-reflection. Once the group has ended, it is nice to have a reminder and follow up to help members stay on track long after sessions have concluded. Remind the group members that skills learned in psycho-educational groups are skills they can take with them the rest of their lives.

Copyright © 2016 Judith Belmont. *150 More Group Therapy Activities & TIPS*, www.belmontwellness.com. All rights reserved.